SAMANTHA ELLIS

How To Be A Heroine

Or, What I've Learned From Reading Too Much

VINTAGE BOOKS
London

Published by Vintage 2015

2 4 6 8 10 9 7 5 3 1

First published in Great Britain in 2014 by
Chatto & Windus

Vintage
20 Vauxhall Bridge Road,
London SW1V 2SA

www.vintage-books.co.uk

A Penguin Random House Company

global.penguinrandomhouse.com

A CIP catalogue record for this book
is available from the British Library

ISBN 9780099575566

The Penguin Random House Group Limited supports the Forest
Stewardship Council® (FSC®), the leading international forest-
certification organisation. Our books carrying the FSC label are
printed on FSC®-certified paper. FSC is the only forest-certification
scheme supported by the leading environmental organisations,
including Greenpeace. Our paper procurement policy can be found
at www.randomhouse.co.uk/environment

Printed and bound in Great Britain by
CPI Group (UK) Ltd, Croydon CR0 4YY

For my mother, and for Emma, top heroines

CONTENTS

INTRODUCTION

A couple of summers ago, I was on the Yorkshire moors, arguing (over the wuthering) with my best friend about whether we'd rather be Jane Eyre or Cathy Earnshaw.

I thought Cathy. Obviously Cathy. The point of this walk (this *pilgrimage*) was to see the ruins of the farmhouse that inspired *Wuthering Heights*, which loomed at us promisingly from the top. We'd both, without consulting each other, worn lace-edged T-shirts in honour of the occasion, and after stopping off for supplies in Haworth, here we were at last, and it was just as I'd imagined: all rain-green moorland, spiky heather, a turbulent waterfall and signs beguilingly translated into Japanese (the Brontës are big in Japan).

It was supposed to be Emily Brontë's favourite walk. She was an inveterate walker, always out, in all weathers. Once, she found a merlin hawk in an abandoned nest and brought him home. She called him Hero. Or possibly Nero. No one can read her handwriting. She painted a watercolour of him, and in her poem, 'The Caged Bird', she imagined him longing for 'Earth's breezy hills and heaven's blue sea'. And in fact he did escape, while she was away studying in Brussels, and when she got back she could find no trace of him.

I hoped we might see a hawk. But I was excited just to be there, on the moor Emily had walked, the moor Cathy spends whole days out on, and haunts after her death. I was just about managing to stop myself from yelling out to Heathcliff that it was me, Cathy, coming home.

So stoic, virtuous, plain Jane was very much *not* on my mind. But Emma argued that Jane was independent, she knew who she was, she didn't suffer fools and she stuck to her principles. 'And Cathy's just *silly*.' Ignoring my howls of fury, she continued, 'She's always weeping and wailing, and she says she loves Heathcliff but she marries the rich boy because she's a snob, and that makes everyone unhappy.'

I defended Cathy. She's passionate and headstrong – and gorgeous. 'You can't like her just because she's pretty,' said Emma. All right, but Cathy doesn't *mean* to marry the wrong man. She's pushed into it. And she regrets it, doesn't she? Emma asked, 'Why not just *not* marry the wrong man?'

I was thrown. Emma had been my best friend since we were eleven, which meant we'd been lending each other books and passionately discussing them for over twenty years. She'd introduced me to J.D. Salinger, I'd introduced her to Antonia White. We had once spent a whole week lying side by side on a beach, both reading *War and Peace*. We didn't always agree. Not agreeing was part of the fun. But this was different.

Cathy's claims to my loyalty were strong. I'd known her almost as long as I'd known Emma; since I first read *Wuthering Heights* at twelve, she had been my favourite literary heroine, the undisputed queen. Cathy and Emma had both been there for me at dark times, and Cathy had even supported some of my more impulsive romantic decisions – which Emma had advised against. I was looking forward to seeing Cathy's house. Yes, it was ruined, yes I would have to imagine the window ledges with her name scratched over and over in the paint, but at least I would feel 'the north wind blowing over the edge' and see the 'gaunt thorns all stretching their limbs one way as if craving alms of the sun'.

But when we reached Top Withens, the skies cleared. The clouds vanished and the sun shone, as if this was the backdrop for some moment of revelation. Which it was. I was wrong.

My whole life, I'd been trying to be Cathy, when I should have been trying to be Jane.

As we leaned against the warm stone, basking – actually basking – in the sun, drinking flasks of tea, I wondered why I'd written Jane off. She *is* independent, and brave, and clever, and she really does stay true to herself. And while Cathy ends up a wandering ghost, Jane ends up happily married. The brilliant sunshine was very Jane weather, I thought; pleasant, clear and rational. It would have rained for Cathy, there would have been thunder and lightning. And (said a small, but firm Jane voice) we would have shivered and eaten soggy sandwiches hunched under the hoods of our waterproofs.

The Brontë Society had put a plaque on the ruin, warning over-eager fans that Top Withens wasn't *actually* Wuthering Heights, and that even before it was ruined, the farmhouse 'bore no resemblance' to the house in the novel – though they did concede that 'the situation may have been in her mind'. It felt like a corrective to romance, a prompt to question old assumptions. I decided that when I got back to London, I would dig out my copies of *Wuthering Heights* and *Jane Eyre* and read them again, with more scrutiny and less sentiment. I would find out how I really felt about Cathy and Jane. But maybe that wouldn't be the end of it. After all, if I'd been wrong about Cathy, had I been wrong about my other heroines too?

Once I'd asked that terrifying question, I knew I would have to meet all my heroines again, every last one. I wanted to think about what they meant to me when I was growing up, and what they mean to me now that I'm grown up, and a playwright and writing heroines of my own.

As a girl, I had thought of myself as being, like Catherine Morland in Jane Austen's *Northanger Abbey*, 'in training for a heroine', an activity I thought both important and worthwhile. I had read to find out what kind of woman I might want to be, lived through my heroines, and rehearsed lives I might live. But I'd also cringed at the moment when Catherine, intoxicated by her beloved Gothic novels, is prowling round Northanger Abbey to see if she can find evidence that her host, General Tilney, has murdered his wife or maybe just imprisoned her in a secret dungeon. She is caught red-handed by droll, charming Henry Tilney, who pours cold water on her lurid suspicions. She nearly dies of shame at how her reading has led her astray. She vows to keep fact and fiction strictly separate. After meeting my heroines again, would I end up making the same vow? Maybe even trying to be 'in training for a heroine' had been a terrible mistake – perhaps the line was Austen's joke against Catherine and never meant to be taken as seriously as I had taken it. I had a chilling image of myself editing my bookshelves, of the gap *Wuthering Heights* would leave when I – what? – put it in the bin? Burned it? Even the idea of giving it away was unthinkable.

But maybe I would have to think unthinkable things. My confusion over Cathy and Jane made me suddenly feel that I didn't quite know how I'd got here, and it seemed important to find out. Otherwise, how would I know where I was going? Next to my heroines, I felt undefined, formless; I had no narrative arc, no quest, no journey. And these are things I have to think about professionally. When I write heroines, I always try to give them strong objectives, burning desires, journeys like the one the archetypal hero is supposed to make. In his storytelling bible, *The Hero with a Thousand Faces*, Joseph Campbell says a hero must cross a border, defeat a dragon and return with treasure that will heal his people. Notoriously, Campbell thought women didn't need to make these journeys. But I think we do. And, having reached my mid-thirties, I didn't know what mine was.

Back in London, a pile of books formed by my bed. They were battered and tear-stained, their jackets scuffed, spines cracked, margins scrawled in; some had flowers pressed between the pages, some bulged from being dropped in the bath. The heroines on their covers were like old friends: there was Katy Carr climbing a fence in a red dress, Sara Crewe in rags talking to a large rat, Nanda Grey backed by flowers and wistfully staring at the sky, Posy Fossil practising ballet in a mirror-walled studio. I hoped I'd still like them. I hoped I wouldn't end up thinking they'd ruined my life.

My reading had sometimes got me into trouble. As when a desire for Scarlett O'Hara's seventeen-inch waist made me crash-diet at sixteen. Or when *The Bell Jar* made me think that suffering would make me a woman. But my heroines had helped me too. Growing up in the Iraqi Jewish community in London, I knew, from early on, that I didn't want the happy ending my parents wanted for me: marriage to a nice Iraqi Jewish boy. Sleeping Beauty made me think I could do something different. Lizzy Bennet gave me hope that that might involve something more interesting than being a princess. Anne Shirley inspired me to become a writer. Franny Glass consoled me for my loss of faith. Marjorie Morningstar made me love the theatre.

Reading that pile of books again, I realised that some of my heroines had misled me, some now seem irrelevant, some I had wildly misread, some I now regret. But many – most – were a pleasure to meet again. I rediscovered the wonder of immersing myself in books, the way I did as a girl. When my heroines confused or disappointed me, I read the writers' diaries, letters and biographies to find out what really happened to the women (they were mostly women) who created my heroines; why they poured their hopes into their heroines, and why they sold them short. I realised how partisan my line-up of heroines was, and how partial, and found myself hungry for new heroines – like go-getting Judy Jordan from *Lace*, and fierce, ambitious Emily Byrd Starr.

And when I went back to *Northanger Abbey*, I found it wasn't nearly as down on reading as I'd feared. Austen stays firmly on her heroine's side. (My favourite authors always do.) Catherine may make wild claims, but Austen backs her up. So, although General Tilney is no murderer, he does turn out to be a villain. He sends Catherine away, extremely rudely, insisting that she leave at once, without an escort, without giving her time to let her family know, forcing her to travel seventy miles unaccompanied. All because he's learned that she is less wealthy than he'd thought.

Catherine was right: General Tilney is a villain. She was right to read life like a book: her mistake was to think she was in a Gothic melodrama when actually she's in a domestic comedy. Once she knows her genre, she gets herself home, not unheroically. Henry eats his words, defies his father and proposes. And Catherine ends the novel ready to embark on the adventure of marriage with a charming, amusing man who likes to read until his hair stands on end and thinks anyone who doesn't enjoy a good novel is intolerably stupid. Catherine has completed her training and become a heroine. I don't think anyone is 'born to be a heroine'. It takes effort, valour, and a willingness to investigate your own heart.

So here I am, showing willing. Because as I started reading again the books that had meant so much to me, I remembered how I'd felt as a four-year-old wishing I was the Little Mermaid, or at twenty, wanting to be Lucy Honeychurch. It was hard to confront my mistakes, and I had to ask myself difficult questions. But I discovered that I did have an arc and a journey after all. I wasn't just reading about my heroines, I was reading the story of my life.

1

THE LITTLE MERMAID

The summer I was four, I got lost on a beach in Italy. I wandered off from my family, and we didn't find each other again for two whole hours. My mother says it was the worst two hours of her life. They had police helicopters out looking for me and everything. But although I knew I was lost, I wasn't scared. It was my first time ever on my own. I walked further than I had ever walked. I made sandcastles with a small Italian boy. I went on past the tourist part of the beach, and it was just me and the sand and the sea and the sky. Walking along the very edge of the sea, splashing through the cool water, I felt amazingly free. When I was reunited with my parents, I cried. I was glad to be safe again. But it had been an adventure. And now it was a story, with me at the centre of it. And even then, I wanted to live a storybook life.

My young, beautiful mother had already *had* a storybook life, with a childhood in Baghdad, then persecution, a failed escape across the mountains of Kurdistan, twenty days in prison, a successful escape to London and a whirlwind romance with my father – all by the time she was 22. She was my first heroine. I thought her life was high romance. My mother did not. She wanted to shield me from suffering, she wanted me never to have to go through what she'd gone through; she wanted me to have a boring life. Throughout my childhood, this outraged me. Never to have adventures? Never to do extraordinary things? Never to take risks? When I once wished aloud that I could go to prison because at least it would be interesting, my mother shuddered.

She wanted my life to have a happy ending: a wedding. Which I thought would be fine, if I could marry a prince. My first fictional heroine, even before I could read, was Sleeping Beauty. I liked her because she was beautiful. I wanted, very much, to have golden hair and blue eyes. My eyes had started blue and gone green, but maybe if I wished hard enough, they'd change back, and maybe my unruly brown curls would straighten and go blonde. Then I'd look like a princess, which was halfway to being one.

It was the end of the Seventies, and Lynda Carter was always on TV, as Wonder Woman, doing her dazzling spinning transformations. I would make myself dizzy in the living room, copying her, hoping my hair would fly free and a mystical ball of light would appear as my clothes were replaced, not by superheroine spangles but maybe by a dancing dress and probably a tiara.

And even though I now regard Sleeping Beauty with the proper feminist horror (her main characteristic is beauty! She spends a hundred years in a coma! She never *does* anything! She never *wants* anything!), I can't help but feel a residual affection for her. Because she was my first fictional heroine and she gave me a desire, an aim, a goal: I wouldn't have a boring life because although I would get married like my family wanted me to, I would marry a prince.

In the 1959 Disney film I watched over and over, the love story is the point. Sleeping Beauty is barely in danger. She's not even asleep for very long. She meets her square-jawed prince *before* she pricks her finger, so the minute she falls asleep, the race is on to find her, kiss her (because only true love's kiss will break the spell) and marry her. It all happens very quickly, and there's a similarly swift resolution of the fairies' argument about what colour Sleeping Beauty's dress should be (obviously, it ends up pink). This all made sense to me, then. And when, a bit later, I read the story in *Grimms' Fairy Tales*, where Sleeping Beauty is asleep for years and years, and the whole palace falls asleep with her, and a forest grows up around them, and it takes a real hero of a prince to hack his way through, I liked that even better.

Now I find the Grimm story a bit prissy. I like the girl stopped in time and the freeze-framed palace servants, and the brilliantly disquieting image of the many sad, young princes who try to get through the forest but die, in the flower of their youth, because 'the thorns held fast together, as if they had hands, and the youths were caught in them, could not get loose again, and died a miserable death'. But the story still hurtles towards a kiss, a wedding and a happy ever after. The version Charles Perrault wrote in 1697, a century before the Brothers Grimm cleaned up the story, is much darker and stranger.

Perrault's story doesn't end with the prince waking Sleeping Beauty with a kiss. Not at all. Instead, he goes on to tell us what happens after Sleeping Beauty gets married. She's out of the frying pan and almost literally into the fire, because her mother-in-law is a jealous ogress who orders her steward to kill and cook Beauty's children, Dawn and Day, in 'piquant sauce'. The kind steward fools the ogress by cooking a lamb and a kid, but when she asks for beauty to be cooked in the same sauce, he panics, because although Beauty is officially 20, she's been asleep a hundred years. 'Her skin, though white and beautiful, had become a little tough, and what animal could he possibly find that would correspond to her?' He decides on venison. But the ogress knows she's been fooled, so she decides to kill Beauty, Dawn and Day herself. She gets a vat and fills it with vipers. Luckily her son returns and catches her red-handed. She dives into the vat herself and is devoured by the hideous creatures inside.

Only then can Sleeping Beauty and her prince and their mawkishly named children get a shot at living happily ever after. I love the fact that Perrault's princess goes on living and struggling after she finds her prince, and that Perrault doesn't shrink from the weirdness of Sleeping Beauty being over a hundred years old but having the body of a lithe young thing. When the prince wakes her, he considers telling her she's wearing the kind of clothes his grandmother used to wear, but decides it's best not to mention it just yet. Oh, and Perrault doesn't specify that Beauty's hair is blonde or straight. She could well be a curly-haired brunette.

Only recently I came across Giambattista Basile's even earlier version of the story, from 1634. His princess, named Talia, is warned that she will be in mortal danger if she ever goes near any flax. Her father duly forbids all flax, but one day Talia sees an old woman spinning, pricks her finger and falls down dead. The old woman is so scared that she runs away and, says Basile, 'is still running now'. Talia's grieving father has her laid out in one of his country mansions. Some time later, she is raped by a passing king and, nine months later, still unconscious, she gives birth to twins. Trying to find milk, the babies mistake her fingers for nipples and suck out the flax. The princess awakes. The rapist king returns and everyone's delighted. The only problem is, he's already married. So he takes Talia and her children to his palace and hides them away. His wife, understandably put out, tries to kill, cook and eat the interlopers. At the last minute she's foiled, Talia becomes the new queen, and the rather queasy moral of the story is that lucky people find good luck even in their sleep.

If I'd read that version as a child, then – like the old woman – I'd still be running now. But now even this nasty tale seems preferable to the mindlessly syrupy Disney film, with its faux-medieval costumes, simpering wasp-waisted princess and long scenes where she charms the forest creatures by trilling the same song over and over. I can't fathom why I ever wanted to be her. Though I still kind-of sort-of want her hair.

I do try to fight this retro-sexist yearning, but a few years ago, already in my thirties, I was interviewing an Orthodox Jewish wig-maker, as research for a play I was writing, and she invited me to try on a wig. I hesitated. She told me to shut my eyes. She pulled my hair taut into a bun at the nape of my neck, covered it in a net and scraped the wig's combs in at the sides to secure it. When I opened my eyes, I couldn't believe it. In the mirror there I was with fairy princess hair – blonde, poker-straight, shimmering to my waist. 'Does it move?' I whispered. She smiled. 'Why don't you flick it?' I did, and there

I was, like the girl in the meadow in the Timotei advert, with my very own cascade of golden hair. Clearly, I hadn't entirely grown out of Sleeping Beauty.

Last year, as I watched Disney's recent film *Tangled*, I longed to have hair like Rapunzel's, not just blonde but so long she can use it to tie a man up, let herself down from a tower, and as a zip wire, lasso and swing. Rapunzel's hair even has magic healing powers. When it is cut and changes to a lovely burnished chestnut brown, she finds out that her tears can heal as well as her hair ever did; because, it turns out, brunettes are magic too. (Also in *Tangled*, when they kiss at the end, *she* dips *him*. Revolutionary stuff!)

Then, though, my hair wasn't the only thing stopping me becoming a princess. There was a bigger obstacle. I loved sitting on the edge of my mother's dressing table, watching her put on her make-up, and playing with the kohl pots she'd brought from Baghdad, two shaped like trees, one shaped like a peacock, with a tail you pressed down to release the stopper. One evening, I confided my life plan, but she said, 'You can't marry a prince.' Just like that. 'There are no Jewish princes.' I was crestfallen. It did not occur to me that I didn't have to marry a Jew, or marry at all. I thought my dream was over. How would I ever become a princess now?

This conversation was the beginning of my realising we were different. My mother would say 'We are Jews. We never know when they might not like us any more and we'll have to get on a boat and just get out.' We had to stick together, we had to be alert, we had to avoid non-Jewish princes. And as Iraqi Jews, we were different even from other Jews. We ate rice instead of gefilte fish, we belly-danced instead of watching Woody Allen. We were a tiny community, a self-contained little world. So rarely did I meet anyone who wasn't an Iraqi Jew that until I went to school, I thought all grown-ups spoke Judeo-Arabic, and that English was just a children's language. I assumed that when I grew up I'd be fluent in Judeo-Arabic, just as I'd be taller. And married. And allowed to drive.

At the weekends, my family would sit around a table at my grandparents' house in Wembley, chain-smoking and talking about Baghdad. Their stories emerged from a grey-blue cloud. One of my earliest memories is of sitting under the table, pulling the stalks off parsley to make *tabbouleh* while above my head, the women made *sambousek bi tawa* (pastry crescents filled with spiced chickpeas), or *purdah pilau* (chicken and rice cooked in a 'veil' of pastry), or *ras asfoor b'shwander* (literally, little birds', heads, actually small meatballs cooked with beetroot in a sweet and sour sauce). Iraqi Jewish food is all mixed up, sweet and sour together, and so were the stories.

They talked about sleeping on the roof in the hot summers and seeing shooting stars, which they thought were UFOs; about the gazelle they kept as a pet; about learning to swim in the Tigris; about eating water buffalo cream for breakfast, sold by women who carried it on their heads in round, flat trays. It was as thick as cake, and the women would slice it with a hairpin for them to take home and eat with warm pitta bread and black, sticky date syrup.

They had ice cream that was chewy because it was made with mastic from crushed orchid roots – I've tasted it in a Turkish café in London so I know it exists. But I've never eaten *masgouf,* the enormous flat fish hauled from the Tigris and roasted on the riverbank, with spices, over an open flame. I've never seen the sandstorms that turned the skies red or the blind master musicians in dark glasses playing languorous songs of lost love.

I desperately wanted to go to Baghdad, preferably by magic carpet. I'd watched *The Thief of Bagdad* and *Sinbad the Sailor*, and I had a very clear image of my grandmother setting off for the copper market (where the banging was so loud you had to communicate in signs) perched elegantly on a fringed rug. But the red-and-blue carpet in our house wouldn't fly, no matter how long I spent sitting on it and wishing.

It was at synagogue, at Purim, that I found a possible solution to my princess problem. A loophole. The festival of Purim celebrates a heroine, Esther, who is Jewish and a queen – which was almost as good as being a princess. Like all small girls, I was less interested in queens than in princesses. Usually once a fairytale princess has married her prince, there's nothing more for her to do and the story is over. But Esther's story goes on after her marriage to King Ahasuerus as she saves the Jews of Persia from the prime minister who wants to kill them all.

At Purim, when we read the story, we would shout, stamp and rattle noisemakers to drown out the baddies' names. Grown-ups were required to drink so much they forgot the difference between good and evil. Iraqi Jews gamble at Purim, so my synagogue would hire baize tables and roulette wheels to become, thrillingly, for just one night, a makeshift mini Monte Carlo. But the best thing about Purim was that it was the festival of fancy dress. All the girls wanted to go as Esther. In Tel Aviv, the whole city celebrates with a boozy, three-day carnival, and in the Orthodox suburbs hundreds of girls dress as Esther, all in white, with sparkly tiaras and wispy veils and bouquets of orange blossom; endless tiny brides. My Esther dress, made by my mother, was cream satin with gold braid and a tiara of silk roses. She zipped me into it and even daubed my eyelids with her best Seventies disco blue. I wanted to be Esther every day of the year.

My Hebrew teachers said I should like Esther for saving the Jews, but I was more interested in the bit before that, where she gets her king by winning a beauty contest. I imagined her as pretty as Sleeping Beauty, but a brunette. With green eyes. All right, I imagined her as a gorgeous, grown-up version of myself. And she *was* Jewish, and she *did* become a queen. (At Hebrew school, we skated over the fact that she married a man who wasn't Jewish. Everything was forgivable in a heroine who saved the Jews.)

Later, in synagogue again as a bored teenager, refusing to dress up and irritated by the noisemakers, I actually read the Megillah myself and I was shocked. There is no beauty contest. Ahasuerus is no doe-eyed prince. He's already executed his first wife, the captivating Vashti, for the monstrous crime of refusing to come when he sends for her. Esther attracts his attention when her uncle gets her to join the sex-starved king's harem.

Once queen, she does save the Jews. But she does it *so* passively. When she hears that the prime minister plans to kill her people, she's too timorous even to go and see the king. Instead she starts fasting. It doesn't say why. Does she fast for luck? Does she fast because thin girls win? No one knows. After three days, she invites Ahasuerus to dinner but the words dry in her mouth.

She invites him again the next night, and finally (with her people facing extinction, now, quite urgently) tells him she is Jewish and can he please not kill her people. He doesn't exactly say yes: he says he can't rescind the order now it's gone out (why not? He's the *king*) but he will allow the Jews to defend themselves. Which is big of him. So they do, killing a lot of Persians in the process. It's not the most unqualified of happy endings.

The less I liked Esther, the more interested I got in Vashti, the dissident queen. I'd been told she was a bad wife, and hideously vain – I suppose, to provide shadow and contrast to Esther's luminous innocence, she had to be cast as the evil queen. My Hebrew teachers had said she refused to answer the king's summons because she had terrible acne and didn't want him to see. Or because she'd been wickedly dabbling in witchcraft and had grown a tail and was desperately trying to magic it away. They didn't tell me that when Ahasuerus sends for her 'in her crown', he almost certainly means he wants her to rock up in *just* her crown, to be leered at by several hundred of his male friends, who have been partying for seven days. When she says no, the king's mates respond like stag-party morons. 'Vashti . . . hath not done wrong to the king only,' they opine, 'but also to the princes.' How has Vashti wronged the poor princes? 'This deed of the queen will come abroad unto all women, to make their husbands contemptible in their eyes.' Spooked by the idea that their wives might stop coming when they call, the louts get the king to issue a command to all women to obey their husbands. And that's it for Vashti. As a teenager, I switched allegiance. Vashti's defiance and pride seemed a lot more interesting than silent, docile Esther resorting to the most tired of feminine wiles (fasting and flirting) to get what she wanted. But now I wonder: if Vashti had stayed queen, would she have saved the Jews? The joke that all Jewish festivals boil down to the formula 'They tried to kill us! We survived! Let's eat!' is painfully true of Purim, and Esther's intervention (however unpalatable in terms of feminism) does save her people. I still like Vashti but I can also see the point of a heroine who stops a genocide by using the only strategies she knows.

Back then, however, Esther was paling into insignificance beside the new star of my heart: the Little Mermaid. In my battered, crayon-scribbled, pink book of Hans Christian Andersen's *Fairy Tales*, she is as blonde as Sleeping Beauty but her hair curls like the waves she lives in. Like me, the Little Mermaid faces impossible obstacles in her ambition to marry a prince. She longs to visit the human world above the sea, but she is too little. Her older sisters used to dream about going too, but once they're allowed to, and can go whenever they like, they become indifferent to it. Not so the Little Mermaid. When she's finally old enough to swim up to the surface, she is dazzled. She sees a ship and, spying through the porthole, she falls in love with the first human she sees, who happens to be a handsome prince. She watches him party on board the ship, wishing she could join him. And when a storm blows up and the ship is smashed up, she risks her life to swim through the wreckage to drag the prince to safety on the shore.

At home in the mermaid kingdom at the bottom of the sea, she gets depressed that her love can never be. (There's a load of gobbledegook here about how mermaids live for three hundred years and then dissolve into spume, while the Little Mermaid would rather have a short human life and be rewarded with an immortal soul. I ignored all this when I was small, and it makes no more sense to me now.) She goes to a witch and gets a potion that will turn her tail into legs. The witch warns that getting legs will be very painful, like a sharp knife cutting into her flesh, and that afterwards, though she'll *look* graceful, she'll *feel* as if she's walking on swords, and there will be blood. And if she doesn't succeed in winning the prince's love, her heart will break and she'll die instantly. Worst of all: the witch wants the Little Mermaid's sweet voice as payment.

Undaunted, inspired by love, the Little Mermaid sticks out her tongue for the witch to cut it out. She swoons in pain and wakes (as all swooning women should) to see the handsome prince gazing down at her. He's probably staring so hard because she's got no clothes on. Andersen is coy about it, but why else would she immediately try 'to cover herself with her long, thick hair'? It seems that Operation Win The Prince is go, but sadly the prince is unworthy of the Little Mermaid's love. He pets her and calls her his 'dear little foundling', but he doesn't twig that she's the one who saved him from the shipwreck, and now that she has no voice, she can't tell him. He doesn't see her as bride material, but that doesn't stop him hugging and kissing her and wishing (aloud! the manipulative cad) they could get married. And then he goes and marries someone else and, rubbing salt in the wound, makes the Little Mermaid a bridesmaid.

Her heart clearly broken, she prepares to die. But then her sisters rise up out of the sea, pale and bald. They've given the witch their own radiant hair, in return for a knife which the Little Mermaid can use to stab the prince. If she bathes her legs in his warm blood they will transform into a new, shimmering mermaid tail and she can come home.

But the Little Mermaid can't do it. She loves the prince too much. So she dives into the sea and sacrifices herself. She turns into foam, as mermaids do. At this point, harking back to the stuff about souls, Andersen bolts on a perplexing Christian salvation message about how the Little Mermaid can earn a soul if she is good for three hundred years, but every time she sees 'a rude, naughty child', she'll get more time in purgatory. Don't be rude or naughty or the mermaids will suffer? *Please.* Even as a child, I knew this was ridiculous.

Now, this seems the least of the problems in this cruel, woman-hating story.

I can't quite believe that I was so keen on a story about a mermaid who *gives up her voice for legs to get a man.* Put as starkly as that, it's obvious what an affront it is. Also, the legs aren't so she can walk. In Andersen's story, mermaids can live on land, but the Little Mermaid's grandmother tells her that while mermaids think their tail is their best feature, humans think it is hideous. So the Little Mermaid submits to horrific pain purely to conform to an alien and incomprehensible ideal of beauty. You don't have to be Naomi Wolf to have issues with this.

And then there's the business about losing her voice. In *Titus Andronicus,* Lavinia has her tongue cut out and her hands hacked off and she *still* manages to tell her father the name of her attacker (so he can avenge her), by writing in the sand, the stick clutched between her bloody stumps. Shakespeare gives Lavinia a bit of agency. Andersen never even lets the Little Mermaid use sign language. Her campaign to win the prince's heart consists of her staring at him mournfully. Of course he goes off and marries someone a bit more lively.

The other stories in my Andersen book are about underdogs too, but they get happy endings. (Andersen's life had a similar trajectory, from grim poverty to literary stardom.) The ugly duckling becomes a swan, Thumbelina marries a miniature prince and even grows wings, Gerda rescues her friend Kai, who has been abducted by the Snow Queen, and melts his frozen heart. And after her dreadful night of pea-induced sleeplessness, the princess passes the test and gets her prince. But not the Little Mermaid.

As I grew old enough to read the stories for myself, I became dissatisfied with princesses. Later, in my teens, I shunned them completely and denounced all fairy tales as instruments of the patriarchy. Andrea Dworkin would teach me to damn Sleeping Beauty as 'that object of every necrophiliac's lust – the innocent, *victimised* . . . beauteous lump of ultimate, sleeping good'. The princesses did nothing. The mothers were evil, jealous harridans, Freud's darlings. The old women were bitter crones. At university I discovered the poet Anne Sexton's take on Sleeping Beauty in her 1971 collection *Transformations*; her Beauty has been abused by her father, and when the prince wakes her with a kiss, she recoils, thinking it's her father, coming back to hurt her again. After this horror, she can't have a happy ending. And her century of catatonia has left her so terrified of sleep that she can't live her life. Sexton tells the story as if it torments her, but she has to tell it, and she ends with a restive uncertainty about what it really means.

It was Angela Carter who started bringing me back to fairy tales. Her revisionist stories, in *The Bloody Chamber* (1979), emphasise how uncanny fairy tales are, with their strange lacunae and unexplained twists. Her heroines aren't innocent good girls: they are complicit, almond-eyed, ripe for corruption. I love her take on Bluebeard. The young heroine (so young she's happiest in faded gingham and serge skirts, like a girl in a Colette story) is fascinated by her rich older husband, a marquis (not de Sade but he might as well be) who walks as though on velvet, smells of spiced leather, smokes cigars as fat as a baby's arm and showers her with presents: marrons glacés, furs and a necklace of blood-red rubies originally made by his aristocratic grandmother who was defying the guillotine. Exploring her new home, she finds erotica that makes her gasp, and then she finds a torture room and the embalmed corpses of his three previous wives. The marquis, of course, plans to guillotine her. But the audacity of Carter's ending makes me laugh with relief and joy because just as the girl faces death, her mother arrives, hair flying, skirts rucked up to the thigh, clutching her father's old gun in one hand, and shoots the marquis dead. Yes, it's a startling reversal but every generation spins fairy tales their own way. It's no more implausible than all those happy-ever-afters. And why shouldn't it be the heroine's gutsy mother who saves her, rather than some handsome huntsman or layabout prince?

As I'm wondering if The Little Mermaid could be rewritten too, I ask my small god-daughter why she likes her so much, and she's indignant. 'It's a happy ending! They get married!'

She introduces me to Disney's 1989 film which does, indeed, have a happy ending. Disney's Little Mermaid has a name (Ariel) and she's an entrancing redhead, and a talented singer about to make her concert debut. Her luscious soprano captures the heart of the prince (incongruously named Eric) when he hears her singing during the shipwreck. So when she gives up her voice, she gives up a potential career, and also the quality that makes her most attractive to men.

There's none of the nonsense about legs like swords; Ariel *is* a bit unsteady on her new feet, but that only gives her the perfect excuse to lean giddily on Eric's arm. And she doesn't get legs for beauty's sake but because she has to *be* a human to woo a human; it is assumed she won't be able to move around on dry land without legs. The witch also persuades her to give up her voice by saying men don't like chatty women. She's wrong, of course; Eric has fallen in love with Ariel's voice. Even the witch knows it isn't true: monstrously ugly, and vain, with a husky rasp, she wants to steal Ariel's voice and use it to attract Eric for herself. This is not a film about women silencing themselves to get a man.

Ariel gets the prince, defeats the witch, gets her voice back and even gets her father to bless their unconventional marriage. Watching the film now, with my god-daughter, makes me wish I'd seen it as a child. Its exuberance totally rejuvenates the story and I can't help thinking my life would be different if I'd known Disney's Little Mermaid, not Andersen's.

And yet I can't shake the Andersen story. I keep returning to his image of the Little Mermaid's sisters rising up out of the sea, like avenging angels. And I wonder if his story could be read as a cautionary tale for women saying: Don't give up your voice! Don't make sacrifices for unworthy men! And definitely don't mutely kill yourself when they go off with other women! Instead, the story (maybe) advocates killing your prince with a knife given to you by the sisterhood (literally), and returning to the sea where, after all, there are plenty more fish. Not to mention attractive, suitable mermen.

That's just the kind of heroine I could get behind now. But it also seems obvious to me why I loved the Little Mermaid as a child. It's nothing to do with her being a princess, or her quest to marry a prince. It's because, like me, she's caught between two worlds. I was homesick for Baghdad, even though I'd never been there and everyone told me I would never get to go. And Andersen lavishes some of his most sensuous and heart-rending prose on the beauty of the world at the bottom of the sea, the world his heroine wrenches herself from, never to return. Painfully he portrays her trying to fit in with the humans, a misunderstood misfit who is no longer a mermaid, not quite a human. She never quite manages it – and Andersen knew that feeling: he never managed to fit into his new, glamorous life. He was insecure, desperate for praise, always fawning on anyone with money, beauty or power. He never found love. And even his friends found him ingratiating. So instead of giving her a happy ending, like his other protagonists, he gave the Little Mermaid those complicated feelings about being an outsider and walking painfully through a world he could never truly communicate with, and never, ever being able to go back home.

The witch spells it out: 'you can never again become a mermaid . . . You may never return to your sisters, and your father's palace.' Then, I read this with a lump in my throat because I knew my family could never return to Iraq. I still well up when I read about how the Little Mermaid creeps out of the palace every night to sit on the marble steps that go down to the sea, to cool her feet in the water; her legs really do feel like swords and only the sea can numb the pain and wash away the blood. Her sisters swim towards her, arm in arm, singing sadly because they miss her so much. They even bring their old grandmother and their father, who are too old to swim close enough to speak to the Little Mermaid. She sees them across the waves and weeps. It's a devastating image of deracination.

When I was a child, this connected with images from the two films my brother and cousins and I watched over and over at our grandparents' house: *The Sound of Music* and *Fiddler on the Roof*. While the grown-ups talked about having to leave their home in Baghdad, we would alternate the videos – Nazis one week, Cossacks the next. I knew that the Von Trapp family walking out over the Alps was somehow the same as the Jews packing up the shtetl, and that both were no different from my family leaving Baghdad, and the Little Mermaid leaving the sea. These stories helped me grapple with fears I couldn't articulate, terrors of displacement and separation and loss. I hadn't lost my home, my language or my country, but I was picking up on the grown-ups' fears. And I was starting to doubt that marrying a prince would solve them. My most tattered and destroyed book, a read-along picture book of *The Story of Henny Penny*, is about a different kind of heroine, a brave red chicken who thinks the sky is falling down and goes on a journey (so there, Joseph Campbell) to tell the king. But a fox gets her friends, and although she survives, she never manages to tell the king. This petrified me. What if the sky really *was* falling down? Didn't the king need to know? Henny Penny is a heroine on a mission, a heroine who *does* something, a heroine with a social conscience, a heroine who knows fear. And she's not a princess, or trying to become one.

Maybe I didn't want to be a princess after all. Maybe, just maybe, there was more to life than that.

2

ANNE OF GREEN GABLES

When I was seven, my grandfather took me aside and told me a secret: 'I'm going to die very soon and you'll have to look after everyone.' I was devastated. I adored my grandfather, and I thought he lived a wonderful life, spending all day in his pyjamas, reading lots of books. Was he really going to die? 'Will I really have to look after everyone?' I asked, wide-eyed. 'Even the grown-ups?' He said, 'Everyone.' We could hear them in the kitchen, talking, cooking, eating. It was such a responsibility. There were so many of them! 'Even Mum and Dad?' I asked. 'Even my uncles?' It seemed impossible. 'Even *Grandma*?' At the news that I would have to look after her too, I burst into tears. My mother heard me, and scooped me up and told me my grandfather wasn't dying. He was just sad, 'because of what happened in Iraq'. Which seemed to be the answer I got to all my questions.

My recurring nightmare is set in a desert. I am running, pursued by dark men with moustaches. My heart pounds, sand flies into my face, hot air scours my mouth, my eyes. And the implacable mustachioed men keep chasing me down. Then, my nightmare desert had cacti in it, and oases, because my only visual reference for the desert was the Westerns we watched on TV. As I learned more Judeo-Arabic, and asked more questions,

I realised I was dreaming versions of my family history: their stories of leaving Baghdad, along with most of the city's Jews. In its Jewish heyday in the 1940s, Baghdad was one-third Jewish; every third shop, every third house. By the Eighties, the population had fallen from around 350,000 to just a couple of thousand. Now, reportedly, there are only seven Jews in Iraq.

The Jews had been brought to Baghdad in 587 BC, as Nebuchadnezzar's captives. He set them to work dredging canals between the Tigris and the Euphrates. At first they wept by the rivers, as per Psalm 137, but later, when they got permission to leave, many chose to stay. Under the Ottomans, Jews were protected – though not equal – but after the First World War anti-Semitism grew, from street violence in the 1920s and discriminatory laws in the 1930s to the *farhud* of 1941, when Baghdad rioted and Jews were murdered, raped, and their homes and businesses looted. The word *farhud* means a breakdown of order; the Jews would never again feel at home in Iraq.

So in 1950, when they were told they could sign up for a mass airlift to Israel, many registered to go. My father's family were among them. They were stripped of their Iraqi citizenship, and the Iraqi parliament passed a secret law to confiscate Jews' possessions and freeze their liquid assets. They left with nothing. After the *taskeet,* the denaturalisation (such a bland word for the destruction of a community), only 6,000 Jews – including my mother's family – stayed. They hoped things would get better.

But when the Baathists came to power, things got definitively worse. In 1967, Iraq sent an army to fight Israel in the Six Day War. In 1969, crowds cheered as nine Jews were hanged in the streets. They'd been imprisoned, tortured and condemned in televised show trials as Zionist spies. One was my mother's cousin; he was only eighteen. By now, many Jews were leaving illegally, smuggled by Kurds over the mountains into Iran. My mother's family tried to escape in 1970 but they were caught at the penultimate checkpoint and imprisoned. They were released after twenty days. When they came out, my grandfather sank into depression. He was a talented doctor, but now he became a hypochondriac, constantly checking his own pulse. When he was arrested again, and kept in prison for nearly four months, his depression set in for good. I never knew him happy, and the reason he stayed at home all day in his pyjamas was that he was too heart-crushingly miserable to go out.

Although I was growing up in London, in safety, I would flinch if a stranger touched my hair, because my mother told me that when they interrogated her in prison they pulled her hair. My grandmother told me about the day in prison when the guards took all the men away. The women were terrified, and to calm them, the guards brought them a watermelon. Eventually the men were brought back. I still don't like watermelon.

What could I do with this difficult, unhappy morass, except have bad dreams? I was also scared of witches, and bats, and vampires, and burglars and whatever else might emerge from the vanishing darkness beyond the edge of our garden. The grown-ups said I had an 'over-active imagination'. It seemed a terrible problem, an unconquerable flaw. Until I discovered Sara Crewe.

The heroine of Frances Hodgson Burnett's 1905 riches–rags–riches novel *A Little Princess* is not actually a princess, but her horrid headmistress thinks that because she's rich she must be as spoilt as a princess (she is not) and the school's downtrodden scullery maid, Becky, thinks she must be a princess because she's so kind and beautiful. Sara's definition of princess is closer to Becky's than to her headmistress's, and she pretends she's a princess to help her behave like one.

Like Sara, I lived in a world of my own, forever daydreaming and making up stories. When Sara's father dies, apparently bankrupt, and she's forced to skivvy alongside Becky, she puts her 'pretending' to good use. The two girls make their rat-infested attic a palace, sturdily believing they can imagine themselves happy. I hoped that if I was ever ripped from all I knew, like Sara (and like my family), my imagination might help me too.

But now, Sara seems a bit insipid. And her imagination is escapist in the wrong way. She uses imagination to forget her troubles, instead of trying to imagine an escape she might actually make. She does get out of the attic, but only because she is rescued. She is as passive as Sleeping Beauty in making it happen. The ending, where Becky becomes Sara's 'delighted attendant', feels like a betrayal of their friendship and a reassertion of the class divide that is deeply unimaginative. Luckily, soon after discovering Sara, I read *Anne of Green Gables* (1908) and its vivacious heroine Anne Shirley showed me that imagination could do a lot more. It could even be heroic.

Anne bursts on to the page, eleven years old, waiting at a railway station, wearing an ugly, tight yellow-grey dress, and a faded sailor hat over two red plaits. Her eyes look green in some lights and moods and grey in others, and she wants to be called

Cordelia, but if that's not possible then 'Anne with an "e"'. No one has come to pick her up, and she decides that, if they never come, she'll scramble up into a wild cherry tree and sleep there among the blossoms, in the moonshine. This is a girl who can even make waiting at a train station an adventure. Her imagination helps her forget her fear that she'll be left there alone all night. So far, so Sara Crewe. But L.M. Montgomery wants to take her, and us, on a much longer journey than that.

Anne's imagination has developed under pressure. Orphaned at just three months old, she's drudged for various hard, unkind women; one of them had three sets of twins and Anne got *dreadfully* tired carrying them about. She's done time in an orphanage. She's *needed* to imagine all her misery away. She even, courageously, declares that there's more scope for imagination in the horrible places she's been. She needs her imagination again when she finds out that the Cuthberts, whom she was waiting for at that railway station and who she thought were going to give her a home, never wanted her. There's been a mix-up and they'd really wanted a boy to help out on the farm.

Anne turns to her imagination to help her cope. 'Suppose she wasn't really going to stay here! She would imagine she was.' She strenuously imagines she's going to stay, determinedly enjoying herself, and is brave and positive in the face of a world that doesn't want her; she refuses to be defined by other people's pinched expectations. When her reverie is broken, she says 'the worst of imagining things is that the time comes when you have to stop, and that hurts'. This line inordinately influenced me. I wanted to imagine and I didn't want to stop. Sometimes I think I became a writer so I would never have to stop.

Imagination seems to be winning the day for Anne, as shy, middle-aged Matthew Cuthbert finds her chatter so interesting that he persuades his sister Marilla to keep her. But then a hurdle: Marilla wants Anne to curb her imagination and be sensible. She wants Anne to learn to keep quiet. And she thinks that when God puts us in certain circumstances, He doesn't want us imagining them away. She's right: imagination does get Anne into scrapes. Daydreaming, she forgets to put flour in a cake. She nearly serves up a sauce a mouse has drowned in. She nearly drowns *herself* while re-enacting 'The Lady of Shalott' in a leaky barge. And, as it did for me, imagination gives her terrors.

Anne and Marilla have their climactic fight about imagination when Anne refuses to run an errand through the spruce grove because she's been calling it the Haunted Wood and filling it with ghosts and now she believes they might actually walk. Commonsensical Marilla makes her run the errand anyway, and cures her of letting her imagination take her places where she doesn't want to go. Anne helped me slowly let go of my fears of witches and vampires. Though she also gave me one fear I didn't have before: I still worry, when I dye my hair, that it might go wrong, like hers did, and turn green.

Anne learns to channel her imagination. She talks less about her imaginings, and starts writing them down. Now that she no longer has to imagine her life away – she *likes* her life – she's free to use her imagination for something better. She's going to be a writer.

That settled it: I would be a writer too. I bought a shiny black notebook, labelled it 'Collected Poems' and started filling it with poems, dashed off in a single draft, in neat, swirly writing in coloured inks. They were terrible. Anne's early writing doesn't sound much better; her first heroines have florid names and purple eyes and meet tragic ends. But she learns to use shorter words, to write simply, and instead of 'love and murder and elopements and mysteries' she writes about things that might happen in her own life. She takes writing advice where she can get it, and strives to be her own severest critic. And so, eventually, I ditched my shiny notebook and my coloured felt-tips and began filling a series of plain exercise books with draft after painstaking draft, with many crossings-out in unromantic biro.

Coming back to Anne now, I was worried I'd find her sugary, that I'd be sceptical about the way she goes through all eight books making friends, winning over crotchety neighbours, cheering the miserable and healing the lonely. But Anne's sweetness and humour still tug at my heart. I thought I'd find Montgomery's prose too purple; and that I'd want to skim the raptures about trees and flowers and clouds. But it is amazing, sinewy, knowledgeable nature writing – and I googled Anne's Prince Edward Island and it really *is* phenomenally beautiful!

And the *Anne* books are *fun*. Anne has a gift for pleasure, whether she's taking apple blossoms up to her bedroom 'for company', signalling to her best friend Diana in made-up Morse code, walking a ridgepole, savouring her first ice cream, reciting poetry or walking in the woods. I find Pollyanna, whose eponymous book came out in 1913 (five years after *Anne of Green Gables* was a runaway bestseller) brainlessly optimistic, with her 'glad game' and her constant exulting over everything. But Anne's joy in life is bolstered by her altruism, her willingness to work hard, and her commitment to friendship – qualities that are mostly rewarded in the *Anne* books, as of course they should be.

Anne does much more with her imagination than just write. By imagining how other people feel, she can love them, and sometimes help them. A case in point is when she and Diana startle Diana's aunt by jumping on her bed in the middle of the night, having no idea the fierce old lady is in it. Bravely Anne goes to apologise (Diana is too scared) and Aunt Josephine severely tells her she has no idea what it is like to be jumped on. 'I don't *know*, but I can imagine,' Anne exclaims. But having empathised with Aunt Josephine, she wants her to follow suit.

'Have you any imagination, Miss Barry? If you have, just put yourself in our place. We didn't know there was anybody in that bed and you nearly scared us to death. It was simply awful the way we felt. And then we couldn't sleep in the spare room after being promised. I suppose you are used to sleeping in spare rooms. But just imagine what you would feel like if you were a little orphan girl who had never had such an honour.'

Aunt Josephine melts. She forgives the girls and admits that her imagination has got rusty from lack of use. As their unlikely friendship blossoms, Anne helps her get it back in working order.

She changes Marilla too. At the start of the novel Marilla is stern, tart and repressed, her body all angles, her hair all pins, her experience narrow, her conscience rigid, her every move dictated by duty. She has been in love, long ago, but she has long since closed off her heart. It is hard for Anne to understand a woman who seems her polar opposite, but she keeps trying. She makes her laugh (so heartily that Matthew is amazed), shows her the beauty around her and keeps loving her, even when she's met by embarrassed, brusque responses. Eventually Marilla becomes 'mellow'. She starts to appreciate Anne's imagination; when she finds herself overwhelmed by love for her, she wishes she had more of an imagination too because although she can hug her, she 'would have given much . . . to have possessed Anne's power of putting her feelings into words'. Now, I find this so moving that I could almost argue that Marilla is the novel's heroine. She shows it's never too late to learn to love again. She shows her brother she loves him before (*sob!*) he dies. And now she's learned to love, she can't stop. She invites her widowed best friend to move in with her (to avoid arguments, they each have their own kitchen!) and she even adopts two more orphans.

When Montgomery wrote this, she had left her teaching job to come back home and look after her widowed grandmother. Her grandparents had brought her up, but they never mellowed. Anne sacrifices a scholarship to look after Marilla too, but only for a year. Montgomery stayed on, and after she got engaged to a minister, at the grand old age of 32, she kept the engagement secret and didn't marry until her grandmother had died and she was no longer needed. So *Anne of Green Gables* is wish-fulfilment. But knowing that doesn't dent the power of Montgomery's argument about the power of imagination. And if this was fiction, I would fulfil some wishes too. I would rewrite the past so that my grandfather found comfort and consolation. I might even cast myself as the heroine who found the right thing to do or say to make him feel better. I wouldn't, if this were fiction, admit he didn't, and I didn't. (Later, much later, I did write a play about a girl who asks why her mother – to distance it enough to free me up to write, I made it her mother – is so sad and is told she left her heart in Baghdad. Being very brave and very young, she takes this literally, and flies to Baghdad on a magic carpet to find her mother's heart and make her smile again. The play, *Operation Magic Carpet*, has a happy ending.)

Montgomery's diary records that she wanted to write optimistically, to keep the shadows of her life out of her work, but in fact the *Anne* books take in mean-spiritedness, sickness, death, financial collapse, blindness, grief, unrequited love, thwarted passion, hatred, cruelty and much, much more, and they are better for it; the darkness makes the happiness seem earned. Even now I cry my eyes out when Anne gets puffed sleeves. And I can't contain myself when she gets together with Gilbert Blythe.

Oh, Gilbert. He was the first fictional boy I truly fell for. Three years older, he's in the same class as Anne because he's been off school looking after his sick father. Diana warns that 'he's aw'fly handsome . . . And he teases the girls something terrible. He just torments our lives out.' Oh to be tormented by Gilbert!

He has roguish hazel eyes and a teasing smile and he likes pinning girls' braids to their chairs. But when he calls Anne 'carrots' (not knowing that red hair is her *greatest* affliction; as great an affliction as my failure to go blonde), she cracks a slate over his gorgeous head. No amount of apologies will melt her heart. She takes a whole book to forgive him, and two more to consent to becoming more than his friend. But they do eventually marry. For me, growing up among a lot of arranged marriages, it was a revelation that you could marry a man who was also a friend – and that a man might want a woman who was his intellectual equal; in the years when they are enemies, rivalry with Gilbert spurs Anne on to work harder than ever at school, and they're always battling to be top of their class. I was already starting to feel that boys were supposed to be clever and girls were supposed to be pretty, so I found this deeply reassuring. And I liked the way that while some of their other schoolfriends thought Anne was odd, with her head always in the clouds and her funny way of expressing herself, Gilbert seemed to really understand her. So dreamy misfits *could* find people to understand them.

I was less happy about how long it took for Anne to realise Gilbert was The One. This is another bit of wrong imagination that she has to grow out of. Her dream man is dark, inscrutable and called something like Bertram de Vere or Perceval Dalrymple. Men like this are thin on the ground in rural Canada. She gets five proposals of marriage, each more ludicrous and disillusioning than the last. Then Gilbert proposes – and Anne says no! He goes white, and Anne shudders at the pain in his eyes. But she doesn't realise she's made a mistake. Instead she blames reality for failing to live up to her imagination: 'There was nothing romantic about this. Must proposals be either grotesque or – horrible?'

Then she meets him. The hero she's dreamed of. Even as a

child I was dubious about Royal Gardner. Anne can call him 'Roy' all she likes, but his name is Royal, and that's only one of the reasons he's wrong. But for pages and pages, she thinks he's Mr Right. They go out for two whole years, until at last he proposes, spouting stock phrases, and finally Anne realises he's a vacant clothes horse. After that, she is glad to have her damaging illusions stripped away. And when Gilbert tells her he dreams 'of a home with a hearth-fire in it, a cat and a dog, the footsteps of friends – and YOU!', she finally knows this is true romance, and says yes.

After this deliciously frustrating delay – *and* a prolonged engagement – it's a let-down when they become what Bridget Jones would rightly call 'smug marrieds'. They're too perfect to be believable. This confused me then, and now it massively disappoints me. Anne and Gilbert are so winning when they're young, yet they grow up bland and unsympathetic. I'm sad to find out that Montgomery couldn't write a convincing happy marriage because she didn't have one. Having waited five years to be able to marry, she became a celebrity author, so the idea of becoming a minister's wife was not so enticing. Especially as her husband resented her success. Duty made her go through with it, and made her stay when she found that her husband suffered from debilitating bouts of 'religious melancholia'; for months at a time he would be convinced he was going to hell. What with that, three difficult pregnancies, the death of one child, her eldest son's hooliganism, and the endless unpaid pastoral duties required of a minister's wife, it's astonishing that Montgomery managed to lock her door every morning for two hours to write. When her husband was really unwell, she put up a screen in a corner of their bedroom and wrote behind that. Whatever happened, she never stopped writing.

But Anne does. Why?

It's wounding to see Montgomery become almost *snide* about Anne's writing in the sequels. I cringe when Diana enters one of Anne's stories in a competition sponsored by a baking powder company: to make it eligible, she blithely inserts some lines about Rollings Reliable baking powder. Anne is mortified to see her baby mutilated but, being a good friend, she forgives Diana and even manages to thank her. Then, I took from this the message that a writer shouldn't be too precious about her writing, but now it leaves a bad taste in my mouth. Montgomery makes it clear that Anne's story, 'Averil's Atonement', is the worst kind of teenage writing – romantic, untruthful and ill-informed. It seems unfair to damn her juvenilia. Anne is learning her craft, and working hard at it. And while Gilbert cheers her up by saying the prize money will come in handy, I wish he had a little sympathy for her. He doesn't seem to understand why she's upset, nor does he seem very supportive of her writing.

Once they're married, Anne turns her back on writing. She meets an old sailor full of fantastic yarns just waiting to be turned into a novel, and instead of writing it herself, she passes the material on. To a *male* writer. She says her writing is 'fanciful . . . fairylike . . . pretty', and that the sailor needs a writer who is 'a master of vigorous yet subtle style, a keen psychologist, a born humourist and a born tragedian'. Because *Montgomery* is all these things, this feels like heavy irony. If it's a joke, it's a joke at the expense of her readers. And it demeans Anne.

It gets worse; when an old rival asks if she's still writing, Anne replies, 'I'm writing living epistles now', by which she means her children. This line is frequently and admiringly quoted on biblical motherhood blogs which advocate women's giving up work to bring up their children. Montgomery, who was managing to write while being a mother and much more, seems to lose interest in her heroine in the later books. In *Anne's House of Dreams*, sullen beauty Leslie Moore steals the limelight. Like Montgomery, she is chained in marriage to a man who has lost his mind, and she is so torn up with envy and bitterness that she can't be happy until she goes through the brave, painful process of admitting her feelings and learning to love. Compared to her, the older Anne just seems drab. She's barely there in the last novel, *Rilla of Ingleside* – her lisping, unambitious daughter has become the central heroine, while Anne is referred to, *in the narration*, as 'Mrs Blythe'. As if that was where she was going all along. As if all eight books have been charting her journey from waif to wife.

It's the same story with *Little Women*.

Having found Anne, I was thrilled to find another writer-heroine. Jo March was fabulously rebellious too, and she had such flair. But I was confused by the end of *Good Wives*, where Jo marries a portly, bearded German professor nearly twice her age, and gives up her literary dreams to run a school.

What a betrayal! Even now when I think about writing, I think of Jo holed up in her attic, in her 'scribbling suit', her hair tucked into a special hat she could wipe her leaky pen on, ready to 'fall into a vortex'. When she's writing, Jo doesn't care about anything or want anything; she's happy with her characters, who are as real to her as friends. Louisa May Alcott made writing sound *fun.* She gave me words to describe the feeling of getting utterly absorbed in an imaginary world, really feeling I was travelling in time and space, and making something on the page.

Jo is a misfit too, not because she's too dreamy but because she wants to be a boy. I liked Jo's style. She's not pretty but she's dashing. When the sisters put on plays, she takes the male roles, in old boots and a slashed doublet, and wielding a foil. Inspired by Jo, I would sometimes borrow my brother's clothes. And Jo taught me that whatever I later heard to the contrary from *When Harry Met Sally*, men and women *can* be friends. I wanted to have male friends too, and especially I wanted one like the Marches' handsome, musical neighbour, Laurie, who calls Jo a 'good fellow' and never treats her like a girl. And why should he, when she's so plucky? What other heroine would raise money for her sick father by *selling her hair*? (Her radical haircut, of course, makes her even more of a tomboy icon.)

From Jo I learned how to read a good book: in a garret, armed with 'half a dozen russets' ready to 'weep a little weep'. So when I come to read *Little Women* now, I stock up on chocolate and hot milk, and I am mostly reading through hot tears. But I don't *like* it.

It's unbelievably preachy. Every page is rammed with endless, intrusive moralising. I never loved Marmee droning on about *The Pilgrim's Progress* but I honestly had no idea that *Little*

Women was so clogged up with homilies. It's like a lightly fictionalised Victorian ladies' conduct book – perhaps not surprising as it was written in 1868, but I am surprised. Because I never realised before that in *Little Women*, each March sister is tamed, one by one, apart from Beth, who doesn't need taming because she is a personality-free doormat. Which apparently is the ideal.

It makes me angry. I start simmering just a few pages in when the March girls get a letter from their father, who is away serving as an army chaplain in the Civil War, saying he hopes they will 'conquer themselves so beautifully, that when I come back to them I may be fonder and prouder than ever of my little women'. His daughters set out to fight their faults. Meg is a tiny bit vain. She lets her friends doll her up for a ball, and is punished when she overhears gossip about herself. No more pretty dresses for Meg. It's pretty harsh – even Anne Shirley gets puffed sleeves! – and poor Meg wasn't interested in much except dresses, so that's her spirit quenched.

Jo's problem is temper. When her youngest sister Amy spitefully burns the manuscript she's been writing for years, Amy, who is a charmed child, gets a mild telling-off. The next day, Jo goes skating with lovely Laurie and Amy tags along. Jo is still so angry that she doesn't look after her properly, and Amy falls through thin ice and nearly dies. She *doesn't* die. Amy always lands on her feet. But Jo is destroyed. Amy *could* have died, and it would have been Jo's punishment for temper. Because in *Little Women*'s skewed moral universe, burning your sister's life's work is bad, but being angry about it is tantamount to murder.

Then comes the most annoying bit. Marmee tells Jo she has

a temper too, but she's learned to hide it. Her husband trained her to suppress her anger by putting his finger to his lips every time she flared up. One day, she hopes to control her temper so much that she won't even feel it. Jo ends this heart-to-heart hoping she too can learn 'the sweetness of self-denial and self-control'; I end it thinking if I ever marry a man who stops me expressing myself, I'll be out the door. When Mr March finally returns, he nauseatingly praises Jo for being 'a young lady who pins her collar straight, laces her boots neatly, and neither whistles, talks slang, nor lies on the rug as she used to do. Her face is rather thin and pale just now, with watching and anxiety; but . . . it has grown gentler, and her voice is lower; she doesn't bounce, but moves quietly . . . I rather miss my wild girl; but if I get a strong, helpful, tender-hearted woman in her place, I shall feel quite satisfied.'

This is particularly repellent because Jo has changed only because she's been through hell, nursing Beth through scarlet fever while her parents are both away. That's why Jo looks thin, pale and anxious. Mr March prefers his daughter when she's traumatised than when she's healthy, whistling, bouncing and wild.

The perfect 'little woman' is Beth. She is pathologically shy. She finds school too alarming so she's educated at home. She's even scared of birthdays. What a wet blanket. And Alcott signals early, a bit wildly, that Beth is doomed: 'There are many Beths in the world,' she writes, 'shy and quiet, sitting in corners till needed, and living for others so cheerfully that no one sees the sacrifices till the little cricket on the hearth stops chirping, and the sweet, sunshiny presence vanishes, leaving silence and shadow behind.' Beth likes playing the piano (so long as no one is listening), but everything else she likes is tinged with sacrifice – like sewing for other people, and setting up a 'hospital for infirm dolls', her sister's ugly, broken cast-offs.

When Beth does have fun, it goes horribly wrong. The girls are forever slogging their guts out doing chores, studying, earning money to contribute to the family finances *and* constant charity work, so they jump at the chance of a week off. Little do they know that Marmee is actually trying to teach them the consequences of all play and no work. To really ram the message home, she retires to bed and gives their servant the day off too, without telling them. Beth finds her canary 'dead in the cage with his little claws pathetically extended, as if imploring the food for want of which he had died'. It's very troubling and Victorian. Beth must surely have assumed that their servant would feed the canary, or Marmee would, as she's sanctioned this holiday. She has no way of knowing that both are out of action. It seems a very harsh punishment for such a tiny lapse from duty. And Marmee does not come out of it well. Why doesn't *she* feed the bird? Why is teaching her daughter a lesson more important than saving the life of the canary?

There are questions to be asked about Beth's death too. It's never clear why she dies – scarlet fever makes her weak, but then years go by before her slow death. And why is she so resigned? Why does she say to Jo, 'it never was intended I should live long' and 'I couldn't seem to imagine myself anything but stupid little Beth, trotting about at home, of no use anywhere but there.' Why 'stupid'? Why 'of no use'? Beth has worked harder than any of them, always helping in the kitchen or sewing for the poor, until, poignantly, her needle gets too heavy.

In their vast, iconoclastic tome, *The Madwoman in the Attic*, feminist critics Sandra Gilbert and Susan Gubar (they wrote together – so sisterly!) call Beth's death a 'prolonged suicide' that illustrates 'the terrible cost of feminine submission'. This may be overwrought, but I see what they mean; when she's ill, Beth is 'cherished like a household saint in its shrine' and afterwards, the Marches preserve her empty chair, her work basket and her beatific picture; and she talked so little anyway that she's as present as she ever was. They probably imagine her happy in some heaven of zither-playing angels and misshapen dolls.

While Meg's not allowed to be pretty, Jo's not allowed to be angry and Beth's not allowed to rest, Amy gets off scot-free. She's a selfish minx, and always gets what she wants. Because she's ladylike and keen to please, their rich aunt takes her to Europe instead of prickly Jo. There she pragmatically abandons her creative ambitions and decides she'll be a patron of the arts instead. She promptly attracts an embarrassment of rich suitors. You'd think this would make her a pariah to the self-denying Marches. But when she coolly writes home saying she's going to marry money, does Mr March send a stern letter? Does Marmee start firing copies of *The Pilgrim's Progress* across the Atlantic? No. Apparently they don't mind Amy being a simpering little gold-digger. When her conscience pricks her, she does nobly reject one wealthy admirer, but then she marries Laurie, who is even richer!

Then, this made me grind my teeth in rage. But now I'm treacherously thinking I might learn something from Amy. She knows what she wants and how to get it. She's pretty, but she works at it. She is the mistress of playing hard to get. When Laurie runs into her in Europe he's so mesmerised, he's practically stammering to find out where she learned to look so stylish. She casually says she's used to making the best of herself, and that she knows how to make cheap flowers look good. Which makes Laurie admire her resourcefulness as well as her style.

Still, Alcott doesn't let Amy seal the deal until she's been broken down. After Beth's death, Laurie finds Amy sad, homesick and grieving. Like a replay of the scene where Mr March praises Jo for being ladylike when actually she's worn to shreds, Laurie falls for Amy's 'womanly pain and patience'. The men of *Little Women* like women better when they're weak. Worse, this storyline makes Beth merely instrumental to her sisters' personal growth.

The other infuriating thing is that Laurie's supposed to marry Jo. I found it very hard, then, to hear Jo turn him down, saying he should find a lovely, accomplished girl to be the mistress of his house. Why can't he marry Jo and have *fun* in his house? They could slide down banisters and sprawl in front of the fire and call each other 'good fellow' and go boating and skating all day long. The line is that Laurie's still too much of a boy for Jo. And maybe she's too complex for him. But why can't Alcott just make him grow up and become good enough for her? Especially as poor Jo is dreading becoming 'a literary spinster, with a pen for a spouse, a family of stories for children, and twenty years hence a morsel of fame'. This doesn't sound so bad. It sounds better, anyway, than hooking up with Professor Bhaer, who makes her stop writing.

When she first meets Bhaer, Jo is writing sensation fiction – the schlocky, melodramatic thrillers beloved of so many Victorian women (and often written by them, too), where passion trumps propriety and no plot twist is too unlikely, no emotion too extreme. Jo's writing helps support her family, but Bhaer doesn't care. He tells her that good young girls shouldn't read, let alone write, such trash. And so she burns her work. In the 1994 film, which tries to square *Little Women* with feminism (Susan Sarandon's Marmee rails against corsets, Winona Ryder's Jo wants the vote), Bhaer is played by a rugged, sexy Gabriel Byrne who isn't nearly so stern. Quizzically, he asks if she's really fascinated by lunatics and vampires (sensation fiction staples), but then immediately apologises for being critical, advises her to write from her heart, and inspires her to write *Little Women.* Alcott's Bhaer is not so twinkly. For me the saddest bit of *Little Women*, much sadder than Beth's sentimental deathbed scene, is when Alcott tells us that 'Jo corked up her inkstand'.

Alcott *didn't* cork up her inkstand. Again, I wonder why she wrote an author avatar and sold her short.

Alcott's publishers were partly to blame: they pressured her to marry off the Marches. But they also made *Little Women* happen. Alcott had been bashing out sensation fiction for years and didn't want to write a book for girls. She claimed she never liked girls, or knew any, apart from her sisters. So when she got the commission, she based the book on them. She was stunned when it made her name. Its vast success warped the sequels. Alcott wrote to a friend that 'Jo should have remained a literary spinster but so many enthusiastic young ladies wrote to me clamorously demanding that she should marry Laurie or somebody, that I didn't dare to refuse and out of perversity went and made a funny match for her.'

Now I can see how conflicted she must have been about it. In *Good Wives*, just after Jo has been doomily predicting that she'll always be a spinster, Alcott strikingly breaks convention to address her readers directly: 'Don't laugh at the spinsters, dear girls, for often very tender, tragic romances are hidden away in the hearts that beat so quietly under the sober gowns.' She goes on to insist that 'Even the sad, sour sisters should be kindly dealt with, because they have missed the sweetest part of life.' Heartbreakingly, she implores 'Gentlemen, which means boys, be courteous to the old maids . . .' She wrote this at 35, a spinster herself. Maybe she felt sad and sour. And maybe that's why she gave Jo the kind of husband she might have liked for herself: Professor Bhaer, pushing 40, gentle, freethinking and clever, could have been a perfect match for Alcott. And even though he's too old for Jo (who is ten years younger than her creator, at only 25), Alcott does her best to make him not *too* perverse and funny a match; I love the scene where he proposes, adorably, ineptly, laden with parcels, hampered by his comical accent, in a storm, and just like in *Four Weddings and a Funeral*, they're so in love they don't notice the rain. However, it is infuriating that Jo immediately promises she'll stick to a woman's sphere from now on, that she uses her inheritance to set up a school where Bhaer will teach and she'll be matron, and, gallingly, only boys will be admitted. And she doesn't write a word through all of *Little Men*.

Alcott never stuck to a woman's sphere. In real life, she, not her father, joined the Civil War; when she was 30, she travelled five hundred miles to become an army nurse and caught typhoid that nearly killed her. Mr March annoys me even more now I know that he monopolises the heroism that, if she was really going to write autobiographically, Alcott should have given to Jo. I didn't know that years later, when Alcott was dying of mercury poisoning, from the medicine she'd taken for typhoid, she decided to give Jo the happy ending she deserved.

As a child, I never got as far as *Jo's Boys*. I wasn't interested in boys, and I'd found *Little Men* depressing. But now I wish I'd ploughed on. *Jo's Boys* is not a wonderful book, but it's the book where Alcott took her gloves off and wrote what she wanted.

Jo starts *Jo's Boys* bursting with pride because her school's one female pupil is studying medicine – and when a boy tries it on, Jo indignantly declares, 'That girl's career shall not be hampered by a foolish boy's fancy'. So much for women sticking to their sphere. This Jo has had a feminist awakening, and remembers the feisty girl she used to be. She reads to her sewing circle from the very latest feminist books – I particularly like the sound of Mrs Duffy's *No Sex in Education* and Mrs Woolson's *Dress Reform*, both of which were real books Alcott was taking the opportunity to champion. She even spells out that they are 'excellent books wise women write for their sisters, now that they are waking up and asking: "What shall we do?"'

And then Alcott plays her trump card. She reveals that Jo has written *Little Women*! She's become a hit writer, and Bhaer is now so supportive that Jo calls him a thoughtful angel. It's a brilliant last-minute save. But it is *very* last minute. Most readers miss it. I certainly did. But I'm glad to have found it now, and glad that Alcott did her best for her heroine in the end.

Montgomery also wanted to go back on her decisions about Anne. So in 1923 she created a new heroine, who was basically a rewrite of Anne. Emily Byrd Starr is another orphan and writer, and she also wins over her guardians and marries her childhood sweetheart. But where Anne is articulate and winsome, Emily is watchful and fierce. Montgomery raided her diaries for material and even gave Emily 'the flash', her private word for imagination. The *Emily* trilogy was written by the flash's uncanny light. The prose is elated, kinetic. The *Anne* books came slowly and non-chronologically but Montgomery wrote the *Emily* trilogy fast and in order. They're so raw and vivid, they make their predecessors feel sentimental and sepia. Montgomery also gave Emily an antagonist – and based him on her own envious, embittered husband.

Dean Priest is a relative who saves Emily's life the first time they meet, and immediately spoils the moment by saying that now he's saved her life, he owns it. To add to the creepiness, he's 36 and she's twelve. Montgomery builds to a scene that is almost the inverse of the one where Anne has to swallow down her disappointment when her story is turned into a baking powder advert. Diana is the wrong person to read Anne's story because she's kind and clueless; but Dean is the wrong person to read Emily's novel because he is a toxic critic, a false friend. His killer

line – 'How could you write a real story? You've never *lived*' –
makes Emily burn her manuscript. Blinded by her tears, she trips
and falls down the stairs and, soon after, agrees to marry Dean.
Thankfully, she does break free of him. And he confesses that
he thought her novel was brilliant, and only lied because he
wanted her all to himself. He was jealous of her writing.
Although Emily finds love in the end, that's not the point of
the story. Her journey is towards learning to put her writing
first. Montgomery evidently wrote the *Emily* books as a sort of
letter to her younger self. They are full of exhortations to keep
writing, and so much writing advice that they almost form a
writer's primer. She makes writing seem heroic – even claiming,
in a very forgivable bit of wish-fulfilment, that the 'violet
shadows [under Emily's eyes] always seemed darker and more
alluring after Emily had sat up to some unholy . . . hour
completing a story'.

As I started copying out my poems and sending them off to
competitions, and dreaming of seeing them in print, it might
have been good to have Emily's example of toughness and
endurance. But I'm not sure she would have eclipsed Anne.
Because I don't think writing is heroic, in itself. And anyway,
the biggest thing Anne did for me was not to show me I wanted
to be a writer but to make me think that imagination, instead
of being a flaw, might be my best hope. The grown-ups around
me might be bewildered, struggling and uncertain, but although
I didn't have to look after them, I could at least try to understand them.

I'd need to – because I was growing up too. Everything seemed
to be happening very fast. When I started my period at nine,

my mother said 'Now you can have babies!' She didn't mean immediately, but still, that *now*! I started to realise that when bold, clever, creative girls like Anne and Jo became women, something happened. They became less themselves. This was a worry because I would soon be a woman myself.

3

LIZZY BENNET

At twelve, I had my bat mitzvah (in ruched fuchsia, and black lace that I thought was totally like something Madonna might wear) and became officially a woman. We saved a tier of the cake, installing it in our second freezer, where it took up a whole shelf (this was one of the reasons we needed two freezers), ready to be eaten at my wedding. If I wasn't going to poison the guests, I'd have to marry young.

My grandmother had had an arranged marriage at eighteen – she met my grandfather for the first time at their own engagement party. He was exactly twice her age. For their honeymoon, they took a train to Istanbul. She came back pregnant. There is a picture of her taken soon after, sharing a hammock with her mother, grandmother, great-grandmother and, incredibly, her great-great-grandmother. Five generations on the one hammock (six, if you count the baby she was carrying). At 45 she had her first grandchild: me. My mother had married for love, at all of 22. She met my father at the Iraqi Jewish social club in London. He had been here for ten years, in business with his brother, importing and exporting everything from fabric to novelty telephones. When they were going out, they would go to Heathrow to watch the planes come in. One evening, driving round and round the airport, he proposed. For their honeymoon, they went to Disney World.

In the late 1980s, as I turned twelve and started wondering how I might get to be a bride myself one day, my community was turning in on itself. Terrified of assimilating and losing ourselves, we clung to tradition. We went from warm, noisy and loving to just plain claustrophobic. I was lost in a maze of codes and values and strictures. And all because I was a girl. When my brother had his bar mitzvah, we didn't save the cake. At parties, men and women sat separately; the men talked business and politics, while the women talked children, food and scandal. At Hebrew school, where once we'd all sung 'We All Live in a House in Golders Green' (to the tune of 'Yellow Submarine') and 'Puff the Kosher Dragon' (in which Puff learns that Jewish dragons don't eat meat that comes from little piggies with their dirty, dirty feet), the boys were now studying fascinating, abstruse Talmud, while we girls learned each festival via its cakes. We baked honeycake for Rosh Hashana, *hamantaschen* for Purim, macaroons for Pesach. One day we left the creamy Shavuot cheesecakes to cool while we went off to learn about the purity laws. We returned to find nothing but crumbs. The boys had eaten the cakes. As we washed up the empty tins, I wondered why no one else was angry.

It was a different story at my school, in the City, where lessons took place to the din of drilling as shiny new skyscrapers shot up around us. We were encouraged to become businesswomen – sharp shouldered, scarlet lipped. In one drama class, we improvised a play about suffragette Emily Wilding Davison throwing herself in front of the King's horse (I played the horse).

At home, my grandmother told me about her mother being taken out of school at fourteen because reading was spoiling her eyes and men seldom make passes at girls who wear glasses. It was confusing. Sometimes the pressure of The Cake would get to me and I'd fantasise about tiptoeing down in the middle of the night, opening the freezer door and letting it defrost.

So while my friends were reading Judy Blume, Jane Austen felt more relevant to my life, and *Pride and Prejudice* was my new favourite book. Like me, the five Bennet sisters were under pressure to marry. Jane was too sweet, Mary too priggish, Kitty too air-headed, Lydia too flirtatious, but I loved Lizzy. I loved her for her muddy petticoats, her irreverence and her big heart. But mostly I loved her defiance of convention. Her cake in the freezer, her ticking clock, is the fact that the Bennets' home is entailed to Mr Collins and will go to him when Mr Bennet dies. So when Mr Collins shows up, wanting to marry her, of course the family all want her to rescue them from the horrid fate of losing their home.

I thought Jane had it easy. She conveniently falls for the man her mother wants for her, wealthy Mr Bingley. But Lizzy can't stand Mr Collins, and nor could I. He is so unctuous, so objectionable in every way that I practically cheered when I first read the scene where he proposes and Lizzy turns him down. It's particularly satisfying because he's so vain that he can't believe a woman would ever reject him, so she has to really *squish* him. It's incredibly brave of her to do it when the stakes are so high. I was sure her parents would be furious. But she's lucky. Her mother screeches and blusters and threatens, but her father supports her.

My first attempt to resist society didn't go so well. I was going to my first henna party – where a bride has henna put on her hands (a fertility ritual inspired by the crashingly obvious symbolism of dry, green henna going soft and red when it is moist). My mother had zipped me into a party dress and spent an hour blow-drying my hair poker-straight and now she wanted to sew salt into the hem of my dress. But I refused.

She always sewed salt into my dresses to ward off the Evil Eye, which we believed was a freewheeling spirit that could possess anyone. It was activated by jealousy. So if someone envied you, the Evil Eye could turn their gaze into a curse. You could ward it off by saying 'seven' a lot, by wearing the blue Evil Eye symbol (which was both obvious and *rude* as it implied you thought your friends might be possessed) or by wearing a symbol of a hand or a foot (ditto). Or you could discreetly carry salt. My mother saved sachets of salt from plane trips and restaurants. That day she had one marked 'British Airways', she had her seam ripper, needle and thread. But I said no. It was superstition, I said. Cool, rational Lizzy would never allow her mother to sew salt into her clothes. I kept saying no, all the way to the party.

At midnight, all the girls were given long candles and we made a circle around the bride. The women were belly-dancing, laughing, ululating, and jamming balls of dark, gooey, glittered henna on the bride's fingers. Her hands shimmered. And then I saw a flame. I realised it was coming from my head. I smelled burning. I saw flames lick and loop through my hair, and started getting hotter – then someone chucked champagne over me, someone else chucked orange juice, and I was wet, sticky, drowned in Bucks Fizz, clutching a clot of singed hair as big as my fist. So much for fighting tradition.

I do still carry salt – on first dates, to stressful meetings; and on opening nights, if the stage manager's amenable (or not looking), I even sprinkle salt on the stage to protect my play from whatever spooky magic might seep out of the audience's eyes. I know Lizzy would laugh at me, but on my first attempt at resisting convention, my hair caught fire. If the same had happened to her when she refused Mr Collins, would she have been able to do it again?

Because she does. I told myself that if Mr Darcy proposed to me, I too would muster the courage to say no. Of course I would. I hated him for saying at the ball that Lizzy is 'tolerable, but not handsome enough'. Ouch! Chubby and awkward, I knew all about being a wallflower. My bat mitzvah, and all the parties I went to, were as ordered as Regency balls, with the dizzying circles of the Israeli hora giving way to Arabic music for the women to belly-dance to, the men relegated to the sidelines to clap or wave handkerchiefs, and finally the disco, where it was fatal not to have a boy to dance with. I often didn't.

Mr Darcy doesn't just insult Lizzy and refuse to dance with her (even though there is a shortage of men at the ball!). He does worse. He separates Mr Bingley from Jane. And then Lizzy finds out he stole fun, dashing Mr Wickham's inheritance, which means Mr Wickham is now too poor to marry Lizzy even though they get on so well. I thought Mr Darcy was rude, pompous and a villain. But I still thought Lizzy was brave to refuse his proposal. Because he's also fabulously rich, and this is her second proposal, and she's not getting any younger. Yet she still says no. It's magnificent. Then, I sneered at Lizzy's friend Charlotte who jumped into marriage with slimy Mr

Collins. I thought Charlotte was a weak, wrong-headed fool, but her acquiescence depressed me too. Would I really have to marry whoever asked me? And if not, would I end up like Jane, pining for a man who had vanished? Or would I get bitter like Lizzy, sniping that 'Stupid men are the only ones worth knowing, after all'?

I was so relieved when it all came right. Yes, Lydia gets a raw deal when Mr Wickham (not so fun and dashing after all) seduces her into an elopement. But Jane gets Mr Bingley, Lizzy gets Mr Darcy, their younger sisters start to blossom, and Mr and Mrs Bennet agree – possibly for the first time ever – that this is all good news.

Lizzy gave me hope that I could find a husband my family liked as much as I did. The crucial thing was not to give in, like Charlotte, and marry any old man. And not to be blinded by charm like Lydia; Austen makes it clear that their marriage is unhappy. I didn't want to be as passive as Jane, who only ends up with Mr Bingley because Mr Darcy engineers it. But if I could be like Lizzy, if I could stay strong, hold my nerve, say no to anyone I didn't like, maybe I could find my own Mr Darcy, square my parents' expectations with my own and make my own kind of marriage.

Ideally I wanted someone just like Mr Darcy. I'm ashamed to admit that I had started reading books not just for the heroines I wanted to be, but for the heroes I wanted to be *with*. Bumbling Mr Bingley didn't appeal at all, but Mr Darcy did.

It wasn't his 'fine, tall person' that captured my heart, nor his 'handsome features'. It was his candour. I'd started to think that being a woman was about deceit – you straightened your curls, you wore clothes that made you look thinner, you used blusher to define your cheekbones, you never, *ever* told a boy you liked him, you played games. But at the same time, my friends and I wanted to be true to ourselves, not like the girls we called 'plastics', who fake-laughed and talked behind our backs and wore eyeliner to school. So when Mr Darcy told Lizzy 'We neither of us perform to strangers', I underlined it so hard the pen went through the page. I longed for someone I could be honest with, who understood the real me. And I thought Lizzy's judgement on Pemberley ('She had never seen a place . . . where natural beauty had been so little counteracted by an awkward taste') said a lot about its owner too. Mr Darcy isn't trying to be anything he's not. And neither is Lizzy. And that's why they work.

I didn't know yet who the real me was, so I wanted someone who could help me find out. And Mr Darcy really does this for Lizzy. I shivered when I read the chapter where Lizzy realises she's been wrong about him, that she has been blinded by prejudice into being cruel. 'Till this moment,' she says, 'I never knew myself.' I wanted to learn what she learns: how to unflinchingly dissect her own behaviour, question her judgements and strive to do better – and to do it without being a goody-goody. Lizzy learns, but she doesn't become sanctimonious about it. And if Mr Darcy helps her overcome her prejudice, she helps him right back, getting him to confront his pride. I loved the idea of a marriage of equals.

Mr Darcy had other, more minor, attractions. As he falls for Lizzy, he starts thinking she's pretty. His love makes her beautiful. He's a good friend too. He wants the best for Mr Bingley, and when he realises he's got it wrong, he rushes to correct it. He's willing to learn – Gilbert Blythe seemed to know everything all along, not to have a journey of his own, but Mr Darcy really changes. When Lizzy rejects him, he shows what kind of man he is by the way he responds. He isn't sceptical and angry and rude like Mr Collins. He takes Lizzy's criticisms on board and tries hard to be nicer to her, which is amazingly unresentful, as she's just rejected him. He also saves her family's reputation; rejection doesn't make him bitter. And he doesn't stop loving Lizzy because she's said no to him. He still cares about her and wants to help her. He is doing his best to change into the kind of man she might want, but he isn't hoping for a reward for saving Lydia's reputation; he's doing it because it's the right thing to do. And he's so good in a crisis! When Lizzy tells him Lydia has run away he says how sorry he is then he heads straight for London and quickly sorts things out with the minimum of fuss. That's a hero.

The best thing about Mr Darcy was that he said his ideal woman had to have done 'extensive reading'. Reading might spoil my eyes, as my grandmother warned me it would, but Mr Darcy showed it wouldn't stop me finding a husband. A gorgeous, intelligent husband, in fact, because real men liked bookish girls. It said so in *Pride and Prejudice*.

But there were perils to loving Mr Darcy. I wish I could tell my twelve-year-old self that not all arrogant men are secretly lovely; some are just arrogant. I had a crush on the coolest boy at Hebrew school. He smouldered (as far as a twelve-year-old could), he was funny, and universally adored. Painfully shy and clumsy, I didn't stand a chance. We danced twice. And once he gave me his jacket to hold. It was a baseball jacket, like the boys wore in *Grease*. I still remember how warm and puffy it felt, and tracing the appliquéd letter with my finger, feeling proud to have been singled out. Later I went to his bar mitzvah – by then, I was taller than him, and he had to stand on an apple crate to reach the bimah, but I fancied him so much that I found this touching. At the party I was sitting at a table full of girls. And he'd kissed them all! Every last one. All I'd been allowed to do was hold his jacket. My heart was grazed.

Lizzy gets over being rejected by Mr Wickham by seeking out fresh air and big landscapes; 'What are young men to rocks and mountains?' she asks. What indeed. But this wasn't an option for me. My family weren't big on the outdoors. We kept the windows shut. Our thermostat was set to Baghdad-hot. So I mostly stayed in my room, playing Strawberry Switchblade's 'Since Yesterday' over and over, singing along to the world-weary chorus about how life's joys are past. Then I realised Lizzy doesn't just cope by climbing mountains; she also uses her wit.

If I'd been in Lizzy's place, hearing Mr Darcy say I wasn't pretty enough to dance with, I would have crumpled. But Lizzy turns it into a funny story to tell her friends, venting her outrage by ridiculing Mr Darcy. Lizzy's wit is her survival strategy. So much so that her aunt says, when Jane's heart is broken, 'It had better have happened to *you*, Lizzy; you would have laughed yourself out of it sooner.'

Lizzy's laughter isn't mindless. Lydia can barely write her elopement letter because she's in such hysterics, but Lizzy's sense of humour never makes her too dizzy to think straight. She's as particular about her wit as Anne Shirley is about her imagination. She tells Mr Darcy firmly that she is no cruel satirist: 'I hope I never ridicule what is wise and good. Follies and nonsense, whims and inconsistencies, *do* divert me, I own, and I laugh at them whenever I can.' When I first read *Pride and Prejudice*, I was more like Mr Darcy than like Lizzy: I was achingly earnest.

But I didn't want to be. At secondary school, I'd made new friends, including Emma, who is not unlike Lizzy. Emma's father is a Syrian Muslim, and her mother's family are Austrian Jews, but she wore her cultural difference lightly. It didn't restrict her, or define her. She seemed to do whatever she wanted. I was amazed when she dyed her hair (all by herself, without asking permission), anxious when it went pink (not as bad as Anne Shirley's green, maybe, but still!) and in awe of the way she styled it out. She seemed so free. And so unworried. She gave me perspective. I started to see that there was life beyond the goldfish bowl of my community. And then as now, like the best best friends, she never just automatically agrees with me. If I need her to hate someone, she does get stuck in but if she thinks I'm wrong, she'll say so. (Hence, among other things, this book.) Our friendship was cemented, one lunchtime, when we were eating our sandwiches (ham for her, cheese for me) and I told her about my hair catching fire. Emma said that it was nothing more sinister than bad luck. I could flout convention again and my hair probably *wouldn't* catch fire. She even pointed out that the product required to straighten my hair may have been a contributing factor. 'Hairspray's flammable,' she said. It made me laugh. Not just because it was funny but because it was true. Maybe I didn't have to worry so much any more. And maybe I would be able to do what I wanted.

Lizzy does the same for Mr Darcy. He has been serious for so long that his friends don't dare to tease him. When Lizzy hears this, she takes it as a challenge. 'Mr Darcy is not to be laughed at!' she exclaims, pretending to be shocked. In fact, she turns him into a figure of fun. She regrets this when she finds out she's been wrong about him. 'It is such a spur to one's genius, such an opening for wit, to have a dislike of that kind,' she admits to Jane. But even though she likes him better now, she's not going to stop laughing at him altogether. When they get engaged, Lizzy still reflects that he has yet 'to learn to be laughed at', and she's the woman to teach him. By the end, she's obviously succeeded, because their marriage is 'lively, sportive' and full of 'liberties'. When I was twelve, it sounded a blast.

It still does. *Pride and Prejudice* is bliss to reread. Lizzy's as funny as she ever was. And so is Austen. It's such a relief, after smiling through my tears at Sara Crewe, Anne Shirley and the Marches with their constant attempts to be good girls, to be laughing out loud at Lizzy, who is just trying to be herself. She's a truly light-hearted heroine, arch, playful and bold. Austen famously said that when it came to heroines, 'pictures of perfection . . . make me sick and wicked', and compared to *Little Women* with its endless Victorian pieties, *Pride and Prejudice*, written 55 years earlier, seems positively amoral. Lizzy is sisterly too, and strong. And is there a better proto-feminist line than 'Do not consider me now as an elegant female, but as a rational creature speaking the truth from her heart'? (Delivered, of course, to Mr Collins, who seems as vile to me now as he ever did.)

Lizzy's freedom seems even more idiosyncratic and extra-ordinary in her closed, difficult world. When Jane is taken ill and Lizzy walks to Netherfield 'crossing field after field at a quick pace, jumping over stiles and springing over puddles with impatient activity', she's as unladylike as Jo March. And there's a new reason to lust after Mr Darcy; I'd forgotten that this is when he really starts to fall for her. While Miss Bingley and Mrs Hurst start bitching about Lizzy as soon as she leaves the room (they are *such* plastics), pronouncing her hair 'so untidy, so blowsy!', her petticoat 'six inches deep in mud . . . and the gown which had been let down to hide it not doing its office', and finding her generally wild and undecorous, and Mr Bingley sticks up for Lizzy, saying she's a good sister to race over to see Jane, Mr Darcy frankly admires her glowing skin and the way the exercise has brightened her eyes. He isn't bothered about decorum and it's not Lizzy's kindness that interests him; he just thinks she's gorgeous. The scene is thrillingly charged – Lizzy radiant in her filthy clothes, with her messy hair and flushed face, and Mr Darcy thinking she looks much better than when she was pretty and pristine in her ball gown. And though I wouldn't ever want to be without Colin Firth's Mr Darcy emerging from that lake in the BBC adaptation, it's worth noting that *this* very sexy scene is actually in the book.

But Lizzy is not as free as she seems. Mr Bennet used to make me laugh. I used to think he and Lizzy were similar. But now, I almost dislike him. He hates society's pressures too, but he's a man and he has his library to retreat to. No one can push him into marriage, or take away his home. He made a mistake in marrying a pretty girl who turned out to be shrill and silly, but instead of making the best of the situation and treating Mrs Bennet kindly, he cultivates a sardonic distance. He laughs at his wife and encourages his children to join in the fun. But it isn't fun. In fact, his sense of humour is snarky and nihilistic; he thinks 'we live, but to make sport for our neighbours, and laugh at them in our turn'. No, we don't. Lizzy knows that her father is improper, even reprehensible, to treat his wife this way. And even if she wanted to live like him, she couldn't. She can't marry whoever she likes, and she can't not marry. I skipped a lot of the talk about money when I first read *Pride and Prejudice*, but now I see it is crucial; even Mr Bennet's supporting Lizzy's decision to reject Mr Collins feels a bit irresponsible. It's all very well to jeer at Mr Collins, but if one of the girls doesn't marry him, they'll all be forced out of their home when Mr Bennet dies.

Now, I feel sorry for Mrs Bennet, mocked by her husband and doing her best to marry off her five daughters, none of whom appreciate her efforts. I don't *like* her exactly, but I do see why she's so desperate to hustle her girls into matrimony. Even a marriage as unsatisfying as hers is better than poverty and homelessness.

I'm still shocked when Charlotte agrees to marry Mr Collins, but I don't entirely agree with Lizzy that Charlotte 'cannot have a proper way of thinking'. Austen is so deft here. Charlotte has always said she's 'not romantic' and she is going into marriage with her eyes open. When Lizzy visits her in her married home, she notices that she's arranged the house so she has as little contact as possible with her husband. She's particularly impressed by one of Charlotte's contrivances: 'The room in which the ladies sat was backwards. Elizabeth had at first rather wondered that Charlotte should not prefer the dining-parlour for common use; it was a better sized room, and had a more pleasant aspect;

but she soon saw that her friend had an excellent reason for what she did, for Mr Collins would undoubtedly have been much less in his own apartment, had they sat in one equally lively; and she gave Charlotte credit for the arrangement.' The prose is a little laboured here because Austen is deliberately slowing us down, making us see how a woman can make the best of a bad marriage. In most adaptations, Charlotte is venal or stupid. But in the book, she is practical. And Lizzy is enough of a realist to learn to admire her for it.

I'm glad I didn't see all this when I was twelve. I didn't need to learn to compromise. I was doing that already. I longed to be bolder. I desperately wanted to shrug off my shyness and worries and I thought Lizzy would help me. But now, one sentence in particular in *Pride and Prejudice* jumps out at me. It comes after Lydia has eloped, and everyone is expecting her to be humble and contrite, but 'Lydia was Lydia still; untamed, unabashed, wild, noisy, and fearless.' And Lizzy is 'disgusted'. But why? It's not so long since she fancied Mr Wickham herself. And having failed to warn Lydia that he was bad news, she surely shares some of the blame for Lydia's elopement. I like Lizzy better when she is pert and valiant than when she is primly advocating restraint. And at twelve, maybe I would have been better off trying to be less tame, less abashed; trying to be wilder, noisier and more fearless – more, in fact, like Lydia.

Though I didn't spot Lizzy's primness at the time, it wasn't long before I started to find Austen's novels a bit, well, tame and the rest. Charlotte Brontë called *Pride and Prejudice* 'a carefully fenced, highly cultivated garden, with neat borders and delicate flowers; but no glance of a bright, vivid physiognomy, no open country, no fresh air, no blue hill, no bonny beck', and I thought she had a point. And I didn't like the story of Austen writing in a corner of the drawing room, hiding her work when she heard someone coming. In my community we were scared of gossip, wary of being looked at because of the Evil Eye, and we didn't raise our heads above the parapet for fear of anti-Semitism. And I was sick of it. It would be years before I fully tried to live *Wuthering Heights* but I had read it and it was working its way into my heart. Would Emily Brontë have hidden her manuscript when people came to visit? Not likely. My favourite story about Emily was the one where she gets bitten by a rabid dog and races home, bursts into the kitchen, seizes a hot iron and presses it to her skin to cauterise the wound. Such courage! How could Austen compete? Plus there was the problem of *Mansfield Park*. I didn't know I'd end up making a life in the theatre, but I knew I hated humourless Fanny Price.

In *The Madwoman in the Attic,* Gilbert and Gubar say that Austen shows 'how to inhabit a small space with grace and intelligence', and that was absolutely what I got from *Pride and Prejudice*, and just what I needed, then. But later I started feeling that a battle was coming, a battle about what kind of woman I was going to be, and that laughter and irony would never win it. Lizzy wins the game of Regency society: she gets a desirable man, and she gets him on her terms. But I was starting to think I didn't want to win my community's game; I didn't even want to play it.

In Shakespeare's plays, which we were reading at school, all the heroines resisted their families and society to marry the men they wanted. They did it not by learning how to win the game, but by breaking the rules. The plays made me ask myself questions like whether, if it came to it, I would have the guts to go into a forest at night with the man I loved, like Hermia and Helena. When a schoolfriend took me to see *A Midsummer Night's Dream* in Regent's Park, I marvelled at their bravery, and kept some of the confetti the actors threw at the audience, tucking it into my copy of the play for luck. All that's left now is fine, sparkly dust.

Next came *Romeo and Juliet* and I thought Juliet even bolder – and so self-possessed! Lizzy says no to two marriage proposals, but Juliet, who is only thirteen, deceives her nurse, marries in secret, sleeps with Romeo, stands up to her parents, plots an escape . . . Even death doesn't faze her. And she's the brains of the operation (not that Romeo is exactly the brawn). And the scheme she cooks up with Friar Laurence, to fake her own death and then run off with Romeo, so nearly works! It was such a proactive subversion of all those Sleeping Beauty stories too. Juliet is going into a death-like state, and she hopes Romeo will be there to kiss her when she wakes up. But she's not swooning because of a curse or a spindle or flax; she's calculatedly (and bravely) taking a drug that will enable her to start a new life. And she's not waiting for any prince to wake her; she'll wake up when the drug wears off. It'll be nice if Romeo is there, of course, but if not she'll surely have the sangfroid to wait for him, so they can escape. She's not trying to become queen bee in Verona either; she wants to elope, to make a whole new life for herself. Her elopement is grown-up, thought-through and desperate, a world away from Lydia's whimsical joke. The only thing I didn't like about Juliet was her choice of man. Romeo was so boring, so inept (forever getting them into danger because he's not careful enough to avoid it), and so fickle; he's only just been saying he's in love with Rosaline, so how can his love for Juliet be trusted? Love poleaxes him, but it empowers her. If I could have an ounce of Juliet's courage, I'd be all right, I thought. And maybe instead of marrying a man my parents liked, I could even consider the radical possibility of marrying someone they didn't like.

Romeo and Juliet made Lizzy's victory feel almost too easy, almost a trick. I'd started to feel Lizzy's happy ending could only happen in a novel with an author on hand to remove the obstacles just in time for the big finish. Without knowing it, I had stumbled upon the marriage plot – the classic narrative where mistakes and misunderstandings are resolved so the couple can marry at the end – and I didn't like it. I was frustrated by the artifice, and by the idea that all a heroine had to do was get a man to marry her.

Unless of course she died. All the heroines' stories seemed to end in death or marriage. It seemed I could either be Lizzy, guided into Mr Darcy's arms by Austen, or Juliet, killed off by Shakespeare, and all for a man who isn't even worthy of her. I blamed Shakespeare for not giving her someone better, and for not saving her life. But not as much as I blamed Charles Dickens for letting Nancy Sykes get bludgeoned in *Oliver Twist*. I wondered, not for the last time, if these heroines were tragic because their authors were men. Dickens, in his readings of *Oliver Twist*, would try to make as many women faint as he could: when I heard that I spent a whole vengeful summer rewriting the book so that girls came out top. My heroine, Olivia Twist, became the queen of the Victorian underworld.

Belatedly, I decided to try to drag my reading into the twentieth century to catch up with what my friends were reading, and to see if I could find a heroine who didn't marry or die. I should have had a lot in common with Margaret Simon, the sweet heroine of Blume's 1970 novel, *Are You There God? It's Me, Margaret.* She is half-Jewish, twelve and as anxious about growing up as she is excited. Like her, I prayed to God for things that probably weren't strictly within His remit, like getting boys to dance with me. But she was desperate for her period to start and I was three years into mine and, unlike her, I didn't want puberty to go any faster.

My mother had just inducted me into perhaps the greatest mystery of Iraqi Jewish womanhood: depilation. The first time, she sugared my legs with a tub of sugar I was sure had come from Baghdad. This seems improbable, but then my family did bring some unlikely things when they left – including two rolling pins – and the sugar was certainly vintage. My mother heated it up and spread it over my legs. After a lot of ripping cotton and not a little pain, I emerged from the bathroom, splotchy, reeking of caramel and determined never to do it again – even if I grew fur like a bear and had to live in a cave. If this was womanhood, I didn't want it.

Compared to Margaret, I was painfully naïve. I would never have dreamed of kissing a boy at a party. When once, at a bar mitzvah, I stumbled into a room where a game of spin the bottle was in progress, I fled. I definitely didn't do any of the things in *Forever,* the Blume book everyone else was reading. The one with all the sex in. The one without God in the title. I was still a dutiful daughter. I confided in my diary that even if it made my friends hate me, I was *determined* not to have sex before marriage because 'that's just what I feel'. Like I said, I was an earnest child. And by the time I read *Are You There God? It's Me, Margaret*, my friends had already moved on to reading Jilly Cooper's *Riders* under their desks. Not me, though. *Riders* was a step too far. I was scared off by the cover, featuring a male hand on a woman's tight white breeches.

Now, curious about the girl I might have been if I hadn't been such a coward, I get hold of a copy. The cover image is the same as in 1987, and the blurb promises that *Riders* is the first, and steamiest, in her series which is called, incredibly, the Rutshire Chronicles. Not that I'd suspected Cooper of subtlety, but *still*. I make a cup of tea and get stuck in.

And I can't put it down. This despite groan-worthy puns, retro-sexism, far too much about horses, and a narrative that stretches out for 918 pages (*Pride and Prejudice* comes in under 300). When Cooper wants to be funny, she's hilarious. When a man strips prawns for his date, she asks 'Do you undress women as expertly?' and he replies, 'Far more expertly, and I don't pull their heads and legs off, either.' The heroines are bewitching and perpetually trolleyed (they're always on crash diets so a sniff of champagne goes straight to their heads), the men are cads, the horses are neurotic, and Cooper writes with such relish that you can't help but warm to her. My friends go wistful when I say what I'm reading. 'I've lost days of my life to Jilly,' they say. 'I've lost weeks.' 'I've lost *years*.'

Discovering Cooper is like joining a cult. There's a drinking game where, as you read her novels, you drink a shot every time a dog or horse dies dramatically, toast the Queen whenever a member of the royal family shows up, have 'a teeny tiny sip' every time you're pained by a pun. The game ends when you're drunk enough to read on without shame. In another writer, the repetition would be boring, but there's a comforting familiarity to the returning tropes: women splashing scent over themselves, the adjective 'bootfaced', wild garlic as a metonym for spring.

The sex is alarming. There's so much of it. When I get to the infamous scene where Rupert Campbell-Black comes like a train, I laugh. And a lot of the sex is played for laughs. When Helen meets Rupert, he's hunting foxes and she's with the hunt saboteurs (caricatured as fat, vegetarian and filthy), and he gets her attention when *he pulls a horn from her cleavage*. If I had been brave enough to read *Riders* when all my friends did, the humour might have made the sex less intimidating. And maybe Helen would have been my heroine. She loves books, especially *Romeo and Juliet*. She even uses the same library as me. In the reading room, quiet and dense with erudition, like me, sometimes, she feels as trapped as a bluebottle slamming into a window. And then *this* happens:

'Have you any books on copulation?' said a voice.

'I'm afraid I don't work here,' said Helen. Then she started violently, for there, tanned and gloriously unacademic, stood Rupert.

If I thought there was any danger of that happening, I'd go to the library more.

But while Austen's humour mirrors Lizzy's, Cooper seems to turn on Helen. She becomes a house-proud neurotic and finds it hard to relax with Rupert, who is flagrantly unfaithful, and who wants her to be as liberated as he is, and even have orgies. He calls her frigid, 'a frozen chicken. Fucking you is like stuffing sausage meat into a broiler. I'm always frightened I'll discover the giblets.' This is even worse than Mr Darcy saying Lizzy is 'tolerable'. Poor Helen does eventually achieve sexual pleasure, but it doesn't last. And she never finishes writing her book. I'm not sure she really *can* be my heroine.

The only feminist in the book is a walking cliché, who doesn't wear bras or deodorant, or eat meat, or shave her legs or armpits, names her daughter Germaine and Kate (after Greer and Millett) and pursues Rupert with nymphomaniac lust. Then there's Janey, who is messy, uninhibited and actually has a job, but is too bitchy and brainless to like. The only heroine who has a proper journey is Fen, who goes from freckled pony-mad child to Olympic showjumping star, but I don't think even as a tween I would have identified with her; she isn't always very kind. I do like Fen's sister Tory, though. She secretly eats cornflakes with double cream in bed (such decadence!), hates being a debutante, and wishes she lived in the seventeenth century and could be painted by Rubens and considered beautiful. She coolly buys a horse for the man she fancies – plucky, brooding Jake, who takes her to bed and finds her 'splendid' without her clothes on. Susie Orbach would be so proud.

But Cooper doesn't let Tory stay splendid. She winds up sad, patient and dull. Jake cheats on her, she poisons herself, and then it's supposedly all OK because depression and attempted suicide have made her thin. What more could a woman want? Body-fascist Jake visits her in hospital where 'she'd lost so much weight since he'd seen her. Her face, still flushed from the belladonna, gave an illusion of health. Long lashes swept her hollowed cheeks. All Jake could think was how beautiful she looked.' So, to keep your husband, you have to starve and poison yourself?

If I had read it back then, *Riders* would have scared me witless. And I'm not sure I would have found it useful to learn what a certain kind of man likes a woman to order for lunch (pâté, steak, green salad); that I should live on grapefruit in the run-up to a date, so I'd be thin and liable to get tipsy and lascivious on one glass of wine, and use freesias to mask the telltale spinster smell of cat. I don't know what I'd have made of the information about how to ice my nipples for a lover, and that when running away from my psychotic showjumping husband with my sexy (but still showjumping) lover, I should make sure to pack hot tongs, heated rollers and hairdryer. On the whole, I'm glad I waited to read my first bonkbuster. (Having started, though, I can't stop. Racing for a train to rehearse a play in Edinburgh, I pick up *Rivals*, and read it all the way to Scotland.)

If I were twelve or thirteen now, I'd be reading the *Twilight* novels. Now, attracted by the book's covers with their campy Gothic script and the image of a blood-red apple in ice-white hands, I tear through all four of them. Vampires fascinate me, but the heroines of vampire novels aren't usually much to get excited about. They seem to waft around a lot, in white. At first Stephenie Meyer seems to have bucked the trend with

Bella Swan. She's angry all the time, hates being the new girl in her dad's rain-sodden town, and falls for the boy I would totally have gone for too. Edward is Darcy-esque in his disdain. But Bella is accident-prone and he keeps on rescuing her, so she knows he must love her! And he does. He loves her so much he can't trust himself to be near her. Not because he might ruin her in the old sense, but because he's a vampire, and if he kissed her he wouldn't be able to stop, and she'd soon be undead too. So she's the one wanting to be kissed and he's the one saying no – an interesting reversal – and Meyer has a lot of fun making Edward a nice vampire, whose family have sworn off human blood. His father's even a doctor, in a hospital, around blood all day long and nobly never drinking a drop. Meyer is very keen on praising his amazing restraint. But as the novels go on, it turns out this is because she's a practising Mormon and she's got an agenda that gets more and more intrusive. Miserably I slog through the last book, the vexing *Breaking Dawn*, bombarded by pro-abstinence, pro-marriage, anti-abortion messages, and some very reactionary views on men and women. Bella is constantly cleaning and cooking for men, and wanting to be rescued and ravished. Edward gets controlling and stalkerish, and Meyer calls this *caring*. He's allowed to patronise Bella because he's a century older. Bella sometimes stands her ground, but only on issues Meyer is interested in. So when her half-vampire baby is drinking her blood from the inside (*ughhhhh*), she goes to the brink of death rather than terminate the pregnancy. By the end she's so abject and smug that I don't care what happens to her or her ridiculously named child, Renesmee.

It's when I find myself wondering what Lizzy would make of *Twilight*, and hoping she'd agree with me, that I realise she's never truly been supplanted in my affections. And a little research in the library (sadly unmolested by sexy showjumpers) makes me see that I misjudged Austen. The reason she preserved her anonymity and hid her writing was that she was shy. Like Mr Darcy, she was awkward, self-conscious and reserved. *She* was the one who didn't perform to strangers.

While she was writing the first draft of *Pride and Prejudice*, she was in love with the charming Irish lawyer Tom Lefroy. That's why the book is so effervescently optimistic. Like the Bennets, the Lefroys had had five daughters, and no money. But their situation was even more extreme because Tom Lefroy's father lived in hope of inheriting from a rich uncle, who he feared would cut him off if he knew he had married a woman without a dowry – unless they had a son. So the Lefroy parents spent ten years married secretly, trying for sons, and only having daughters, before finally they produced Tom.

He needed a rich wife. But that didn't stop Austen from hoping he'd defy his family and choose her. And maybe they did consider doing something rash. His parents had married secretly, after all. Austen's juvenilia is full of elopements. She and Tom Lefroy almost certainly never set off for Gretna Green, as Anne Hathaway does in *Becoming Jane*, but maybe it crossed her mind. Maybe she knew how it felt to be Lydia.

Much later, between writing the first draft of *Pride and Prejudice* at 20, and rewriting it when she was 37, Austen got two proposals, one from a man as rich as Darcy and the second from a perfectly respectable clergyman. She refused both men, even though she was in dire financial straits. I wonder if writing Lizzy gave her the guts to reject those two wrong proposals. I wonder if Lizzy made her brave.

4

SCARLETT O'HARA

The main thing I remember about Scarlett O'Hara is the measurement of her waist: a cool seventeen inches. When I first read *Gone With The Wind* at sixteen, I raided my mum's sewing box for a tape measure and checked. My waist was 26 inches – *nine* more than Scarlett's, and we were the same age! I started skipping breakfast and feeding my lunch to the ducks. I ate whole sticks of celery because of the negative calorie myth (that eating it burned more calories than were contained in the celery itself). Later, I would decide dieting was for retro-sexists and give up celery in disgust; later still, I would discover it's actually quite delicious. Then, I didn't know a seventeen-inch waist was impossible without luck, starvation and aggressive corsetry; I didn't know even tiny Vivien Leigh's waist was 22 inches. The damage was done. I had started worrying about what I looked like.

Luckily, I also got something better from Scarlett: the strength to fight for independence. On any normal index of teenage rebellion, I would score very low. I was a good girl. But I was the only girl I knew in my community who wanted to go away to university rather than stay at home and go to university in London, so I became, if not quite a rebel, a pioneer. I started having secrets. I started writing my diary in Cyrillic so my parents couldn't read it. (The joke's on me because now I can barely read it. My Russian teacher was right when she said Cyrillic looks like chestnut hedges.) I got angry.

Recently I was watching *The Taming of the Shrew* and when the shrew, Kate, raged across the stage, her father shrugged and threw up his hands as if to say 'What can I do with such a daughter?' This was how I felt at sixteen, except that no Petruchio turned up to tame me or save me (depending on how you interpret the play). My parents wanted me to get a degree, but they wanted me to do it at home, where they could keep an eye on me, and send me on dates with their friends' sons. They didn't want me to risk my safety, health and reputation to go God-knew-where, and study God-knew-what. For my sixteenth birthday my mother filled my bedroom with pink helium balloons. I woke in a thicket of ribbons topped with fluorescent clouds. Her own sixteenth had not been sweet, so she was determined mine would be fantastic. And it was. But I also felt trapped by her expectations.

Scarlett O'Hara has similar issues with her mother. Ellen O'Hara is a saint, scented with lemon verbena, dressed in silk, always doing good deeds. Her back never touches the back of any chair, and like all great ladies she knows how to carry her burden while retaining her charm. But Scarlett has always 'found the road to ladyhood hard'. I passionately identified with this, and felt vindicated when later in the book Margaret Mitchell reveals that Ellen too chafed at ladyhood, and only got married after her first love, her wild, flashing-eyed cousin, was killed. When she dies calling out his name, poor Scarlett has no idea who he is, or how much she and her mother might have had in common, if only she'd known.

I found Ellen a cold fish, with her austere beauty, strict morals and 'utter lack of humour'. But I understood Scarlett wanting to live up to her, deciding, like some hoop-skirted St Augustine, that she *will* be a great lady, one day . . . but not yet.

I also read the book for tips on how to flirt. Scarlett 'smiled when she spoke, consciously deepening her dimple and fluttering her bristly black lashes as swiftly as butterflies' wings'. I tried this in the mirror but it didn't work, so I went back to putting toothpaste on my spots as advised by *Just Seventeen*. Perhaps this would get me closer to a relationship with someone like Ashley Wilkes, the object of Scarlett's flirtation.

Ashley seemed a noble figure, then, but he's not. He's a milquetoast. Even Scarlett admits to herself that his conversation bores her. Then, I foolishly thought he wouldn't bore *me*, because unlike Scarlett, I liked talking about books. In truth, I was less like Scarlett and more like her rival, Melanie, who talks Thackeray with the boys – which makes Scarlett giggle and scoff that she's a bluestocking. Scarlett later turns out to be dazzling at maths and business, but she's careful to hide her cleverness from men. And she has no time for literature; she's much too hard-nosed.

There were other things I had in common with Melanie. She looks like 'a child masquerading in her mother's enormous hoop skirts' and I was, and am still, shy and self-conscious about dressing up. Melanie seeks and nurtures her female friends, but Scarlett pursues men and sees all women as enemies. I could never be that ruthless: I could never try to steal a man from someone else – but Scarlett does, brazenly declaring her love for Ashley and fully expecting him to break his engagement to Melanie for her. I would never have her confidence, or her gall. She's not even that mortified when she realises that someone has overheard the whole thing. And not just anyone; a man.

But what a man! Rhett Butler still makes me flutter. He's thirty-three, tall, swarthy and apparently almost too muscular to be a gentleman. He's got a scandalous past, he's surprisingly metrosexual (he adores fashion), and he's a darling with children. And may I just say here that I don't care that Clark Gable apparently had bad breath in the film. In fact, I don't even believe it. I might even have kissed him in *spite* of it. Because Clark/Rhett is a stubbly, six-foot, barrel-chested sex bomb – have you seen him banter with Claudette Colbert in the best screwball ever, *It Happened One Night*? Have you seen him crack into tiny pieces under Marilyn Monroe's tortured, luminous, lostness in *The Misfits*? (In which he did all his own horse stunts. At fifty-nine.) It's unsophisticated to conflate the actor with his role, but in this case, who can help it?

Rhett tells Scarlett straight out she's 'no lady'. He's like her *anti*-mother. Because not only does he not care that she's not ladylike, he likes her for it. He salutes her as 'a girl of rare spirit'. Scarlett flounces off: she doesn't want to be a girl of rare spirit, and she's not going to let anyone say she's not a lady. I *longed* for someone to call me a girl of rare spirit. I wanted to liberate myself. (Or, as I put it in a terrible poem I wrote at the time, my pink bedroom was a womb I would smash my way out of.) So I knew it was a dreadful mistake for Scarlett to do what she does next: she walks away from Rhett and coldly, out of spite, marries Melanie's boring brother Charles. This only makes her even less free, even more subject to her mother's strict code of behaviour. And within two months, Charles has been killed in the Civil War and she's a widow and not allowed to do anything. Rhett points out that the way the South treats widows is deeply unjust. He rails against women being immured in crêpe and forbidden enjoyment. Like a consciousness-raising Seventies feminist, he makes Scarlett question the rules of her society, tempts her into breaking them (by dancing!), and applauds her daring: 'Bravo! Now you are beginning to think for yourself instead of letting others think for you. That's the beginning of wisdom.'

Mitchell got her feminism from her mother, a suffragette who wrapped her baby daughter in a VOTES FOR WOMEN banner and took her to rallies. When, at six, Mitchell said she didn't want to go to school, her mother took her to see the derelict mansions just outside Atlanta, where impoverished former belles still lived like wraiths in the ruins, and warned her that one day her world might explode and only education would save her. Mitchell often said that *Gone With The Wind* is all about survival, but she didn't think it was education that helped people survive; she thought it was gumption. She felt that she was living in a world destroyed. There are many problems with the way she writes about the Old South – she perpetuates damaging myths about slavery and justifies the Ku Klux Klan as a tragic necessity – but she does write powerfully and honestly about being torn from your roots. Which was another reason *Gone With The Wind* was my new favourite book.

It had became clear that I would never go 'back' to Iraq. The 1990 Gulf War made Iraq front-page news. We watched it on

TV, late at night, all sitting on my parents' bed. They pointed out landmarks: 'That's Al Rashid street! That's the river!' It was the first time I'd seen Iraq moving and in colour. 'If the camera turns left, we'll see my school!' And then we realised we didn't want the camera to turn, because it was on a bomber plane, identifying targets, and if we saw the school it would be bombed. At first we thought that after the war Iraq would be safe to visit. We were wrong. And the more we saw footage of Baghdad, the more we became aware that the city my family knew had vanished. And of course things have only got worse since then. So I understood Ashley's nostalgia, his longing to go back in time.

Scarlett is the opposite of nostalgic. She's fighting to survive. She looks forward, not back. She resents her friends and family, she sees them as burdens, but she doesn't shirk. She doesn't let them starve. When the Yankees are coming and everyone flees Atlanta, she stays with Melanie who is too pregnant to move. She delivers the baby herself. Only then does she ask Rhett for help. He's so overcome by her bravery that, having promised/threatened to kiss her ('you need kissing badly . . . by someone who knows how') he finally does. Mitchell's overheated prose makes it clear he *absolutely* knows how. He even admits he loves her – but he's not going to fight at her side. He leaves her on the road to Tara and goes to join the losing Confederate army. He's not immune to nostalgia, and besides, he knows she can handle herself.

This is where Scarlett's struggle really begins – and her ladyhood only gets in the way. She's never been out in the sun without a hat or veil, never handled reins without gloves, she's always been clean and neat and protected, and now she's driving an old wagon, she's filthy and hungry, and she is responsible for keeping the others safe. She gets home to find her mother dead, her sisters ill, her father out of his mind and Tara pillaged by the Yankees, so when Mammy complains that Scarlett's blistered hands and sunburnt face are unladylike, she doesn't listen. She can't afford to.

You could tell the whole story of *Gone With The Wind* through Mitchell's descriptions of Scarlett's hands. They start out white and folded in her lap. Later, after she swears she will never be hungry again, Ashley calls them 'the most beautiful hands I know . . . because they are strong and every callus is a medal, Scarlett, every blister an award for bravery and unselfishness.' As she goes from spoilt belle to ruthless survivor, she finds her mother's advice increasingly irrelevant: 'Nothing, no nothing she taught me is of any help to me! What good will kindness do me now? What value is gentleness? Better that I'd learned to plough or chop cotton like a darky. Oh, Mother, you were wrong!' She does chop cotton, and work the fields. She even kills a Yankee soldier.

But though Scarlett commits the murder, it's only now that I notice how brave Melanie is in this scene. Weak from childbirth, she appears at the top of the stairs, in a ragged chemise, carrying a sabre. She can barely lift it, but wow! Even Scarlett grudgingly admits that Melanie may be soft on the surface but underneath she's steel. It's Melanie's idea to go through the dead man's pockets for money – the money that saves them from starving. And when Melanie covers up the murder, Scarlett frankly admires the cool way she lies under pressure.

Why did I miss Melanie's heroism? Why did I ever dislike a woman who talks books instead of batting her lashes? I think I was scared that I was too much like her. I didn't want to be long-suffering, or to love a man who's always flirting with someone else. Because, forget Scarlett being no lady, Ashley is no gentleman! Why does he tell Scarlett he cares for her but they're just too different? He's engaged. He shouldn't say he cares for her at all. Why does he keep taking Scarlett in his arms and kissing her when he's married and knows she loves him? Why does he bang on about honour when he's being dishonourable? And he's pathetic. He's so bad at farming and so hopeless at business that Scarlett is driven to try to sell herself to Rhett, even though she hates him for leaving her, just to get money to keep her many dependants alive.

As Scarlett heads for Atlanta, Mitchell doesn't mince her words. Scarlett is proposing to commit fornication, a mortal sin, and her crime is 'doubly prostitution' because she is in love with Ashley. Ashley, blind as ever, thinks Scarlett's being gallant. He doesn't see that she's having 'a complete moral collapse', in her dress made of curtains, laughing as though she doesn't have a care in the world, playing the belle she hasn't been for years. Her desperate act nearly succeeds, but she's betrayed by, of course, her hands. When Rhett sees that her hand is scarred, rough from work, sunburnt, freckled, the nails broken, palm calloused, thumb blistered, he spits, 'These are not the hands of a lady.' (The most direct result of reading *Gone With The Wind* again is that I have become more assiduous about using hand cream.)

After Rhett rejects her, the novel takes a really dark turn. Scarlett has to get money somehow so she steals her sister's rich beau. She's had to be so strong that she's lost herself and become hard and unfeeling. As I was fighting my parents for the right to leave home to go to university, I felt myself becoming hard too. I made myself stop feeling so I wouldn't see how much I was upsetting them. Like Scarlett, I thought some day I'd be nice again . . . but not yet.

Scarlett has to cope with the consequences of marrying Frank. Her sister now hates her but that's nothing compared to being tied in marriage to a man she doesn't like. Again. In *Little Women*, Jo sells her hair for the Civil War; Scarlett sells *herself*. It's chilling to see Frank reflecting on how much he likes her sitting on his knee and tweaking his beard and flirting and joking with him. It's repellent that she has to do this, let alone sleep with him. Maybe this is why her spirit is so crushed that she is genuinely shocked to find out she's better at business than Frank and most men. She finds it 'revolutionary'. And she gets a real kick out of making money. But when Frank gets killed, trying to lynch a man who's assaulted her, she tells Rhett she's glad her mother can't see who she's become: 'She didn't raise me to be mean.' I used to read this after arguments about leaving home, where I'd been shouty and bullish, and I'd feel sick.

But now I'm more surprised by what happens on the next page. Rhett proposes, saying it might be fun, but Scarlett says marriage is never fun. I used to be as fooled as anyone else by Scarlett's coquetry, but the sad fact is she's never enjoyed sex. Even Melanie is 'shyly happy' when she goes to bed with Ashley, but Scarlett thinks of sex as 'servitude to inexplicable male madness, unshared by females, a painful and embarrassing process that led inevitably to the still more painful process of childbirth'. Then Rhett kisses her again – yet more hot, purple prose – and she says yes. But she still thinks she's in love with Ashley.

Then, I sympathised. I was in love with Ashley too. But now

this is horrible to read. Scarlett has fun with Rhett, but she thinks it doesn't count because he's not Ashley. For pages and pages, they misunderstand each other, hurt each other, taunt each other, destroy each other, and you can't do anything to stop them.

And then there's the staircase scene. Some readers call it the rape scene. Rhett is drunk and hurt, and he wants to crush Scarlett's head between his hands, like a walnut (*vile* image) to stop her thinking about Ashley. He seizes her and carries her up the stairs. She screams. He kisses her savagely. They go to bed. In the morning she feels she's been used and hurt and humbled – and she's 'gloried in it'. In the film, Vivien Leigh wakes up purring with happiness. Did he rape her? Did she like it? She's been so strong all the time, and now, writes Mitchell, she's found Rhett is 'stronger than she, someone she could neither bully nor break, someone who was bullying and breaking her'. It's not easy reading for a feminist.

I don't know what happens when they get upstairs. I don't know if there is a moment when Scarlett consents. But I do know that Rhett's always trying to have a grown-up, honest, passionate, fun relationship with Scarlett and she can't see it because she's dreaming of Ashley. He wants them to be equals, intimates, to talk. He values her gumption and her mind. He wants her to stop hanging on to an infantile idea of true love as perpetual yearning and flirting and hiding your heart and playing hard to get to the end of time. (Just like in that awful book *The Rules* where they say you should keep playing games with your husband even after you're married, and for ever, because then he'll value you, and send you roses after sex. As if a few flowers would make up for a lifetime of having to lie about who you really are.) Before Rhett, Scarlett has never had fun with a man. And *she wakes up happy*. She's had fun with him, just like he promised. So I don't read it as rape.

It's also why I think the novel ends hopefully. Because Scarlett finally understands that Ashley does love Melanie, he's been keeping her, Scarlett, dangling, and *she* loves *Rhett*. As a teenager I thought the best love was unrequited, so I preferred Scarlett/Ashley to Scarlett/Rhett. The dream of love was fine, but I wasn't so ready for the real thing.

There was a time when, unable to see what a tool Ashley is, I thought impossible love was the best kind. But I hope I'm braver about love now, and I'm tempted to make a rule that any heroine who spends a whole novel in love with someone who can't or won't love her back is not truly a heroine. Because unrequited love is delusional, thankless, and boring. It's also a misuse of imagination – like Anne Shirley fancying all the wrong men before she learns what real romance is, Scarlett wastes so much energy fantasising about Ashley that she can't see him as he really is, and she completely misses Rhett's charms, which are *legion*.

Now I hope that, after the novel ends, Scarlett gets the love she's finally ready for and wins Rhett back. I bet she does, too. She vows to get him back the same way she vowed to never be hungry again – and she wasn't. And Rhett says his love's worn out but I don't believe love ever does wear out. Anyway, before he leaves, he *gives her a handkerchief.* Scarlett's mother told her, way back when, that she should never accept a handkerchief from a man; it would be far too intimate. But Rhett is always giving Scarlett handkerchiefs – and teasing her for never having her own. This last, intimate gift makes me think they will surely get back together. They must. Because you don't find true love very often. I know that now.

Mitchell always claimed Melanie was the book's true heroine. And Melanie *is* heroic, I realise. But I still don't want to *be* her. I wouldn't want to live such a narrow life – even if she is loved, and loving, and mostly happy. At sixteen it would have been fatal to be Melanie; it would have meant staying at home. I needed to leave. And Scarlett's courage, common sense and optimism helped me do it. I still say 'Tomorrow is another day!' to myself when things are hard. I still admire Scarlett's style: compare her curtain dress to the curtain dresses in *The Sound of Music* – Scarlett wins, hands down. And I still try to face my troubles with gumption.

Vivien Leigh's feverish, transcendent performance in the film is dazzling but it doesn't quite get across just how strong Scarlett is in the novel. She's one of the toughest heroines I know. But as I turned seventeen, strength wasn't quite enough. I wanted heroines who were self-aware too. That's how Scarlett, though not herself a feminist, inadvertently led me to feminism.

I first read *The Female Eunuch* in the school library, because its cover, with the limp, hollow skin of a female torso hanging off a clothes rail, was too racy for home. It took me several awestruck lunch breaks. Here was a writer who could marshal science, economics, maths, logic and autobiography to show how women were 'castrated' by the patriarchy. Germaine Greer said liberating ourselves would not be easy but it might be interesting. She challenged us to taste our menstrual blood; if it made us sick, we'd know we weren't emancipated. She claimed that Mary Quant had her pubic hair shaved into a heart shape by her adoring husband – a startling glimpse of what a feminist relation-ship might look like. She confidently said that many things I'd thought were immutable were just conditioning, that women were being sold a story that we could rip up and rewrite. Like Scarlett learning she could dance while in mourning, chop her own cotton, beat men at business and recognise another woman's strength, my eyes were opened.

From Greer, I learned that there was a stereotype of female beauty and I didn't have to conform to it – and that anyway, it might be fun and liberating to 'undress with éclat'. I learned to stop laughing at men's bad jokes. She said powerful women were using masculine methods while playing the feminine game, and I thought about Margaret Thatcher, still inexplicably prime minister, saying she owed nothing to what we still called 'women's lib'. Greer's analyses of pop culture made me see misogyny everywhere. And when she showed how housewives were isolated and mired in repetitive work (she was writing in 1970, but in my community, at the start of the Nineties, nothing had yet changed), I felt even more determined to get away.

Greer demolished my romantic fantasies: 'I cannot claim,' she admitted, 'to be fully emancipated from the dream that some enormous man, say six foot six, heavily shouldered and so forth to match, will crush me to his tweeds, look down into my eyes and leave the taste of heaven or the scorch of passion on my waiting lips. For three weeks I was married to him.' Now, this makes me laugh out loud. Luckily I am reading it at home and can laugh as noisily as I like.

I don't love every line of it. I wish Greer didn't imply that women bring domestic violence on themselves, and I wish she wasn't so peculiar about transsexuals. But it's brilliantly defiant, bracing polemic – and practical too. I don't mean the final, slightly unsatisfying chapter on 'Revolution' but her mischievous injunctions to women to try to be whole people, to love from fullness instead of from inadequacy, to be self-reliant and to hope that people will need our joy and strength.

After *The Female Eunuch*, I started powering through feminist novels, hoping to find a heroine more awake to the world than Scarlett. Postfeminism was just hitting its stride, but I didn't feel *post*; in my world, women stayed at home and men earned money. The fractious second-wavers made more sense to me. But their novels depressed me.

I thought if I had a name as fantastic as Isadora Wing, the heroine of Erica Jong's 1973 novel *Fear of Flying*, I could do *anything*. Isadora is 29, a writer and already on her second marriage, to a psychiatrist (the novel is stuffed with psychiatrists) but she wants out. She's been fooled by 'soupy longings' into marrying but now she longs for other things – to travel, to be alone, to think for herself, not always about another person. She's annoyed that no one told her that even if you loved your husband, sex eventually became 'bland as Velveeta cheese'. (On a trip to Florida that summer I bought Velveeta cheese to see what she meant – it really is astonishingly bland.) She wants a 'zipless fuck' – 'Zipless because when you came together zippers fell away like rose petals, underwear blew off in one breath like dandelion fluff. Tongues intertwined and turned liquid. Your whole soul flowed out through your tongue and into the mouth of your lover.' She tries to find it with another psychoanalyst, lumbered with the surname Goodlove, and they travel and she reminisces about her previous relationships. The smut scared me, the chapter titled 'Arabs and Other Animals' mightily offended me and the final chapter, 'A 19th Century Ending', annoyed me. Why does Isadora go back to her husband? Why not have a twentieth-century ending?

And what was the point, anyway, of liberation that was purely sexual? Predictably, Isadora's biggest fans are men. Like Henry Miller, who said the book would spark a revolution. Of course men love the idea of the zipless fuck.

I think I *envied* Isadora. She seemed liberated already, with her frustrated-artist mother urging her to write, and her analysts and her lovers, and everybody talking about books and sex all the time. She's madly self-aware, she sees herself as a heroine, and ruefully realises she's hamstrung by guilt. 'I feel guilty for writing poems when I should be cooking . . . Show me a woman who doesn't feel guilty and I'll show you a man'. Reading *Fear of Flying* now, I recognise how much I've internalised this voice – guilty, self-conscious, self-deprecating, capricious, extravagantly candid, struggling to be hopeful.

Now I'm more aware of how women flee in guilt and anxiety from their own pleasure, I've got a lot more time for Isadora. What a headlong, unblushing libertine she is. She's not tormented like the old adulteresses of fiction – and when Goodlove leaves, she doesn't throw herself under a train like Anna Karenina or poison herself like Madame Bovary. Instead, she tracks down her husband to a hotel and runs herself a bath. She looks at her body (including, because she has not lost her sense of humour, 'the Tampax string fishing the water like a Hemingway hero' – how Hemingway would have *hated* that line), and realises she no longer feels scared. Goodlove has been her Rhett. He's helped her be adventurous and brave and she's not going to stop now.

Mira Ward, the heroine of Marilyn French's novel *The Women's Room*, is even harder to like. The book came out four years after Jong's, in 1977, at the height of the Struggle, and it feels uncompromising and endless. Actually at 516 pages it is almost half as long as *Riders*, but instead of larks and frolics and frisky horses, French is committed to exposing the grinding tedium of being a 1950s housewife. I would still give the page where she describes Mira's cleaning routine to anyone who styles herself a 'domestic goddess'. *The Women's Room* shored up my determination never to have a traditional marriage.

It might seem odd that I was reading all these books about how to put down your dishcloth and leave your husband. I didn't have a husband. It was my mother's life I was trying to leave. I should have given her the books and got on with studying for my A levels. But as I was fighting for the right to leave home, it helped to have my choices reinforced. Later, I would be ready for postfeminist heroines like Fevvers, the loud, earthy high wire artiste in *Nights at the Circus*, six foot two in her stockings, with a mouth like a shark and wings (God, I love Angela Carter for literally *giving her heroine wings*. The *chutzpah* of it! The nerve!). Later still, I would fall for Virginia Woolf's shape-shifting hero(ine) Orlando. But then, I needed to read about women who struggled to evade the same fate I was struggling to evade. I wanted to learn how not to become a housewife and mother: it helped to read about women who had tried it and wished they hadn't. Watching Nora in Henrik Ibsen's *A Doll's House*, being patronised by her husband, forced to pretend to be a featherbrain and an angel, a lark and a squirrel, while all the time she'd saved his life, I thought nothing was as satisfying as her slamming the door to leave him at the end of the play.

Mira has already left her husband at the start of *The Women's Room* and is hiding in 'the ladies' room'. French never lets the story get in the way of the consciousness-raising, so Mira immediately notices someone's crossed out 'ladies' and written 'women's' instead. It's 1968 and Mira is 38, a student at Harvard, and my struggle to get to university is peanuts next to hers. We appraise Mira via a narrator who sounds much more cool. Mira hides in bathrooms, talks in a high, brittle voice, totters about on heels and sprays her hair till it's as stiff as a helmet. The narrator teaches literature in Maine and walks the beach in jeans splashed with paint from decorating her flat, an embroidered poncho a friend brought from Mexico and, in the winter, a heavy nylon jacket. People call her mad, but she doesn't care. She sounded free and fun to me. 'All of the women I know feel a little bit like outlaws,' she says. It made me want to be an outlaw too.

She goes back to chart Mira's journey from being 'an independent baby, fond of removing her clothes' to a repressed unhappy woman. Her mother tied her up to stop her stripping off, and 'It worked. Mira had trouble removing all her clothes on her wedding night.' Her mother is also firmly against Mira's crossing her legs at the knee, climbing trees with boys, playing tag, raising her voice, wearing more than three pieces of jewellery at a time, and mixing silver with gold. My mother was teaching me never to mix blue and black, or brown and black or brown and grey, and not to wear grey anyway before I was 40. Like Mira, I felt stifled.

Mira acquires a freethinking boyfriend, but he and his friends nearly gang-rape her. Defeated, she marries Norm, who is as boring as his name. He's also smug, and a bully. He won't teach her to drive. He says it's fine not to use condoms (he's a medical student!) then blames her for getting pregnant. Slowly, her identity is eroded. In a notorious paragraph, the narrator says it's easy 'to destroy a woman. You don't have to rape or kill her; you don't even have to beat her. You can just marry her.' Mira finds pregnancy hard, childbirth terrifying, housework a drag, and sex a chore. Her female friends live similar gruelling, endless soap-operatic lives. Even the narrator says she's bored with writing about domesticity – but it's a great strength of the novel that she doesn't stop.

The Women's Room made me respect the hard work of bringing up children and making a home that 'hummed and sparkled' the way Mira's did, the way my mother's did. It also made me sure I didn't want that. Reading it now, I look around my messy flat and feel like a slattern. I'd like my home to hum and sparkle, but I want other things more. Mira's clean house is her defence against the pain and chaos of her friends' lives. Their husbands beat them, betray them, ignore them, commit them to asylums. Mira thinks her trouble is nothing, in comparison; at least she's not banged up having ECT. But when Norm won't let her lend money to a friend of hers who is in need, she realises she's just as oppressed as her friends. By the way, the narrator knows it's unfair to call him 'Norm', and that she hasn't really given him a character, but she says he *has* no character. Or at least, his behaviour is incomprehensible to her because he's a man, and maybe that's the root of the problem.

The lack of understanding between the sexes is what makes *The Women's Room* pure tragedy. After Norm divorces Mira so he can marry his mistress, she presents him with a bill for her work during their marriage (including cooking, cleaning and childcare but also prostitution). She survives a suicide attempt, goes to Harvard, befriends empowered women and falls in love with a male feminist, but she *still* doesn't find happiness. Because her new boyfriend wants her to follow him round the world and have his babies too. In this novel, society is too broken for a feminist to be happy; the battle of the sexes always gets in the way. The toughest woman, Val, a woman given to pages and pages of clunky vitriol, goes mad after her strong, beautiful daughter is raped, and ends up killed in a hail of gunfire by police. There is almost no light in this novel. Mira's consciousness has been raised – but to what end?

For years I pushed *The Women's Room* on women I knew. I thought it told the unpalatable truth and we should all confront it. Then in my twenties, I got my book group to read it. We were all women, all feminists, but they didn't love it like I did. They found it too despairing, too bleak. They said the men were cardboard cut-outs and the politics were glib. Brought up in more liberated homes than me, they didn't understand why I was so moved by Mira overcoming her inhibitions or why I was so exhilarated by the revelation that Mira *is* the narrator: she has become the woman on the beach in the poncho, independent and free (if a little lonely). I didn't read it again for years, but coming back to it now, I don't know if it *is* too bleak. Now I've seen women I know get married to men who seem lovely but still think they can get away with barely contributing to housework or looking after their children. I don't think the double standard ever went away. Reading it now, it still feels hopeful that Mira has at least left behind her parents' house and Norm's house and has stopped hiding in the ladies' or even the women's room. French was surely playing on Virginia Woolf's *A Room of One's Own* with her title, and she gets Mira that room. Mira ends the novel able to enjoy her own company and earn her own living, walk on that beach, wear what she likes and tell her own story.

Which is more than Scarlett can do. She can't be alone; she needs admirers and haters, people around her she can use as her mirrors, to avoid having to look at and get to know herself. I was too late for those Seventies consciousness-raising groups where women went round the circle, telling their stories and being listened to. If I ever tried to take Scarlett to such a group, she'd be bored out of her mind and probably cause a riot, but sometimes I think she and Melanie and Greer and Isadora and Mira *are* my group, my circle. They helped me, anyway, see that part of being able to, as Nora Ephron so brilliantly put it, 'be the heroine of your life, not the victim' is not allowing anyone else to define you, which means coming up with your own definition. Which means knowing yourself. As Melanie does, and Scarlett doesn't: that's her sorrow.

Yet I feel that more heroines now are Scarletts than Melanies. Melanie's quieter virtues have got a bit lost, and many heroines now seem to be defined mainly by their strength. They're warriors, not worriers. They avenge abused women, like Lisbeth Salander in *The Girl with the Dragon Tattoo*, or hunt and kill like Katniss Everdeen in *The Hunger Games* (before she lets herself do more than survive, before she lets herself love and fight injustice and occasionally, just occasionally, be vulnerable). If she were writing *Gone With The Wind* now, Mitchell might make her heroine Grandma Fontaine, Scarlett's tough old neighbour who has no fear since, when she was young, she saw her house burned and her family scalped. 'I don't like hard females, barring myself,' she tells Scarlett. 'But I do like the way you meet things! . . . You take your fences cleanly, like a good hunter.' I would love to be told I take my fences cleanly like a good hunter. Yet I also like Grandma Fontaine's other bit of advice, that Scarlett should 'always save something to fear – even as you save something to love'; Scarlett only really becomes brave when she lets herself feel vulnerable, and allows herself to risk her heart.

In the seven seasons of *Buffy, the Vampire Slayer*, Joss Whedon (who became something of a feminist hero when he was asked why he writes strong female characters, and replied, 'Because you're still asking me that question') investigates how heroines can be strong but not heartless from every possible angle. Buffy is a tough, kickboxing superheroine, but that's not how she defeats the forces of evil. She believes that slayers are stronger if they know how to love. So in the final season, when she is offered more strength, at the cost of becoming more demonic and less human, she refuses. She wants to keep being able to rely on (and love) her lover, her mentor, her sister and her friends. And she gets more strength by breaking the rule, instituted long ago by men, that there can only ever be one slayer. She turns other girls and women into slayers: she shares her power. Watching the very moving final episode reminds me of Scarlett and makes me sad that she doesn't truly value Melanie until she's lost her; if she and Melanie had been a team, Scarlett might have been so much happier.

In *The Taming of the Shrew*, Kate chooses to be shrewish in a society that buys and sells women. And maybe she's lucky to find, in Petruchio, someone who, as Greer puts it (she got there way before me), 'is man enough to know what he wants and how to get it. He wants her spirit and her energy . . . and she rewards him with strong sexual love and fierce loyalty.' Kate stops rebelliously ramming her head against walls, becomes softer, more graceful, more open to joy; in her word, she becomes less *froward*. While I was trying to leave home, I argued vehemently with my parents, yelling and sulking and glowering about the house. Then my teachers suggested that I apply to Cambridge, and my parents agreed that if I got in there, it would be an exception: I could go. If not, I would stay in London. I settled down to work hard and see if I could make it. And with that battle over for the time being, I stopped having to be so froward, and I fell in love.

5

FRANNY GLASS

He was tall, dark and handsome but not inscrutable. He had very long eyelashes. He was amazingly clever. And he was not Iraqi; his family were Ashkenazi Jews. It wasn't much of a rebellion but he was thrillingly different.

Our first kiss was awkward – all clashing glasses and bumping chins. Our subsequent kisses were not much more abandoned. I was absurdly naïve for seventeen. We went for walks in Golders Hill Park, round the pergola and the petting zoo. We watched the flamingos. At parties we danced shyly, or talked in corners. We curled up on his parents' sofa and watched *Cinema Paradiso*. I drove us around, with my brand new licence. We had our first row in that car, in a storm, and I was so unhappy (and so melodramatic) that I couldn't tell the difference between my tears and the rain lashing the windscreen.

It was only meant to last three months. He was about to ace his A levels and go to Israel for a year of travelling, studying and picking oranges. But we fell in love. And anyway, I wasn't the kind of girl who could have a casual relationship, and he wasn't the kind of boy. We were both yearning for something bigger. It turned out he was mostly yearning for God.

Although his parents went to a much more liberal synagogue

than mine, he was moving towards Orthodox Judaism. He had stopped writing, driving and turning on lights on Shabbat. When we walked through north London on a Friday night, he knew the location of all the movement sensor lights and he'd guide me across the street and back again, to avoid turning them on. It was romantic. And kissing in the dark was easier than it had been in the light. I even liked it when he talked about God. Since Hebrew school, I'd been longing to talk Talmud with the boys, and this was my chance.

When he took off for Israel, the distance didn't matter. Having my first relationship was less scary at a distance. We were doing *Antony and Cleopatra* for A level and I thought Cleopatra, the greatest man-eating vamp in history, had it all wrong, ordering her women to bring her something to help her 'sleep out this great gap of time / My Antony is away.' Instead I knuckled down to an epistolary relationship modelled closely on Anne and Gilbert's in *Anne of Windy Willows*. Anne said it was impossible to write love letters with a scratchy pen so I got myself a fountain pen. I sprayed the letters with Chanel No. 5, and stuffed the envelopes with love poems (my own, cringeworthy efforts) and clumps of grass (which I thought he'd miss, out in the desert). We made each other mixtapes. There were dark moments – he sent me the entire text of Ecclesiastes ('all is vanity and vexation of spirit'), and I sent him a poem comparing myself to an empty eggshell – but mostly it was lovely. Soon I had a shoebox full of pale blue aerogrammes, the latest of which I would wear next to my heart (all right, in my bra). Long-distance love was a lot like unrequited love: he was two thousand miles away so our relationship consisted mainly of yearning for each other. Just like Scarlett and Ashley.

And when he wrote to me about his growing faith, I was fascinated. I felt connected to heroines who believed in something bigger than themselves: heroines like Nanda Grey, the nine-year-old protagonist of Antonia White's autobiographical 1933 novel *Frost in May*, whose complex feelings about faith informed all of mine.

At the start of the novel, Nanda's father, who has recently converted to Catholicism, taking his wife and daughter with him, is about to enrol Nanda at the Five Wounds convent school. On the horse-drawn bus to the convent, on a fog-shrouded road, they meet an old Irish woman who says it would be wonderful if Nanda became a nun. And although Nanda knows this would be an appropriate, poetically just sacrifice for the daughter of recent converts to make, she doesn't want to cut off her hair and live in a cell far away from home. The whole novel is powered by her attraction to faith and her terror of what it might ask of her.

She desperately wants to fit in with the cradle Catholics at Five Wounds who eat bread that's been dropped on the floor, dirt and all, as penance (and not even for any particular sins – just in general), sleep with their hair scraped into painful plaits and their hands crossed primly over their chests, put salt instead of sugar on their stewed fruit (to mortify the flesh) and talk knowledgeably about doctrine. She also wants the ecstasy of conviction. But she's often disappointed. At her first communion, as the wafer touches her tongue, she waits to feel Christ is actually present, in the flesh, inside her, but feels nothing. I sympathised. I'd hoped my bat mitzvah would make me feel certain and connected, but instead it had marked the start of teenage self-consciousness and confusion.

At least I wasn't a Catholic. I was petrified of the astringent, sarcastic nuns in *Frost in May*. They hate life outside the convent. They believe 'no character is any good in this world unless that will has been broken down completely . . . Broken and re-set in God's own way'. Nanda's (very slightly) rebellious nature dooms her. She doesn't do anything *so* bad. She starts writing a novel, all about shocking sinners, and of course she plans to redeem them spectacularly at the end. But a nun finds the manuscript and Nanda is expelled. Worse, her father says that 'if a young girl's mind is such a sink of filth and impurity, I wish to God that I had never had a daughter'. She bursts into hysterical tears, and the nuns tell her that now she's been broken, now she's humble, she'll become a good Catholic. Nanda accepts this. It's a dark, dark, ending.

I too thought God might want some kind of sacrifice. Or at least, I thought He wanted me to feel perpetually guilty. I still get angry when people say patronisingly how comforting it must be to believe in God. The God I sometimes believe in (I seesaw endlessly) is not a jolly old white-bearded man sitting on a cloud but an Old Testament scourge, jealous (He admits it Himself), opinionated, disapproving. My Hebrew teachers had given me the impression that our relaxed Orthodox synagogue where most people drove but parked around the corner and semi-pretended we walked, and where married women sometimes wore fascinators instead of hats, was not as good as an ultra-Orthodox synagogue. Like Nanda, I was half attracted, half repelled by the idea of a more austere faith. So, when my boyfriend wrote to ask if I'd be prepared to become more Orthodox, I was open to the idea. He asked if I'd be willing to keep a kosher home, to live in Israel, to cover my hair. We talked about *shomer negiah*, 'guarding the touch', where men and women don't touch before marriage, and I was mainly sad we'd have to give up holding hands. But I imagined myself, married, in one of those fabulous Farrah Fawcett wigs some Orthodox Jewish women wear, slinky in a long-sleeved dress, and fearsomely erudite about kashrut. I entertained the thought. I wasn't saying no.

Nanda wasn't the only heroine slaking my spiritual thirst, though. I also loved J.D. Salinger's enchanting Franny Glass. Emma had given me the slender, perfect novella, *Franny and Zooey*, when we were fourteen, to fortify me for a field trip to freezing wet Snowdonia (she had wisely chosen *not* to do geography GCSE). I first read it by torchlight in a cold, narrow bunk bed at the youth hostel, and in the morning I wanted to discuss it with Emma so much that I skipped breakfast to beat the payphone queue. The sorry state of my pale pink paperback betrays how many times I've read it since. When I wasn't taking inspiration from Anne Shirley, I tried to write my boyfriend versions of the wise, allusive, funny letters in *Franny and Zooey*.

Franny is stylish, in a silk-lined sheared raccoon coat her boyfriend kisses as though it's as desirable as she is. She's cool enough to order a chicken sandwich and a glass of milk in a fancy restaurant where everyone else is eating things with tentacles, yet so wildly enthusiastic she doesn't bother with bourgeois things like spelling. She carries a gold swizzle stick around in her bag because it's a gift from a corny boy and she doesn't have the heart to throw it out, and she's super-bright. She and her siblings are veterans of a radio quiz show called *It's a Wise Child*.

And she's a bit ditsy, a bit scattered, but never so quirky as to be annoying.

And though I loved Franny, I was *in love* with her older brother Zooey, who looked like 'the blue-eyed Jewish-Irish Mohican scout who died in your arms at the roulette table at Monte Carlo'. A heroine to admire and a hero to fancy: what more could I want in a book? (It's also, by the way, hilarious.)

All the Glass siblings have a difficult relationship with faith. The two eldest, Seymour and Buddy, conduct an educational experiment on the two youngest, Franny and Zooey, teaching them Eastern philosophy and metaphysics because they believe the quest for knowledge should begin with no-knowledge. But by the time Franny and Zooey come of age, Seymour has killed himself and Buddy lives like a hermit in a cabin in the woods. Zooey, a successful actor, used to meditate for ten hours straight, still swears he had a small glass of ginger ale with Jesus when he was eight, and can't eat without first reciting the four great vows of Zen Buddhism. And now it's Franny's turn to confront God.

She visits her boyfriend Lane at his Ivy League university, and is disgusted as he goes on obnoxiously about Flaubert's lack of 'testicularity'. He wants Franny to dress appropriately, order the right meal, so they can be correct and admired and aggressively normal. Franny is anything but. She's odd and she knows it; she made me think it might be cool to be strange. As a stroppy teenager I sympathised with her hatred of pseuds and charmers (the same people Holden Caulfield, the anti-hero of Salinger's novel *The Catcher in the Rye*, calls phonies). She's disgusted by the ambitious people around her. And there is something revolting about the way Lane dismembers his meal of snails and frogs' legs, and suggests sneaking into Franny's boarding house even though she's clearly not up for it. Lane is fatuous, try-hard, unattractively uneasy in his own skin. And he can't understand Franny's latest obsession: a small book called *The Way of a Pilgrim*. It is about a nineteenth-century Russian pilgrim who wants to find out what it means in the Bible when it says you should pray incessantly. He discovers that if you constantly say the Jesus Prayer ('Lord Jesus Christ, have mercy on me'), eventually it synchs up with your heartbeat and becomes unconscious. Lane doesn't see the point of this, but Franny does: 'You get to see God.'

This line destroyed me. I was craving something more, something *beyond*. I was reading the medieval poets, who wrote about loving God as though they were writing about loving a chaste, cold, unattainable fair lady in a tower, and I was reading John Donne begging God to 'Batter my heart'. (When I read the 'Holy Sonnets' now, though not insensible to their passion and wonder, I also think how much I'd love to open a Batter My Heart Chip Shop.) So I got it, about the Jesus Prayer. I saw why Franny would want to *see God*, even if it got in the way of her life. I thought seeing God would be infinitely better than seeing a bore like Lane. Luckily, my boyfriend was not a bore and would talk religion by the hour if I wanted to, and even if I didn't. It was the perfect romance for a God-struck teenager, love and yearning, temporal and spiritual, all mixed up.

After he'd been away ten months, I went to Israel. I packed a romantic wardrobe, including a wide-brimmed straw hat, a polka-dot ra-ra skirt and a swooping maxi dress. Endless practice in front of the mirror had helped me perfect a sort of extreme winged eye, in the manner of Cleopatra. (I'd decided maybe she *did* have something to teach me about relationships.) I'd taken the precaution of acquiring waterproof mascara, because it wouldn't be the big reunion without a few tears. In case he didn't know he was supposed to have a handkerchief for me (perhaps, I reasoned, he hadn't read *Gone With The Wind*), I brought my own. I was ready.

At the airport, I did the rom com run and launched myself into his arms – and he took a step back. He almost flinched away from me. Apparently he was thinking more seriously about *shomer negiah* than I'd realised. He had a beard. He looked like an Orthodox Jew. Over the next few days, he talked with the zeal of the newly religious. He was interested in Kabbalistic numerology and predicting the future by looking at significant Torah passages and adding up the numerical values of the Hebrew letters, words or phrases. I asked if he could predict my A-level results, but he said I was being flippant. I wasn't; I was frantic to know if I'd got the grades that would get me away from home. In a deserted playground on a hushed Shabbat in an Orthodox suburb of Tel Aviv, we sat on the swings and talked about the messiah. It was exciting, he said, because our messiah hadn't come yet. It was all to play for. He could come at any time. And then what? The dead would rise, starting at the Mount of Olives in Jerusalem, wickedness would end, there would be peace. I didn't want to talk about raising the dead; I wanted to swap gossip about our friends, eat falafel, and get to the beach in time for sunset. I was starting to feel that all this talk about faith was cutting us off from talking about anything real. And it panicked me.

Franny's Jesus Prayer is supposed to be a refuge but it sends her into breakdown. She cries her eyes out in the restaurant, faints and winds up on the sofa at her parents' New York flat, weeping, mouthing her prayer, refusing to eat, getting pale and thin and resisting Zooey's attempts to argue her out of it.

I couldn't argue my boyfriend round either. I tried to convince him he could be Orthodox without being esoteric and separate, and certainly without his politics veering to the right. And I didn't think the dead would rise. He liked me arguing back. He said I was his anchor, connecting him to the real world. But I didn't want to be a deadweight, stuck in the mud, dragging him back. I was on my own journey.

Back in London, I put aside Nanda, I turned my back on Donne. I didn't want to read about yearning for God. Not when that yearning might lead to living in Jerusalem, in a wig, with two kitchen sinks and many children. I was scared of committing to living in a way that was even more constrained. And that's when Franny really came into her own. Because her story is really the story of losing faith, not hanging on to it. When her fanatical faith drives her to breakdown, she is rescued, not by a knight in shining armour, not by a boyfriend or a husband or a lover, but by her brother Zooey.

What he does is truly beautiful. Franny is still stuck on the sofa, and every time he tries to talk to her, it goes wrong. So he goes down the hall to Seymour's old room, where there's a private phone line no one can bear to get rid of because it would be too final. Zooey does a funny voice and calls her, pretending to be Buddy. This doesn't work either, but it breaks the ice. Somehow the phone gives them enough distance to speak honestly. He tells Franny that while she's repeating the Jesus Prayer, she is ignoring the really spiritual stuff, like the 'consecrated chicken soup' their mother keeps bringing her. He tells her to drink the soup. He tells her that she can't live a detached religious life because she has desires – she wants to act – and it's wrong to repress those desires. And anyway, she doesn't have to. She can have faith *and* art. According to him, 'the only re*lig*ious thing you can do, is *act*. Act for God, if you want to – be *God's* actress, if you want to. What could be prettier?' Then he quotes Seymour telling him, when they were all still performing on the radio, to shine his shoes for the Fat Lady. Franny remembers Seymour telling her to be funny for the Fat Lady too. And Zooey tells her the Fat Lady is Christ.

Some critics think Salinger's spirituality mars his writing; they're wrong. In *Franny and Zooey*, he takes a heroine who thinks she has to shun life to serve God and he shows her that she doesn't. Vocations aren't just for pilgrims or nuns: her vocation is to act. This felt like the answer I'd been looking for: maybe I didn't have to turn Orthodox. Maybe my vocation was to write. And I still love the consecrated chicken soup. This is a half-Jew being told that her Catholic mother's quintessentially Jewish soup is holy and transcendent. It's ebullient, it's radical *and* it chimes absolutely with one of the few beliefs I still hold: that there's nothing as healing as food cooked by someone you love. At the end of the book, Salinger sends his readers out into the world. And he insists this is worthwhile because we can find meaning *everywhere*. (He is also the writer responsible for my *extravagant* use of italics.)

I worry I'll respond differently to *Franny and Zooey* now I know that Salinger became a recluse, sequestered in deepest darkest New Hampshire, writing but never publishing again. I also know other things about Salinger, things I wish I didn't. I know he behaved questionably to women, drank his own urine and breakfasted on frozen peas. Emma says I shouldn't know all this prurient stuff. It gets in the way. Emma is right.

But it does help to know that, like Franny, Salinger was half-Jewish, half-Catholic, so he felt doubly an outsider. And that he had a very bad war. When the Japanese invaded Pearl Harbor he'd already started writing, and publishing. He spent 1942 and 1943 at US army bases, and in 1944 he lugged his typewriter to Europe where he wrote in between fighting the horrific Battle of Hürtgen Forest (in a swamp full of landmines and exploding trees) and the Battle of the Bulge, as well as taking part in the Normandy landings (where two-thirds of the men in his regiment were killed) and the liberation of Paris. One of the first to enter Dachau, he later said he could never get the smell of burning flesh out of his nose. At the end of the war, he had a breakdown serious enough to get him hospitalised in France.

For a while I thought Franny was cute and precocious and unknowable. Now I think that, like Salinger after the war, she knows too much, she's seen too much, she's understood things that other people deny or ignore. So of course she wants to flee the world. She knows she can never be complacent again, she can never fit in. Zooey shows her that even misfits ('We're freaks, that's all') can be at home in the world. No one is as influenced by Salinger as Wes Anderson. His film *The Royal Tenenbaums* is practically about the Glass family (Margot Tenenbaum is Franny's celluloid double), and in *Moonrise Kingdom*, his twelve-year-old heroine is like a younger Franny, composed, mysterious, alienated, flamboyant and morbidly sensitive. She and another outsider, a twelve-year-old orphan boy, run away and set up camp in a remote and beautiful cove. He has survival skills, she has a suitcase crammed with adventure novels and a record player but most of all they have love, and that's what they plan to live on. But by the end of the film, the most tender and romantic Anderson has made, they find a way to live in the world. Just like Franny does.

I'm sad that Salinger didn't find a way of living in the world, that he retreated into seclusion, guarding his privacy with a shotgun and many lawyers. But I'm very, very glad he gave me *Franny and Zooey*'s positive philosophy that I might be able to find meaning outside religion.

As I was beginning to say some of these things to my boyfriend, I was also searching for some kind of safety net; Salinger leaves his heroine on the brink, but if I was going to leave my boyfriend, if I wasn't going to become Orthodox, I needed some idea of what might happen after. So when I found that White had continued Nanda's story past *Frost in May*, I read all three sequels feverishly, looking for options and answers. White changes Nanda's name to Clara, and rows back slightly from the despair of *Frost in May*'s ending. But Nanda/Clara will never quite get free of Catholicism without 'a sense of mutilation' and, although I know it's illogical, I will probably always feel a tiny bit guilty that I am not living an Orthodox life.

Clara has to struggle to define herself against other forces, as well as the Church. In *The Lost Traveller* she battles her parents, in *The Sugar House* she escapes an unfortunate marriage, and in *Beyond the Glass* she faces her own demons, endures a breakdown, is committed to an asylum, and emerges shaky but optimistic.

Clara is not a winning heroine. She's short on charm; difficult, isolated, introspective and sometimes terrifyingly blank and disengaged. But White doesn't give us time to like or dislike her. Instead she plunges us deep into her tangled interiority. This is confessional writing at its most complex – never maudlin, never wallowing, even though White was mining her own life, and that life was, at times, unbearable.

I learned a lot from Nanda/Clara. I learned that I would probably always be wrestling with angels, that guilt would be a constant. When a friend asks Nanda how many venial sins there are, she replies gloomily, 'Hundreds. Almost everything's a venial sin, in fact. If I don't eat my cabbage, or if I have an extra helping of pudding when I'm not really hungry, or if I think my hair looks rather nice when it's just been washed' – and she lists all the ways a Catholic can be implicated in someone else's sins: 'By counsel, by command, by consent, by provocation, by praise or flattery, by being a partner in the sin, by silence, by defending the ill-done.' I always think of Nanda at Yom Kippur when I'm in synagogue atoning not just for things I know I've done but also for sins committed 'under duress', 'inadvertently', 'unintentionally', 'unknowingly' and 'by a confused heart'. And when, years later, I first ate a prawn, I thought of Nanda. I felt so guilty about eating something non-kosher that I made myself throw up. The friend who had cooked me prawn curry (by mistake, he said, but then provoked me to eat it and 'stop believing in nonsense laws created by a tribe in the desert trying to separate themselves from other tribes') stood in the doorway saying 'I'm not holding your hair!' And I got rid of the prawn (but not the guilt), and wished Zooey was there instead. He would have known how to make me feel better.

From Clara, I also learned that I would eventually lose the agonising self-consciousness of being a teenager. In *The Lost Traveller*, White calls Clara 'unformed', 'skinless', 'silly', 'stiff', 'embarrassed', 'half-baked', 'pretentious', 'deceiving', 'crude and priggish and unfledged'; she's always blushing or speaking in a 'high, artificial voice' and giving a 'silly, nervous smile'. It takes going mad, losing her reason and coming out the other side for her to be her real self. To believe in herself, in fact, which is the point.

She has to walk through fire first, though. She has to learn to mistrust charm, and specifically charming actors, like one silver-tongued seducer who is flagged up early on as a Bad Man when he says women can't write and claims Branwell Brontë wrote *Wuthering Heights*. She has to learn to pit her true stories against the false ones she is told, to keep reminding herself that women can write, that she can write, that Emily wrote her own novel. (And not to be too swayed by charming actors. A lesson I have tried to learn myself.)

She has to learn that living in a rackety, bohemian area and wearing rumpled clothes doesn't make you an artist. And that if you feel so high and joyous you can't believe it's real, it probably isn't. But she also finds that she can do extraordinary things 'when the brakes are off'; leaving the asylum, she is told that while in the grip of madness she not only ripped up a fur coat with her bare hands but also sang quite beautifully.

Most of all, Clara taught me to always try to find my own way. Clara tells her father, 'All my life, you've wanted me to think as you thought and do what you wanted and made me feel guilty if I didn't. Why shouldn't I live as I want to?' Yes, and why shouldn't I eat prawns? I don't know. I can, but only sometimes, when I'm feeling particularly robust. But not always. Not usually.

Despite valiant efforts, Clara never quite ditches the guilt. Nor did White; after *she* left the asylum, she had a roller-coaster life, including many tempestuous affairs and more than one flirtation with madness. She suffered terrible writer's block (she called it 'The Beast', and because of her, so do I) which years and years of analysis couldn't break, and which she traced back to what had happened to her at the convent, the story she'd told in *Frost in May*. But in her fifties, having reconverted to Catholicism, she found out the truth. She hadn't been expelled. The nuns had read her manuscript and summoned her father, who really did say that if her mind was such a sink of filth and impurity he wished she'd never been born. (Fathers! Do not say this to your daughters.) The nuns had been willing to let her stay. But her father, who had wanted to tutor her at home instead, to try to get her into a good university, used her disgrace to force the issue – and never told her. It blighted her whole life. Even after she got the truth, she never managed to continue Clara's story, to get her beyond being 24, just out of the asylum, to show her breaking free from her father's unforgiving, hypercritical (and, if you ask me, hypocritical) glare, let alone from God. In 1977, though, when White, in her seventies, was still tormented by this failure, Carmen Callil read *Frost in May* and loved it so much that she started a whole new imprint, Virago Modern Classics, to get it back into print. Her edition is the one I first read, and when I found out how it came to be, I was glad to find that I was reading the evidence of White's late bloom.

Even truncated, Clara's story, like Franny's, helped me see that staying with my boyfriend would mean going from the Iraqi Jewish community to an Orthodox community, from the frying pan into the fire. It also made me see that I needed to hang on to my freedom so I could see who I could be by myself before I hitched a ride with anyone else, and that a heroine should keep believing in herself (and not in anything else).

ESTHER GREENWOOD

Sylvia Plath was the whole reason I went to Cambridge. My Plath obsession had started when I'd bought her *Journals* in a bookshop in Florida. I was sulking my way through a family holiday (the Velveeta one), dressing only in black, wearing my Stygian eyeliner down to a stub, and generally casting as much gloom as I could on the sunshine state. Plath gave my wordless misery a voice. My copy of the *Journals* is a mess: battered, obscurely stained (with tears? with wine?) and frenziedly annotated. Every line felt ripped from the heart. Here was my guide to being a woman and a writer. And although she did her first degree at Smith College in Massachusetts, Cambridge was where Plath's poetry took off, and where she met Ted Hughes, so of course I had to go there too.

My parents and brother drove me up on my first day. We lugged my stuff up to my room, in an ugly Seventies concrete box named after the manufacturers of Velcro. They helped me unpack and still they didn't leave. And suddenly, the door opened, and my whole family – uncles, aunt, cousins, grandma, even my baby second cousin – were there. Surprise!

They'd brought many Pyrex dishes of food, as though I was in imminent danger of starving, or being besieged. We couldn't squeeze even one into the tiny freezer shelf of the shared fridge. And we couldn't fit into my tiny room. We were spilling out on to the staircase. A porter came to see what the commotion was. He was wearing a bowler hat.

We tipped out, all fourteen of us, got lost, got laughed at for pronouncing Magdalene how it looks instead of 'maudlin' (still one of those quirks of the English language that makes me feel foreign) and celebrated with pizza. It was wonderful, it was awful, it was overwhelming. When they left, I locked my door, and leaned against it. It was a room of my own! I blew a kiss to Virginia Woolf. And then I put on more mascara and emerged: it was Freshers' Week.

We were told the college was founded in 1448 and to bring our own Blu-Tack and never walk on the grass. We were told Newton didn't really build the Mathematical Bridge without any bolts. We were told May Week was in June. We were told to mind our apostrophes – Queens' for the college, Lane and Green, named after two queens, and Queen's for the Road, which was Victoria's alone. We were told the food was bad because our college had supported Richard III and paid the price after Bosworth. We were told it was so cold because there was nothing between us and the Urals. We were told when to wear our gowns, and which way to pass the port. We were told that only John's students could eat swan, and only once a year. We were told cleaners were bedders, rowers were boaties, scientists were natscis, computer scientists were compscis, comedy gigs were smokers, parties were bops or squashes, the Porters' lodge was the Plodge and the terms were Michaelmas, Lent and Easter.

That first night there was a party in a room with mullioned

windows set into walls that were two feet thick and four hundred years old. Clutching sherry schooners, we talked about God and children's TV and what A levels we'd done. Suddenly, a deep, plangent voice declaimed, 'I saw the best minds of my generation destroyed by madness.' It was a blue-eyed second-year in a white shirt and battered cords, sitting, lit by a moonbeam, in a wingback chair. He paused for laughter – ironic laughter, because we didn't really think we were 'the best minds' – and then he recited the whole of *Howl*, off by heart. What a rush! Allen Ginsberg's rhapsodic, rangy epic poem was written in 1955, the year Plath arrived in Cambridge. It felt perfect.

For a while I didn't really see the city, just ran around recognising places she'd been. My college had the bridge she'd climbed over late one night. At Pembroke I saw the cobbled court and Gothic keyhole windows that made her feel she should be wearing Elizabethan silks. At her pubs – the Anchor and the Eagle – I drank whisky macs, which were red and gold, just like she'd said. When it rained, I bought chips and, like her, I sprinkled them with vinegar and warmed my hands on the paper bag. I went on the same walks, following the river through meadows and fields to Grantchester, noticing the rooks and hawthorn hedges she had told me would be there. I can't recite *Howl* but I could probably have a stab at Plath's description of the party where she met Hughes, with someone playing the piano and lots of people talking poems, and boys in turtlenecks and girls in blue eyeshadow and the 'big, dark, hunky boy, the only one there huge enough for me' taking her off into another room. After he kissed her, she bit his cheek, and drew blood. I wondered what the callow first-year boys would say if I tried biting them.

Not that I was planning to. My boyfriend and I were still together, just. Our letters had started flying back and forth again. And anyway, I was still a good Iraqi Jewish girl. In that hectic first week, very late one night, a boy passed out and hit his head. There was blood everywhere. The medical students took charge. Lectures hadn't started yet, so they knew as much about medicine as I did, but I didn't have the nous to do what they did, administering water and painkillers, making up a bed for him on someone else's floor, putting him in the recovery position so he wouldn't choke. I was shocked. I'd never been drunk before. It was only because of Plath that I even recognised 'that strong, silted-up force that makes one move through air like swimming'. Everyone else was so confident and capable. I was frozen in his doorway, the room full of blood and vomit like a crime scene.

Then all at once I knew what to do. I got the bucket of cleaning products my mother had packed – enough bleach and antibacterial spray to deep-clean a hospital – and set to work. I cleaned the blood off the walls. I stripped the bed and scrubbed the headboard. I mopped the floor, and cleaned the mop, and washed out the bucket. I boil-washed the sheets. Dawn found me sitting in the hot, empty laundry, waiting for the dryer to finish its cycle. I was so totally my mother's daughter. When in doubt, clean.

Plath would have understood. She articulated, more than any other writer, how the pressure to be perfect can break a girl. Maybe Fifties America – her crucible – was not so different from Iraqi Jewish London in the Nineties. I'd had so many good girl heroines. In her novel, *The Bell Jar*, Plath gave me a heroine who was anything but. Esther Greenwood could even be called an anti-heroine. And *The Bell Jar* is the girls' *Catcher in the Rye*, the stroppy teens' manifesto. It's the book Julia Stiles's truculent Kat curls up with in *10 Things I Hate About You*, and in *Sabrina the Teenage Witch*, Melissa Joan Hart's Sabrina pulls her baseball cap down low and gulps the book down in the school cafeteria, along with the three puddings she's eating instead of lunch.

Esther wants to be a poet and she has a dream summer job, interning at a New York magazine, but she hates the fashion, the make-up, the martinis and the men. She wants to be 'wise and cynical as all hell', she wants to feed her writing with extreme experiences. She's avid for car crashes, street fights, babies pickled in jars. When she sees her first fingerbowl, with cherry blossoms in it, she assumes it's some kind of Japanese soup and drinks it down, blossoms and all. As she starts losing her mind, and her inhibitions, things go grotesque. Esther feasts on caviar and crab and gets violent food poisoning. She dates a misogynist who growls 'Pretend you are drowning' as he sweeps her into a rough tango, tries to rape her and, after she punches him in the nose, smears her face with his blood.

Her medical student boyfriend (cruelly named Buddy Willard) has slept with a waitress but he wants Esther to be pure. She meets his hypocrisy with withering second-wave feminist scorn. When Buddy takes his clothes off, she sees 'turkey neck and turkey gizzards'. When he predicts she'll stop wanting to write after she has children, she decides marriages must be tiny dictatorships where women are brainwashed and enslaved.

As she gets suicidal, she also gets *mean*. She releases her inner bad girl – she picks up sailors, reads scandal sheets, howls at her father's grave. She gives up trying to be perfect, or pretty, stops washing her clothes, stops washing her hair because it's all too much effort, and anyway she doesn't care. After a black comedy of failed attempts to end it, she does what Plath did: leaves a note that she's gone for a long walk, swallows a bottle of sleeping pills and waits for death in her house's basement crawlspace. Plath was found two days later. She was hospitalised and given electroconvulsive therapy.

In hospital, Esther is nastier still. She kicks a nurse, smashes a box of thermometers, doesn't bother to hide her yellow, flabby, stubbly legs from visitors, throws her mother's roses in the bin. And her psychiatrist is pleased. It's as if meanness is part of the cure. Maybe when the pressure to be perfect makes you crazy, the only way to get better is to be as imperfect as you can.

Plath recovered from this first serious depression, emerging a few months later to return to university and to life. *The Bell Jar* ends with Esther about to leave the hospital too:

> My stocking seams were straight, my black shoes cracked, but polished, and my red wool suit as flamboyant as my plans. Something old, something new . . .
> But I wasn't getting married. There ought, I thought, to be a ritual for being born twice – patched, retreaded and approved for the road.

I thought this was a brilliant twist on the marriage plot. Instead of the heroine going through trials and being rewarded with a ring on her finger, she could be reborn as her real true self. To find out what happened to Esther next, I read Plath's poetry, her *Journals,* her letters, and every biography I could find. I thought Esther would probably have married someone ruinously gorgeous and off-the-scale talented like Hughes. I don't know why some Plath fans chip his name off Plath's tombstone; I read so much about her falling in love with him that I was besotted too. I revelled in his poetry, so different from Plath's, so huge and rugged and mystical. I started to wish my boyfriend was more like Hughes. The idea of becoming an Orthodox Jewish wife was losing what small appeal it had had. I got a poem accepted in *The May Anthology*. It would be in print; people would read it. And living in the city where Plath and Hughes had fallen in love, I couldn't help but wonder what it might be like to fall for a poet and build a life on 'Books & Babies & Beef stews'. If he was fanciable enough, I might even stop being a vegetarian. And if it fell apart, I could become Lady Lazarus, the fearsome virago of Plath's late poem who rises out of ash, with flame-red hair. My hair was brown, but no matter. Plath was a brunette too, but for most of her adult life she was a bottle blonde.

Her picture disappointed me. I thought a poet should be a severe, wan beauty, but Plath was laughing, voluptuous, scarlet-lipped, with masses of platinum hair. Towards the end of her life, she looked more as I imagined her; Al Alvarez described her, then, as resembling a priestess, her hair unbleached now, long, dark, pungent and unwashed.

It wasn't just Plath's hair that had changed. She'd left behind her early, mannered villanelles for the wild freedom of *Ariel* where she stopped painstakingly looking up every word in her thesaurus and let rip. In 'Fever 103°' she wrote about 'My selves dissolving, old whore petticoats', just like Esther in New York, standing on the roof of her hotel and throwing all her fashionable clothes into the night wind, where they scattered like ashes over the city.

Hughes also thought Plath had transformed. In his 1982 foreword to the *Journals* he describes how she destroyed her early work, and her early self, to become new. He calls it a violent, primitive sacrifice that might lead to suicide but might also lead to the birth of one's real self. In his poem 'The Minotaur', he describes his savage admiration as Plath smashes up his desk, cheering her on with 'That's the stuff you're keeping out of your poems!'

I wanted to cast off my false self too, to ditch my old whore petticoats and find the real me. I could leave behind the girl who felt maladroit in pretty dresses, the girl who argued sullenly with my family, the girl flirting with Orthodox Judaism, the girl in the college laundry. None of these girls were the real me.

I don't know if *The Bell Jar* has a happy ending. Esther is cured, by a maverick lady psychiatrist who bans Esther's mother from visiting and breezily sends Esther off to get a diaphragm so she can go forth and have sex. 'I was my own woman,' says Esther, before wrecking it: 'The next step was to find the proper sort of man.' The problem's right there; she is barely herself before she latches on to a man. And she's a bad picker. The professor who plies her with wine and carries her into his dark bedroom is no good. She loses her virginity with a sharp, sudden pain, and starts to bleed. At first she feels part of a great tradition of brides and their bloodied sheets. But then she's haemorrhaging dark, sticky blood and she's almost more pleased, proud to be extreme, glad to find this happens to one in a million women. She's worse off than all those brides of history. She's unique because she suffers.

This is, above all, what I got from *The Bell Jar*: the idea that you had to suffer to be a woman. I'd written lots of poems about exquisite suffering, but I hadn't really suffered. I arrived in Cambridge waiting for the harrowing, transfiguring experience that would make me a woman. Like Esther, I courted suffering. She has a warped relationship with pain from the start. She's obsessed with the Rosenbergs being electrocuted, she interprets her skiing injury as punishment for being mean to Buddy, and his TB as punishment for his hypocrisy. Plath, too, seemed to dive headfirst into her own pain.

I wondered how much I'd have to suffer, how far I'd have to go. Plath's poem 'Edge' suggested that only death would suffice. In a play I saw in my first term, a woman played Plath in smudged mascara and lots of black. She leapt off a table shouting that she was 'perfected' and threw a black shoe at the actor playing her father, who stepped smartly aside to reveal (of course) the actor playing Hughes. Angst was everywhere. That same year, Susanna Kaysen's *Girl, Interrupted* came out, a memoir set in the mental hospital Plath went to. In 1994 came Elizabeth Wurtzel's *Prozac Nation*, with the author on the cover, hair tousled, pouting sulkily, fenced in by barbed wire made of pills. Courtney Love's band Hole released *Live Through This* that year too, just after her husband Kurt Cobain had killed himself, and I was stunned by her anguished performances and her train-wreck interviews. These women wore their suffering like fairy princesses wore tiaras. They were beautiful and sad and angry and liberated. Who wouldn't want to be them?

It looked as if I was getting there. My boyfriend and I broke up. It was my decision, and it was awful. We tried to work things out by letter – we had always been best on paper – but now it seemed the worst form of communication. I braved the college computer room to read my first ever email (it was 1993!) and it upset me so much that a compsci took me to the college bar for my first whisky. A lot of firsts that term. Finally, my boyfriend came to visit, and we agreed that it was over.

At home, my parents were in conflict – by my Finals they'd be getting a divorce. Iraqi Jews didn't really get divorced, so the usual shock, anger and distress were magnified by everyone judging and gossiping like mad. I hated seeing my parents so unhappy, and I felt that all my certainties were disintegrating; I had never imagined they wouldn't stay together. An early casualty of the divorce was The Cake, saved from my bat mitzvah. No one knew how it happened, but in the chaos of things the freezer door was left open, and it defrosted. It was unsalvageable. It ended up in the bin. And even though I'd hated it, for years, it still seemed that something had ended.

So suddenly there was suffering, and plenty of it. And then I started to reel.

It came on suddenly, halfway through my second term. I'd feel heady, spinny, as if I was tipping back into a void, or deliquescing. I'd grab a chair, a bed, a friend's arm, and wait for everything to come back into focus.

Ever the romantic (eat your heart out, Cathy Earnshaw) I diagnosed heartbreak. My heart was broken and I was reeling and melting. My heart was broken *so* I was reeling and melting. Maybe this was it, the moment I'd been waiting for. But by the end of term I was trailing off mid-sentence, my eyes going dead, slurring my words and falling. It wasn't heartbreak.

The specialists wouldn't name it. They talked about *events* or *episodes* or *funny turns*. They held my head and spun me round, poured hot and cold water in my ears, held up pencils for me to follow with my eyes, and gave me travel sickness pills – which seemed appropriate, because sometimes it felt like stepping on a boat and sometimes it felt like waves rising up and washing over me. They said it was an inner ear infection, they said it would be gone in six weeks. But it wasn't. And I couldn't stop crying. I'd had a bad reaction to the pills, so they took me off them and promised I'd be fine, in six months tops.

The crying stopped but the falling got worse. I fell harder, faster. I couldn't grab a chair quickly enough. I fell out of bed, I fell down stairs, I fell on the cobbled streets. I was always covered in bruises. I don't remember when I started flailing and spasming, jerking and rolling. Now the doctors said it could be narcolepsy. Or cataplexy, or migraine, or peripheral vestibular dysfunction, or benign positional paroxysmal vertigo. They said the brain was uncharted territory and they were explorers, embarking on dangerous journeys to the edges of the maps where there were dragons. When I went for my first MRI scan, and they strapped me down and slid me into the white, coffin-like tube, I remembered Esther going in for ECT. It was cramped inside the tube, and dark, and the walls vibrated as though the doctors were hammering and drilling at them. Esther thought she must have done something terrible to have ECT, and in that tube, I thought the same. But I had something to comfort me that she never had; unlike her, I had *The Bell Jar.*

I'm embarrassed now that I thought this was my rite of passage, my equivalent of Esther/Plath's breakdown. I'm ashamed that I thought I was finally living an interesting life, suffering as (it was scarcely comparable) my family had in Iraq. I lumped it all in together, such was my confusion, and just because I thought that suffering might have *value*. The insidious idea was everywhere, in the music I listened to and in my favourite books. And maybe it had been imprinted even earlier by one of my favourite childhood novels: Susan Coolidge's *What Katy Did*.

I thought Katy Carr, the heroine of this 1872 book, was a carefree rebel, her hair, like mine, 'forever in a snarl', always having adventures with her five younger siblings, and getting into trouble with her strict Aunt Izzie, who is helping their distracted, widowed father bring them up. I remembered Katy falling off a swing and being horribly injured, but if you'd asked me where this came in the book, I'd have said near the end. I blanked out the rest of the book – the *bulk* of the book – in which Katy comes to terms with being bedridden. It reads very differently to me now I've had seizures for nineteen years. (They never did go away.)

Even the healthy Katy of the book's beginning is a drip. She's supposed to be a writer (yes, another writer-heroine) but all she writes is a religious newspaper about her boring resolutions to be good. Her siblings gleefully burn it in the kitchen fire – the only instance of a heroine's work being burned that I can unreservedly support.

Like the girls in *Little Women*, when Katy does any slightly wayward thing, she is crazed with contrition. So when Aunt Izzie tells her not to go on the swing, and she does anyway, well, you can imagine. It's worse than Beth's dead canary. Katy lies there, weak, frightened, paralysed, sobbing with pain – yet Aunt Izzie and Katy's father's top priority is to get her to apologise for being disobedient. Which she does. She doesn't scream at her heartless relatives, she doesn't rail against the gods, she meekly says she's sorry. And, by the way, Aunt Izzie never told Katy *why* she shouldn't go on the swing. It was broken, but she didn't say that because she expected blind obedience. But she doesn't feel bad about this, not at all. Maybe that's why, having made her apology, Katy is a bit sullen. Well, wouldn't you be? She can't move. She may never be able to move again. She's only twelve.

Then Cousin Helen visits. There should be a special place in hell for Cousin Helen, a saintly invalid who wafts about in ruffled lace nightgowns, is gracious at all times, and thinks illness is an opportunity. Yes, an opportunity. Now Katy's spine is injured, she promises Katy that 'God is going to let you go to *His* school – where He teaches all sorts of beautiful things to people.' Reading it now, when Helen starts calling God's school The School of Pain I hurl the book at the wall. Because although I wanted to suffer, believed it would be transfiguring, internalised this message from Plath, and (as it turns out) from Coolidge, when suffering came, it didn't teach me, or liberate me.

It took years to get a not-implausible diagnosis; I have (probably) seizures, caused (probably) by a basilar migraine which itself is (probably) caused by a throbbing in the basilar artery that runs up the nape of the neck into the brain.

This is what happens when I have a seizure. First there's a flicker, like a moth going in and out of the light. The colours are suddenly too bright, the noises too loud, it's all too much. My arm's moving. I didn't tell it to; it's moving of its own accord. It doesn't feel like my arm. It doesn't feel like an arm at all. There are tiny tremors going up and down it. Rising panic, rising nausea. If people are talking, they stop making sense. If there's music, it contorts. The beat throbs in my head. Phrases and patterns repeat, nonsensically. I feel fuzzy. Sick. My ears ring loud. I'm spinning, so's the world and not in the same direction. Everything goes blurry. Colours seep. Things are big that should be small, close up that were far away; they loom. The world goes Cubist, goes to bits. I try to grab something but my hands lose their grip. They float up. They feel enormous and light, like balloons. And I feel a terrible sense of doom. The world is ending and there's nothing I can do about it. Sometimes there are hallucinations. My hands disappear. The lower part of my face dissolves. Dark figures close in on me. My arms fly up, and I feel the itch of wings sprouting at my shoulders. Or I'm a fish, bucking and flailing on a wooden deck. My muscles go, my legs go to jelly, I open my mouth to say something and my mouth's gone slack, no sound comes out. I fall. My arms and legs jerk. I kick, I twitch. I melt and then I vanish altogether. I'm at the bottom of a well. It's dark down here and I can't hear anyone, see anything. And then it starts to recede. And I'm back. Until the next time.

My seizures haven't made me virtuous or cheerful. Fretful, yes. And cross. And self-pitying. But not virtuous. There is no School of Pain. There is just the tedious business of getting through suffering, day after day, and trying not to hope too hard that it will ever stop, because the harder you hope, the more disappointing it is when those hopes are dashed. So it's hard for me, now, to read the manipulative ending of *What Katy Did*. Katy recovers. It's her reward for becoming so cheerful and capable; she's gone from tween tearaway to angel of the house. But she wasn't such a tearaway in the first place. At least *The Bell Jar* doesn't advocate self-sacrifice and selflessness. Esther would laugh at Katy's vapid, goody-goody pieties. Maybe we *have* moved on a tiny bit.

As I ploughed through my first year, I don't think I read a single book by a woman, but I read a lot about women suffering. There was Samuel Richardson heaping pain and indignity on Clarissa and calling her 'an Exemplar to her sex' as though learning to suffer well made us exemplary. There was August Strindberg implying Miss Julie wanted a bit of rough (or just to cut to the chase and shag Death himself), and Thomas Hardy throwing things at poor Tess until she collapsed under the weight of it all.

Or so I thought. Now I think in *Tess of the d'Urbervilles* Hardy tied himself in knots trying to show the plight of a poor Victorian woman while making her feisty enough to be actually interesting. Tess's family are pretty much ready to sell her to louche Alec d'Urberville who they think might be a distant relative (he isn't) and who only has to open his mouth for it to be clear he's a lying womaniser (and not just because the first thing he does is get Tess to open *her* mouth so he can feed her strawberries). Hardy wanted to put Tess through the mill but didn't want her to be a victim. He wrestled hardest with the crucial seduction scene set in the forest, The Chase. In the first draft, Alec tricks Tess into a sham marriage, and quickly consummates it. But Hardy wanted to make Tess more innocent, so in his second draft, Alec drugs and rapes her. Then Hardy changed his mind again. In his final draft there's no mock marriage, no drugs, and it's not a rape but a seduction.

It's a deep and churning novel. On the surface, Tess is submissive and passive, an exemplar like Clarissa. But underneath she's shrewd, sharp, strong-willed and sensual too – strawberries are never innocent again once you've read *Tess*. She lets Alec seduce her but she doesn't let him master her. She refuses to become just another fallen women. After her child dies, she considers pretending it never happened and trying to start over, but instead she bravely confesses to the man she loves, Angel Clare. She hopes he'll accept her as she is – just as she's fine with him having had an affair. 'Forgive me as you are forgiven!' she says. But Angel's just another Buddy Willard. 'O Tess, forgiveness does not apply to the case!' he says. 'You were one person; now you are another. My God – how can forgiveness meet such a grotesque – prestidigitation as that!'

Angel wants her to be Artemis, or a daughter of nature, or an angel. He can't cope with her honesty, her courage or her past. But she won't be his possession, trophy, saint or doll. The day after their wedding, she doesn't make a scene. And in refusing to faint, or weep hysterically or beg him to stay, she makes it easy for him to leave her. Poverty and censure only make her stronger. She runs into Alec again and rages at the sexism of society: 'Once victim, always victim – that's the law!' But she's not a victim. She's tough, and she's a realist. At the end of the novel, she goes back to Alec to keep her family from starving. And when she can take it no more, she stabs him to death. Hardy calls the bloodstain she creates 'a gigantic ace of hearts': he's saying she's a winner. The winner of the novel. She's an avenging angel, she's Lady Lazarus, and Hardy rewards her with a few pages' grace, where she and Angel have a kind of belated honeymoon. She goes to her arrest like a goddess.

Hardy cried when he killed Tess off. I'd cry too, if I'd written her. She's amazing. And I love her wishing her mother had warned her about men: 'Ladies know what to fend hands against, because they read novels that tell them of these tricks; but I never had the chance o' learning in that way, and you did not help me!' – Hardy is justifying his novel: novels show women that men are dangerous. Therefore novels are good! But what resonates is the force and clarity of Tess's anger.

Blinded by the idea that real women suffer, I never noticed this. I brought the same misreading to *The Color Purple*. Its heroine Celie is raped by her father on the first page. He sells or kills the two children she has by him, and abuses her so monstrously that she becomes infertile. He beats her and denies her education. He forces her to marry a man almost as brutal. Her sister disappears. *The Color Purple* is like a black hole you fall into. Misery and more misery.

And then, things change. Celie meets a woman who should be her enemy: her husband's lover, Shug. But Shug turns out to be Celie's fairy godmother. A voluptuous lounge singer, all sequins and laughter, she gets Celie to put a mirror between her legs and see her own 'wet rose'. I still remember the anxious thrill this gave me. By the end of the book Celie has experienced sexual pleasure (with Shug), she's been reunited with her sister, she runs her own business (designing and making trousers, despite her husband's view that 'Men spose to wear the pants') and she's the centre of a happy, messy, noisy, dysfunctional family. Alice Walker gives her unprepossessing, poor, black, gay heroine an ending fit for a princess.

For years I thought this happy ending was Celie's reward for suffering. But now, I realise it isn't. Not at all. She gets her happy ending because she learns to be strong, and she learns to demand pleasure from life. It's the opposite of a suffering heroine novel. The only problem is – and I'm gutted to admit it – Celie's no fun. She's steadfast and patient and dignified, but those aren't the kinds of qualities that make me want her to be my new best friend. Critic Trudier Harris famously exploded about Celie that she 'just sat there, like a bale of cotton with a vagina, taking stuff from kids even and waiting for someone to come along and rescue her'.

Luckily, Shug, the book's other heroine, enjoys life and makes other people enjoy it too. Even Celie's brutal, unimaginative husband is nicer when Shug is around. Shug won't let *anyone* get away with being horrid or boring. Not even God. In fact, she's reinvented Him as a loving, pantheistic joy-giver: 'One day . . . it come to me: that feeling of being part of everything, not separate at all. I knew that if I cut a tree my arm would bleed.' It's incredibly moving. And I like the schmaltzy ending because I think Walker was so brave to write it. In her 1976 essay 'Saving the Life That is Your Own', she writes, 'It is, in the end, the saving of lives that we writers are about . . . We do it because we care . . . We care because we know this: *the life we save is our own.*' It's a radical fairy tale she's writing, a dream of how things could be.

Realising how wrong I was about Tess and Celie makes me think it's time to go back to Plath. I rejected her at the end of that sad first year. I put her books away. I was sick of suffering. I thought Plath was navel-gazing, luxuriating in her own misery. I didn't want to do that any more.

I thought perhaps, like Catherine Morland, I had got my genres mixed up. I'd been trying to be a tragic heroine, and it was making everything worse. I didn't have to be tragic. If I couldn't change what was happening to me, I could at least change my response. Rather than see my seizures as a dark fate, a necessary suffering, or even (in my more Nanda-esque moments) as being struck down by God, I could decide to be a survivor, to keep getting up again every time I was knocked down.

When I was temping over the summer, my boss took me out for lunch and patronisingly said, 'You like white wine now, and milk chocolate, and Shakespeare's tragedies, but when you grow up you'll like red wine, dark chocolate, and the comedies.' I wish he wasn't right, and every time I drink red wine or eat dark chocolate, I feel irked. He was right about wanting less tragedy, too. So I'm scared, now, to go back to Plath.

When I do, the first thing I notice is that lots of the suffering she writes about is not her own. Sometimes it's problematic – as in 'Daddy' where she identifies with the victims of the Holocaust because she's angry that her father, who happens to be German, died when she was eight. But sometimes her empathy is so powerful it transcends the self. Famously, in 'Ariel' she merges with the horse she's riding till they become an arrow, the dew and the morning. And in 'Cut' she even gives voice to the blood pouring out of her cut thumb: 'A celebration, this is./ Out of a gap/ A million soldiers run,/ Redcoats, every one.' It's not macabre; it's the jaunty, euphoric voice of a writer who wants to see everything, feel everything. And by stripping emotion out of some things while empathising furiously with others, Plath makes you see the world fresh.

But it's hard to separate her from her myth. Her readers are so personal, so biased, so devoted. Women post their tattoos on the Sylvia Plath Ink blog – elongated images of her face, or the quote from *The Bell Jar*, 'I am, I am, I am', inked into a heart monitor's squiggly red line. One woman has the line tattooed next to an image of a heart, not cutesy but anatomical, all ventricles and muscle. At the churchyard in Heptonstall in Yorkshire, I find Plath's grave by following the women in black. Their eyes are smoky, their lips blood-red. They leave pens on the grave, and lipstick. There's a plastic mermaid and a gaudy theatre mask. The flowers are fresh. As I read the inscription, I feel desperately sad. Plath was just thirty when she died.

In *The Bell Jar*, I notice a line I've always missed. It's on page three. Esther describes the gifts she got during her internship, including a plastic sunglasses case decorated with a starfish. She says that for a while she hid the gifts, but now she feels better and 'last week I cut the plastic starfish off the sunglasses case for the baby to play with'. This is a massive relief. It means Esther's all right in the end. All right enough to make her peace with her nightmare in New York, optimistic enough to start a family. She has survived.

The *Journals* are a bit jejune in places (whose diaries aren't?), but they're full of Plath's omnivorous curiosity, her frank sexuality, her hunger for 'a life of conflict, of balancing children, sonnets, love and dirty dishes; and banging banging an affirmation of life out on pianos and ski slopes and in bed in bed in bed'.

When suffering comes, she meets it with anger and with strength. It's got to be worth something that she's such a fighter.

One evening, walking around Primrose Hill, my gaze is caught by a lit window. The blue plaque says it's Plath's, but it seems the wrong house. I remember an address round the corner, on Fitzroy Road. I check Frieda Hughes's moving, restrained introduction to the restored edition of her mother's *Ariel*, and find that Fitzroy Road was where Plath spent her last eight weeks, wrote thirteen poems, and, in February 1963, put milk and bread by her sleeping children, sealed off her kitchen and put her head in an oven. The house I saw, on Chalcot Square, was where she lived with Hughes for nearly two years, gave birth to Frieda, published *The Colossus* and wrote most of *The Bell Jar*. Her daughter insisted that the plaque should reflect Plath's life, not her death.

Her edition reinstates Plath's original selection and arrangement of the poems, and has a very different arc to the book I first read. The bleak, chilly 'Edge' is not even included – immediately making *Ariel* less like a suicide note. In fact, the collection begins with the word 'love' and ends with the word 'spring', and it feels like the story of a woman recovering from a break-up and looking forward to the future. I wish I'd read this cathartic version of *Ariel* when I was unhappy about my parents' divorce. It's the version I'll read from now on, a version that allows me to think that Plath wasn't advocating suffering: she was struggling and heroically wishing for rebirth and giving her readers that possibility too.

LUCY HONEYCHURCH

It's embarrassing to admit how wildly I misread *A Room with a View* when I was 20. Though I'm beginning to think all readings are provisional, and that maybe we read heroines for what we need from them at the time. And what I needed from Lucy Honeychurch then was an idea about becoming an artist and living an artist's life. It was because of her that I started writing plays.

First, she took me to Florence. In E.M. Forster's 1908 novel, Italy opens Lucy's heart, shakes up her assumptions and changes her life. So, channelling Helena Bonham-Carter in the luscious Merchant Ivory film, I cultivated bird's-nest hair and set off for a month in Florence, just before my final year. I was there to learn Italian, but the classes at the fusty stuccoed British Institute were just in the mornings. The sun-drenched afternoons and the cool, lazy evenings were for awestruck wandering, gazing at frescoes and eating gelato. I tried to give myself up to beauty, as Forster advises. He sends Lucy to Santa Croce without her Baedeker guide, and at first she's frustrated by not knowing which tomb is the most beautiful, which most praised by Ruskin. The church feels enormous, and cold. (It is.) Then suddenly 'the pernicious charm of Italy worked on her, and, instead of acquiring information, she began to be happy'.

Lucy's big moment comes when she strays, unchaperoned, into the Piazza della Signoria. There's a fountain, there's the Loggia, it's twilight, but she wants more. Just as she's complaining, 'Nothing ever happens to me', something does. Two Italian men quarrel and one stabs the other. As the blood spurts, she swoons. Straight into the arms of George Emerson. Confused, questing George Emerson, who is staying at the same *pensione* as Lucy and her spinster cousin Charlotte Bartlett. After much tomfoolery and turmoil, Lucy and George finish the novel back in Florence – on their honeymoon.

My Florentine landlady thought I'd found my own George. She thought he was sneaking nightly into my tiny room. In fact she knew he was. The crystals had told her. She was a clairvoyant. Every afternoon, she'd drape shawls over the lamps, sheets over the mirrors (which spooked me – it's what Jews do in a house of mourning) and sweep the crumbs off the kitchen table to accommodate a Ouija board and a jagged stack of crystals. I'd come in to find her weeping with her clients as she called up their dead, her mascara running in inky streaks – another reason to prefer churches full of frescoes to her flat. And the crystals were wrong: I didn't have a man in my room. I had a script: the first play I'd written by myself. It was a Generation X melodrama, heavily influenced by Edward Albee's *Who's Afraid of Virginia Woolf?* which was then my favourite play (*obviously* I wanted to be Martha, wanton, manic, wistful, and for Elizabeth Taylor to play me in the film). My play involved self-harm, bad puns, Barbie dolls, and in the second act we made Angel Delight live on stage. It was called *The Candy Jar*.

Theatre was new to me. At school, I'd played a duck in *Noye's*

Fludde, but I couldn't keep my beak down. I'd done some ballet, feeling like a pink lump, sitting in a circle of girls, in blush-pink leotards, wrinkly tights and irritatingly see-through georgette skirts, while our teacher (sleek and lissom in black, no transparent pink for *her*) yelled 'Good toes! Bad toes!' as we pointed and flexed. And that was more or less it. I hadn't even *seen* that many plays. So when two random boy freshers asked me to write a play with them, I nearly said no. I didn't know about theatre, and I didn't want to. But then they said they needed 'a girl to write the girls'. How could I resist?

I hadn't tried to write a heroine since the summer I'd messed around with *Oliver Twist*. And my first two stage heroines were not my finest. They were a drunk French girl and a buttoned-up forty-something. When we got the play on, a casting mishap meant I had to play the forty-something. It taught me a lot about how *not* to write a heroine; there's nothing like having to perform your own lines for calling your bluff. And even if the writing had been better, I would still have hated being on stage. There was the panic that I might forget what I was supposed to be doing, the self-consciousness of pretending to be someone else and – my worst nightmare – being looked at. I had salt in all my pockets and an extra sachet in my bra too, but I still felt unsafe. I vowed never to perform again. Nevertheless, I was hooked on theatre. Poetry suddenly seemed sterile next to the *liveness* of theatre, where you all came together – writers, actors, director, designer, even the audience, especially the audience – to believe in something. My poems had come out of my own neuroses, but now I could write different voices, live different lives, write my own heroines (and maybe, one day, heroes too).

Cambridge turned out to be a brilliant place to find out about theatre. It was rammed with thesps (we used the word only *semi-*ironically) in black polo necks, and comics in thick-framed glasses. I spent whole lost days talking about Shakespeare and *le nouveau cirque* and Peter Brook over pots of tea and rounds of cinnamon toast in the English Department buttery. I stayed up one night to read Brook's *The Empty Space* as if it was a thriller; he made theatre seem important, human and alive. A dazzling *Private Lives* was so vivid and hazardous that I felt I was in the room with its heroine Amanda, laughing at her jokes, watching her sabotage her life and holding my breath as I hoped she'd find a way to be happy with her sexy scoundrel of a husband. At an elegiac *Uncle Vanya* I realised theatre could make me feel things and know things before I really felt or knew them in real life. I co-wrote a play with a Ukrainian mature student who'd worked in an abattoir and smoked like a chimney; it was about two psychopaths who destroy a family, and we called it *The Nutter.* I directed it too; my first go at getting something from page to stage. With a Sondheim-obsessed mathematician I wrote a musical about vampires and small-town racism called *The Suckers.* As a publicity stunt we carried a coffin through the market square.

And now I'd written one on my own. A friend was passing through Florence, and we took the orange bus out to Fiesole, in the hills above the city. It's in those hills, covered in violets, that George kisses Lucy. We made for the Roman amphitheatre and sat on the stage, and read out my play. He read the boys, I read the girls. We had the whole arc of honey-coloured stones to ourselves, the whole blue sky. Later I'd direct it in Cambridge and on the Edinburgh Fringe, but that afternoon in Fiesole was where it startled into life. At Fiesole, Lucy sees the violets and feels spring, *really* feels the sun and the flowers blooming and opening, and suddenly feels that she can see the world 'beautiful and direct' – and then George kisses her. Because of Lucy, and because of Fiesole, I felt that too; that things were clearing, that I could see.

From *A Room with a View*, I got the idea that the best kind of life was an artist's life. When Mr Beebe, the socially astute clergyman, fails to stop Lucy going out unchaperoned, he puts her rebellion down to 'too much Beethoven' and speculates that 'If Miss Honeychurch ever takes to live as she plays, it will be very exciting both for us and for her.' I loved this. Too much Beethoven! Too much Beethoven could catapult you into the arms of George Emerson, too much Beethoven could catapult you into *life*. Beethoven wasn't my favourite composer (and anyway in the film, which I've seen too many times, Lucy's liberation is underscored by Puccini), but I did want to live as I played. To be brave on and off the page. I thought this would save me from a lot of things: falseness, lies, repression, propriety, primness, delicacy, denial, abstraction, prudishness, artfulness, self-consciousness, pretentiousness, peevishness, sanctimony, and most of all from Forster's bugbear: *muddle*.

Lucy starts out so conditioned that she thinks the proper response to the stabbing is to pretend it never happened. Never talk about it, never let herself feel anything. But George knows something huge has happened. He wants to examine it, feel it, understand it. He wants to *live*. Lucy runs, scared, in the opposite direction, into the stiff, awkward arms of repressed and repressive Cecil. Cecil consumes art only so that he can twist it into puns, evasions and put-downs. He doesn't let it make him feel anything. Cecil would never care about a character in a book the way I care about Lucy. Cecil would hate *this* book. He'd be cold, supercilious, condescending about it. But then, I hate Cecil, so we're even.

Cecil wants Lucy to be reticent and mysterious – basically he wants her in a veil. Forster makes the metaphor explicit when George's father talks Lucy into clarity again and she feels the darkness being 'withdrawn, veil after veil'. She elopes with George. Finally she's doing it; she's living as she plays. But is Mr Beebe happy? No. He's disappointed because what he really wanted was for her to be celibate. So much for living by his credo. It's very flummoxing.

But now it seems I misread the novel, or took what I wanted from it, because Lucy doesn't want to live an artist's life at all. She's not trying to become a concert pianist. Her piano-playing isn't what attracts George (though Cecil loves it. Surely a bad sign). The only artist in the novel, the writer Eleanor Lavish, is roundly mocked for being pretentious, wearing ridiculous clothes and calling stinking alleyways the real Italy.

And Forster doesn't show us Lucy living as she plays. After she admits she loves George, he skips to their honeymoon. We don't see her battle her family and society to marry him, and we don't see her make the bold decision to elope. There's no running-away-in-the-dead-of-night scene, no secret marriage, no journey to Florence pursued by angry relatives. The drama is all off stage. This really annoyed Katherine Mansfield, who cattily said Forster only ever got as far as warming the teapot, but never made the tea.

For most of his life, Forster didn't live as he played. He wrote intrepid heroines who put love first (I also have a soft spot for Lilia, the middle-aged English widow in *Where Angels Fear to Tread* who rushes headlong into marriage with an Italian hunk), while all the time he was living with his finicky, proper mother and putting love very low on his list. He didn't lose his virginity until he was 37, when he was living away from his mother for a while because the Red Cross had posted him to Alexandria. After that, he wrote just one more novel (1924's *A Passage to India*) and then stopped publishing fiction. He lived on for another forty-six years, and there were no more novels, no more stories. He said he'd dried up. But after his death, from his letters and diaries came the heartbreaking revelation that he had stopped writing fiction because he didn't want to write about heterosexual love. His one gay novel, *Maurice*, was written in 1913, but published posthumously: at first, he withheld it because it might upset his mother, and later because he was seeing a married man and had to be discreet.

So Forster wrote *A Room with a View* when he wished he could write heroes instead of heroines. And when he imagined Lucy finally being able to stop lying, he was writing about the kind of honest love affair he wanted himself. And I never noticed before how sympathetically he writes Charlotte. I used to hate her for squelching George, for encouraging Lucy to lie, for her 'barbed civilities', her awkwardness, her obsession with correct behaviour. But in a devastating passage Forster explains why she is how she is. Lucy is lying, claiming she doesn't love George. And Forster writes 'The night received her, as it had received Miss Bartlett thirty years before.'

So it seems Charlotte had a chance at happiness, perhaps at

love (perhaps even with a woman; there's definitely a flirty vibe to her friendship with Eleanor Lavish), and she fluffed it. Now Lucy has broken up with Cecil, claims she doesn't love George and is planning to go away with two fussy, fidgeting spinster sisters she met in Florence. To Charlotte, it looks as if Lucy is on course to become her. And she knows what that's like, and wouldn't wish it on anyone. So, having been a ninny for most of the novel, she sees her chance to cut through the muddle and bring Lucy and George together. And she jumps at it. She rises to the occasion. She becomes heroic. Lucy can't believe Charlotte's done it, but George can. He's read Eleanor Lavish's tacky novel and found that the bit where the heroine is kissed on a hill of violets has a curious power, which can only come from Charlotte describing Lucy and George's kiss to her friend. 'The sight of us haunted her,' says George, 'or she couldn't have described it as she did . . . There are details – it burnt . . . She is not frozen, Lucy, she is not withered up all through.' Reading this now, maybe because I'm older and more sympathetic to maiden aunts, eternal chaperones and companions to the younger, friskier, more skittish heroines, I find it unbearably moving. And I hope if I ever get my call to adventure, I'll say yes. Charlotte showed me it's never too late to become a heroine.

Bertolt Brecht, who my theatre friends quoted incessantly, said that we should always see the choices characters *don't* make, as well as the ones they do. Forster shows how Lucy nearly becomes Charlotte. She swerves at the very last minute on to another path, but she could easily have been lulled into thinking there was no other path. In Brecht's plays no actions are inevitable. Instead of allowing us to suspend disbelief, he keeps us awake, keeps showing the characters' choices and their alternatives. It's not always the most relaxing theatre to watch but it's hugely empowering. Then, I was excited by following Lucy's path. Now I find Charlotte's late flowering into heroism just as inspiring. And maybe Forster was rehearsing his own choices too, maybe it was writing Charlotte that made him seize his chance at happiness when, at 51, he met the love of his life.

Before leaving Florence, I went to Fiesole again with some other students. This time, we read Euripides' *The Bacchae* and I got the plum role. Agave is the queen that Dionysus lures to the mountain. Seduced into reverie, Agave and her women wear snakes in their hair, suckle wolves and gazelles and make wine, milk and honey spring from the earth. When the men try to force them back to civilisation, the women tear a herd of cows to bits with their bare hands. Agave dismembers a lion – and when the trance fades she looks down at her hands and sees it's not a lion's head she's holding, but her son's. Sitting in that amphitheatre, reading from my shared and tattered Penguin Classics copy of the play, I looked at my hands and saw the lion's head transform into the head of my son. I had a seizure, a bad one, and got the bus back with blood pouring from my cut knees. But I had been Agave in that moment, really been her, felt what it might be like to go madly, dangerously wild, and how hard she has to fight to hang on to her reason when she gets it back again. And felt again how theatre was giving me a chance to really *be* other women, to try out their choices and see how I liked them.

Back at Cambridge for my final year, I was facing some choices too. At the end of the year, I'd be moving back to London, where all the expectations I had been avoiding were waiting for me. And, strange though it was to be thinking about marriage while my parents were in the throes of their divorce, on my weekends back they even arranged for me to go on a couple of dates with boys from my community, including one who had gone away to university himself but told me that everyone knew the first thing a girl did when she went away to university was take drugs and spread her legs. My mother said he was testing me, and now he knew I was a lady, he'd treat me beautifully. But Esther Greenwood had shown me I was done with the double standard and anyway, thanks to Scarlett O'Hara, I didn't want to be a lady. At least now I had more of an idea about what I did want: to make a life in the theatre.

Theatre gave me a new community, one that suited me better than the one I'd grown up in. Yes, Franny was right, in *Franny and Zooey*, about theatre people: 'All those egos running round feeling terribly *cha*ritable and *warm*. Kissing everybody and wearing makeup all over the place'. But I also met people who were open about their ambitions, ready to live with thin skins and open hearts, to try to do what Franny's brother Buddy says and aim to make something 'beautiful . . . nameless and joy-making' on stage. Buddy promises that if Franny succeeds, he and the much-mourned Seymour 'will both rent tuxedos and rhinestone hats and solemnly come round to the stage door with bouquets of snapdragons'.

Franny wasn't my only actor-heroine. Looking back it seems obvious I would end up in the theatre; so many of my heroines had preceded me there. Antonia White's Clara had done time in a travelling theatre troupe in the 1920s and she, and the theatrical memoirs I was hoovering up, gave me an enduring fantasy about playing the ingénue in a creaky farce, living out of a suitcase in digs cluttered with aspidistras and fleas (to be dispatched with a cake of soap) and bedbugs (beyond the pale), living on sausages, strong tea and grilled herrings, sticking telegrams in my dressing-room mirror on first nights, and knowing how to apply panstick, combat stage fright, drink men under the table and do an impromptu cabaret turn, all high kicks and silk stockings. Most of this would turn out to be wildly out of date, but I do still think of Clara sometimes, when I'm in a dressing room full of the warm rose smell of cold cream, or picking up post at the stage door, and when once I popped out of a last night party to watch my play's set being sawn up and chucked in a skip and remembered that one thing you have to know about theatre is how ephemeral it is.

But my first and best guide to the theatre was *Ballet Shoes*, Noel Streatfeild's 1936 story of the Fossil girls making their way on the stage. When I first read it, at nine or ten, not knowing I would end up writing plays, I didn't want to be able to act like Pauline or dance like Posy; instead, when gawky, down-to-earth Petrova asks, at the end of the book, 'I wonder, if other girls had to be one of us, which of us they'd choose to be?', my answer was you, Petrova, only you.

The sisters – all unrelated orphans adopted by an absent-minded palaeontologist – only go on the stage to earn their keep. (They also have to take in boarders and share frocks and make do and mend. I love how practical Streatfeild's book is, packed with details about dressmaking and household accounts; she even includes a performing child licence in the book!) But once they get started, Pauline (the blonde) and Posy (the redhead) love it. But Petrova (the brunette – another reason I loved her), hates theatre. She can't think of anything worse than becoming a dancer or an actor. She wants to be a chauffeur or a mechanic or an aviatrix.

Streatfeild takes the girls' vocations totally seriously; this seriousness is part of the book's charm, and its strength. The sisters are loyal and selfless. Even Posy, who can be a brat and is always in disgrace for putting her ambitions first, is funny and sweet. And she's only ever tough because she's following her talent; she doesn't have an ego about it, really. She just knows she has to dance, and so she does.

From *Ballet Shoes*, I learned how stage fright feels in the pit of the stomach ('very queer – like when you miss a step on the moving staircase and think you are going to fall to the bottom'), and that it's normal to cry after the show is over. I learned that being grand will get you nowhere: when Pauline puts on airs, her understudy is sent on in her place. I learned that you're only as successful as your latest show. I learned that stage flying is really being wheeled about on wires, and to beware of modern costume design – cast as fairies, Pauline and Petrova hope for frills and wings and glitter but get nasty yellow skintight all-over leotards instead. I learned that attitude is as important as talent: Petrova works hard and becomes technically proficient but while she never complains about it, she is bored, and it shows. And that hard work is crucial – the girls slog away to get where they get. I hated John Keats saying 'if Poetry comes not as naturally as the leaves to a tree it had better not come at all' (sorry, Keats). *Ballet Shoes* taught me I'd have to work hard.

And – the biggest lesson of all – although theatre is probably the most passionate, hopeful and consistently romanticised art form there is, if I was going to become a playwright I would have to become pragmatic. Pauline is going up for the same roles as Winifred, who is more talented and clever but doesn't have Pauline's beauty or her sweet, unworried nature. Winifred is desperate to earn money, to help her sick father and her impoverished family, but her anxiety shows on her face, and her clothes are dowdy, and she wears them like a frump, and so while Pauline gets to star, Winifred is doomed to be the understudy. Streatfeild knew about the compromises and hardships of theatre because she'd spent ten years as a jobbing actress before, sick of touring, she holed up in a London hostel and sat down to write a book on her father's typewriter. But that book was not *Ballet Shoes*; it was *The Whicharts*.

It's a very odd novel to read if you know *Ballet Shoes*. It feels like an edgy, grown-up version of *Ballet Shoes,* but in fact it's the other way around. *The Whicharts* was Streatfeild's first hit. Seven years later, and a confirmed success, she was surprised to be asked to write a children's book. But like Louisa May Alcott before her, she wasn't one to turn down a commission, so she set out to rehash *The Whicharts* into *Ballet Shoes*. She gave herself three months, most of which must have been taken up with excising all the sex and swearing. She had to cut the storyline about the Whicharts being three illegitimate daughters of the same philandering brigadier, and she couldn't let them be brought up by his first, neglected mistress. But she kept the idea of two girls loving theatre and one hating it, and Tania (the original Petrova) pursuing her dream to fly planes is a rare burst of optimism in this dark, dark book. Because *The Whicharts* is not starry-eyed about theatre; it is cynical and pessimistic. Maimie slips from legitimate theatre into becoming a venal chorus girl, only in it for the men and the money. Daisy loves dancing as much as Posy but when she is offered a comfortable home in the suburbs, she gives up her ambitions – and why shouldn't she, when her older sister has shown her just how tawdry and sordid theatre can be?

Reading *The Whicharts* does tarnish *Ballet Shoes*: it makes it feel a bit sanitised and marshmallowy. But it doesn't stop me loving it. Not at all. Although *Ballet Shoes* may have started as a bowdlerised version of the earlier book, I think that in those frenzied three months, when Streatfeild was lifting whole paragraphs from *The Whicharts* and cutting and pasting character names, something amazing happened: *Ballet Shoes* became the book *The Whicharts* should always have been. I think Streatfeild just started loving her heroines and let them take flight (literally, when it came to Petrova); and that she got over her bitterness about theatre and remembered why she'd loved it in the first place, why it had seemed so alluring, such an escape from her stifled childhood as a vicar's daughter. It strikes me now that in *Ballet Shoes* Streatfeild wrote a version of the kind of relationship she might have liked – she never found love, but the two lady doctors who board at the Fossils' and later move to a charming flat in Bloomsbury could well have been her image of an ideal relationship. And although she was surprised *Ballet Shoes* was such a hit, she embraced it, writing more children's books and becoming a real cheerleader for children's fiction. She may have retired from the stage but she never stopped being a trouper.

I still feel completely pure about *Ballet Shoes*. It's a book I'd give my daughter if I had one. All the best women love *Ballet Shoes* – Nora Ephron obviously did, because when she wants us to root for Meg Ryan's character, Kathleen, in *You've Got Mail*, she has her say how much she loves *Ballet Shoes*. Because of *Ballet Shoes*, I've done my best to be a practical dreamer, as theatre demands I must. I've found a use for my love of pretending (still going strong, ever since Sara Crewe). And through Pauline's discovery that acting is not about mimicry but about 'feeling a part', I learned the most important thing I know about writing heroines: that they don't live on the stage, or on the page, unless the writer cares enough to breathe life into them. (All right, the same goes for heroes.)

In my final term at Cambridge, as I was deciding I was really going to try to be a playwright, I was still searching for a heroine who would take me by the hand and show me how. The eponymous heroine of Herman Wouk's 1955 novel *Marjorie Morningstar* seemed to be The One. She is a naïve, neurotic Jewish girl who escapes her cosseted childhood in the suburbs to follow her dream of working in theatre. She's American, not British, and an actress, not a playwright; she's coming of age in the 1930s not the 1990s, but let's not quibble: she is me.

She begins the novel as Marjorie Morgenstern, the pretty, spoilt daughter of a feather-importer. He and his wife met through a matchmaker, the old way, but things are different now. They hope their daughter will marry someone rich and suitable. (And Jewish, obviously, of course Jewish.) But on page five, Marjorie decides she wants to do something else with her life: she's going to be an actress, and her stage name will be Marjorie Morningstar.

Soon, she's ditched her decent-but-dull Bronx boyfriend and is hanging out with theatre-mad Marsha, learning her craft and falling for the gorgeous cad Noel Airman, a talented composer who warns 'I eat little girls like you'. (If the story of a naïve Jewish girl falling in love with a handsome man on a summer camp entertainment team seems familiar, it's because it's also the plot of *Dirty Dancing*.)

Noel says Marjorie's a 'Shirley', a Nice Jewish Girl who claims she's ambitious when really she wants the suburban dream of a diamond sparkler, nice house, children and a fur coat. She says *he's* a 'Sidney', a Nice Jewish Boy who promises adventure but ends up working for his father. But as their on–off relationship blooms and withers (and blooms and withers, and blooms and withers again), she also learns about theatre.

Marjorie taught me that it's wise to learn about everything – lighting, sound, set-building – because you never know what you'll need, and theatre is as much a craft as it is an art. She taught me that the best way to learn is to watch rehearsals. And that theatre is full of sharks. And that it involves a lot of compromise, but also the knack of knowing when a compromise is a compromise too far.

But in the last nine pages of the book, there's no nice way of putting it: Wouk betrays her. We've suffered with her and dreamed with her and suddenly she gives up theatre and Noel and marries a nebbishy lawyer and moves to the suburbs.

I hated that ending. I made up my own. In my version, Marjorie becomes a star and marries Noel – a man so charismatic that even Marjorie's conventional, suspicious mother melts when she sees him in a toreador costume. A man with an infectious laugh, a man who knows how to enjoy life, and likes other people to enjoy it with him. The 1958 film, with Natalie Wood playing Marjorie to Gene Kelly's sexy, charming Noel, rewrites Wouk's ending and gives Marjorie a romance with another talented, successful Jewish writer who loves her, the unfairly named Wally Wronken. Usually I resent Hollywood happy endings but this one feels like justice. And until now, I've been able to read *Marjorie Morningstar* and just ignore the inexplicable ending.

But now, I'm devastated to say that from its opening pages *Marjorie Morningstar* feels irredeemably snide. It's not quite satire but it's unkind writing. And I don't like unkind writing. And Wouk's agenda is clear from the start. I don't think he's really a storyteller; he's a moralist. So his novel hammers home his reactionary message that you can never find your own way.

All Marjorie's adventures are shadowed by Wouk's gloom about them. He grimly describes her liberation from her traditional parents. When she eats a lobster it's the end of the world. (And of course it doesn't taste nice. How could it, when she is denying who she is and eating sin?) Wouk also seems to regard theatre, in its entirety, as sinful. He marshals dodgy actors to tell Marjorie that if she stays a virgin she will never have the emotional range she needs to be a good actor. She is told this so often that when she's not getting the roles she wants, she considers having an affair, to see if it will help. The moral is clear: don't put your daughter on the stage, or she'll end up a slag.

Yet Marjorie is confident and kind. She wants to be an actress *and* a dutiful daughter. She holds on to her ideals, she works at her craft, she resists her bad critics. She enjoys the raffish Greenwich Village world Noel shows her, but she's not dazzled by it. And he broadens her horizons. Yes, he can be caustic and rude, know-it-all, feckless and unstable, but they are in love. And he's talented. At least he is at first. But then Wouk reneges on that too.

Marsha, Marjorie's old theatre pal, has given up her dreams and is marrying a nice, Jewish man. But he's old, and uninspiring, and at her wedding she sobs hysterically in her bedroom and, red-eyed and tragic in her rucked-up dress, rages at Marjorie: 'I don't have a Noel Airman in love with me. If I had I'd follow him like a dog.' When Marjorie asks if she should agree to sleep with Noel, Marsha screams 'YES, God damn you, YES! . . . *Live* your life, you poor boob.' She advises Marjorie to stop worrying and see what Noel is really like, let him see what *she's* really like, and maybe in the end she'll get her Prince Charming. And if not, she'll have the memories.

This makes sense to Marjorie (as it does to me) and she leaves the wedding to go to the dress rehearsal of Noel's first Broadway show then back to his hotel for an all-night session of Chinese food, coffee and notes with the producers. She forces down a bite of pork, and feels so liberated that once the producers have gone, she goes to bed with Noel. (If only my prawn experience had been so catalysing.)

Wouk can't decide what he's writing here. One minute Marjorie's detached and uninterested; the next minute trembling with desire. But then Wouk reasserts control of his text and his heroine. He sits morosely on the edge of the bed daring his readers to cheer in the face of his solemn, judgmental prose. Marjorie is, he says, 'moving towards her first sex act . . . like an asteroid moving to collide with a comet'. The next line asks, absurdly, 'What of her mother, her father?' The actual sex is 'rough and strange. She was powerless to stop it . . . she was very uncomfortable and unhappy. It became rougher and more awkward. It became horrible. There were shocks, ugly uncoverings, pain, incredible humiliation, shock, shock, and it was over.'

Why, though? If Wouk had been writing a scene where Marjorie had sex with one of her nice Jewish men on their wedding night, would it have involved roughness and shock and incredible humiliation? Noel isn't the kind of man who would misjudge the situation so drastically that he wouldn't be tender and gentle. And Marjorie wants him. She's wanted him for years. But it doesn't matter what the characters are like because Wouk isn't letting them live. He's pushing them around. And he fatally loses this reader by adding maliciously, 'So it was that Marjorie qualified at last to portray true emotion on the stage.' All right, Wouk, I get the message. A nice Jewish woman who tangles with theatre will inevitably shove pork down her throat and shag around. To underline the point, Wouk throws in an eclipse of the moon. As Marjorie loses her virginity, the sky is drained of light and the moon goes the colour of blood.

I can scarcely bring myself to report what happens after page 417. Noel's musical dies on stage. (Of course. Wouk can't let Noel be a success.) Noel leaves Marjorie. She pines and repents, and whenever she remembers her night with Noel, she feels shamed and tormented.

Then Wouk gives Marjorie another chance. Her parents are on side this time, and they encourage her to go to Paris and win

Noel back. She goes to Paris. Noel proposes. In Montmartre! With champagne and candlelight and everything, and what does she do? She says no.

Again, Wouk is unclear. Sometimes Marjorie seems to be saying no because Noel is looking a bit older and more tired than he did. Sometimes it is because she's met a man she likes on the ship to Paris. (I do *not* like this man. He's a pill-popping skeeve who works in pharmaceuticals but claims he is secretly saving Jews from the Nazis.) Wouk also suggests that Marjorie has become bored by what Noel offers – travel, adventure, bohemianism, and that Lucy-ish idea of living as you play. According to Wouk, when Noel takes Marjorie to the hottest *boîtes* in Montmartre, she complains that the smoke makes her cough. They go for a walk and she says her feet are sore. They sing in the rain and she says her hat's getting soggy and the curl is coming out of her hair. She doesn't see any of the romance of Paris; none. And I don't believe it. I think Marjorie would have been as excited by Montmartre as Lucy was by Santa Croce. It just shows, again, how little Wouk cares about his heroine.

Back in New York, she has another chance to marry Wally. He's like a less sexy Noel – talented but he loves his mother – yet she runs away because she can't face telling him she's not a virgin. I don't believe this either. Wally knows Marjorie's been seeing Noel for years. And he's an open-minded young man who works in the theatre. He wouldn't mind, and Marjorie knows it. But Wouk minds. And his characters have stopped being alive and he's just shlepping them from one page to another. So he finds Marjorie a nice Jewish lawyer and they get engaged. *Mazel tov!* But when she confesses she is not a virgin, the lawyer can't cope. She runs away to a hotel, spends six days in bed with a high fever (the fever of sin, perhaps? Wouk doesn't specify) and comes home twelve pounds lighter, like a medieval saint who has fasted away her crimes. Then the lawyer consents to take her 'with her deformity, despite it. For that was what it amounted to in his eyes and in hers – a deformity: a deformity that could no longer be helped; a permanent crippling, like a crooked arm.' Thanks, Wouk. Thanks a lot.

Of course, she has to give up theatre too. She has to be ashamed of her ambitions. She has to conform totally to her parents' out-of-date ideals, and count herself lucky to have snagged a nice Jewish man who will forgive her for having had a life.

Cut to some fifteen years later and Wally, now famous, goes to see Marjorie. He is shocked to find her grey and dull, claiming to be content but knocking back highballs and waltzing tragically by herself.

I can't ignore this ending any more. It doesn't feel inexplicable; it's where Wouk has been going all along. He didn't want me to dream, after all: he wanted me to stop fantasising and grow up, and knuckle down to being a Nice Jewish Woman. I feel angrier than ever about the ending of his book now that I realise that he stacked the deck against Marjorie from the start. He could have made her a gifted actress who became a star, or a gifted actress who sank without trace. Both are good stories. Anyone who works in theatre has seen talented people fail as many times as they succeed; theatre is tough. But instead, he makes Marjorie a vain little Jewish girl who deludes herself into thinking she might become a star.

There's another story Wouk could have told about Marjorie,

the story in which she becomes a working actor, never gets a big break but enjoys her sustaining, challenging work in the theatre. This is the story Streatfeild might have told about Marjorie, the story of a work ethic, a dream and a determination to see life as an adventure. It was the story I wanted for myself – and in choosing to write plays, maybe I was also spiting Wouk and keeping Marjorie's theatrical dreams alive. After Cambridge, I took my play to the Edinburgh Fringe, and there were no rhinestone hats, no snapdragons, but it was thrilling. On the night coach home to London, we swigged from a paperback-sized bottle of whisky, ate a block of Dairy Milk, sang all the songs from *The Sound of Music*, read aloud to each other from *The Portable Dorothy Parker* and finally got out a prop blanket (smeared in Angel Delight, but warm nevertheless), curled up in it and talked about the future. We didn't expect it to be easy. We knew we'd have to work. But we were absolutely going to try to live as we played, and play as we lived.

THE DOLLS (FROM THE VALLEY)

First, of course, I had to get a job. All my ideas about being a young woman at work came from *Valley of the Dolls*. Which was and wasn't useful. But at least it was a book by and about women. After three years of English at Cambridge, being force-fed literary theory, I was almost convinced that literature was all coded messages about Marxism and the death of the self. I crawled out of the post-structuralist desert thirsty for heroines I could cry and laugh with. I was jaded. I craved trash.

So I picked up Jacqueline Susann's salacious 1966 bestseller, which I'd first read in the sixth form. On the cover of my edition was a photograph of a squat glass pillbox, in sharp focus and, behind it, a woman so blurred it was impossible to tell if she was reaching for the pills or lying there, already dazed and strung-out, or worse. It should have been a warning that this wasn't a chic, fun, frothy read. The dolls are pills – downers to sleep, uppers to stay skinny – but they are also the heroines, so objectified by men and by each other that they seem more like dolls than women.

At 21, I adored *Valley*'s non-stop storytelling, the gossipy, succulent, exclamation-mark-studded prose and the glamour. I felt as though I was eavesdropping on the stars – and I more or less was, because Susann spent most of her life chasing fame and knew everyone in showbiz New York, and all their secrets. She spills them all on the page. She holds nothing back. Despite all attempts to drown it in kitsch (Russ Meyer's soft porn melodrama, *Beyond the Valley of the Dolls*, is a spoof and a travesty), there's something weird and brilliant and lasting about Susann's novel.

The heroine I liked best was Anne Welles, an elegant beauty, described as 'classy' on practically every page, who can't wait to leave her stodgy Massachusetts town. She's getting out of Lawrenceville and she's *never going back*! I was back home in London where my parents' divorce was in its final, painful stages, and I felt more disillusioned with my community and its values than ever. I too wanted to get out and *never go back*. The novel runs from 1945 to 1965 but Anne had many issues that were also mine. Her mother wants her to marry her childhood sweetheart and become a housewife and mother. She has brought her up to be a lady. But Anne doesn't want to be a lady. She wants to be a working girl. In New York.

There, she meets Neely, a spitfire of a girl, freckled, clumsy, stubborn and, at seventeen, already a veteran of vaudeville. Endearingly, Neely's perfect night is an evening in with a quart of milk, a box of cookies and *Gone With The Wind*. But when she needs a stage name in a pinch, she steals Scarlett's, and as Neely O'Hara she'll become just as ruthless as her namesake.

And oh, I wish I'd had the wit to learn from her. Anne gets a job as a secretary in a theatrical law firm, and that is the end of her ambitions in New York. She's got her good black dress and her good black coat, and her tweed suit, and her nice manners. She's tasteful, she doesn't mix business with pleasure, she doesn't drink too much, or flirt, she spends her money wisely and she always gets enough sleep to save her energy for the office. And maybe because she has no ambitions of her own, she is always attaching herself to careless, driven, charismatic people. First she becomes the person Neely turns to in every crisis, and then Anne falls for her boss like some 1940s dollybird.

His very name indicates he's trouble. Lyon Burke is a dreamboat – tall, permatanned, with ink-black hair, a clipped English accent, a heroic war record, and sheer animal magnetism. He's good at his job but he tells Anne that his secret dream is to 'Be dreadfully rich . . . Sit in some lovely spot in Jamaica, have several beautiful girls who look exactly like you to look after me and knock out a best-selling novel about the war.' Anne doesn't find this off-putting and smug. She doesn't hear the warning klaxon of *several* beautiful girls. No. She starts egging him on to write, slavishly typing up his manuscripts, and gazing into his sad, tormented eyes as he tells his boring war stories.

She nurtures him in other ways too, and there are compensations: when she has her first orgasm, she squeals, 'I function, Lyon – I'm a woman!' But when she inherits her childhood home and he demands that they turn it into his perfect writing retreat, with Anne cooking his meals and washing his socks, she sees that he's about to perpetrate muse abuse, and she says no (because Anne has left Lawrenceville and she's *never going back*!) Lyon promptly crosses the Atlantic, hoping to marry 'the first plump English maiden who will cook and tend for me'. It gives me great pleasure to report that he doesn't marry any English women. Perhaps we are immune to his charms. (I confess that I was *not* immune to Lyon's charms but I am all grown up now.)

I was astonished when I made a brief foray into internet dating to find how many men contacted me saying they were looking for a muse – even though my profile said I was a writer, which surely would indicate that I might have been looking for a muse of my own. (I wasn't.) Maybe those men were picking up on something about me, maybe they knew Anne was my heroine at the time. And Anne's way of doing things *was* useful in my temping: as a PA, as a receptionist (when we were nominated for Reception Desk of the Year, it was time to leave), and when I got a job in charity communications. In my early twenties, I was doing jobs that required Anne qualities – diligence, punctiliousness, patience – instead of doing what I should have been doing: writing my plays and getting them put on. At the flat I'd moved into with a playwright friend, I often slipped into Anne-like roles. I would cook dinner for everyone, then wash up while they went off to the pub to talk theatre. And when my flatmate and I put on a double bill of our plays, I took the thankless role of producer, which meant I was too busy sourcing props, painting sets and rigging lights to go to rehearsals, or write something new. One rainy afternoon I tramped from charity shop to charity shop, trying to find a cheap wedding dress for the heroine of my play. When finally I found a rack of white dresses, I grabbed the one in my size, which was also the actress's, and hastily tried it on. I emerged from the changing cubicle, hair soaked, a grim and martyred look on my face, to find the shopkeeper offering me a mug of tea, the use of a hairdryer, a pair of heels, and even a bouquet of silk flowers 'to get the full effect, dear'. Only then did I realise she thought I was shopping for my own special day. I was so embarrassed I went along with it. But afterwards I had to laugh, because even writing plays had landed me in a wedding dress – and I was still so eager to please that I had ended up lying about it. So much for shrugging off the good girl, the dutiful daughter and the pseudo-wife.

Neely would have given me the same advice she gives Anne. She constantly tries to get Anne to be more savvy and less nice. When Anne prissily worries about pulling strings to get Neely a part, Neely warns, 'Those fancy manners are gonna stand in your way. You gotta go in a direct line for the thing you want. Come right out and ask for it.' Neely gets into the show. Anne wants her to dress soberly, but Neely wears purple taffeta so she'll stand out in rehearsal. And she does – so much so that the star, brassy battleaxe Helen Lawson, feels upstaged and gets her fired. But Neely doesn't lie down quietly and take it. She turns up at Anne's office, in floods of tears. Anne wants her to calm down, control herself, stop making such a fuss. Neely's loud, ugly tears catch the attention of Anne's boss, who gets her back on the show, in a bigger role than before. It's a brilliant lesson in negotiation. And while Neely's tears are genuine, she's not above faking them if necessary. She knows it's the squeaky wheel that gets the grease.

Once in the show, Neely's a sponge, learning everything she can from Helen, while never trusting her an inch. It would be a more heart-warming story if Helen became Neely's mentor, but Susann isn't interested in heart-warming, she's interested in telling the truth about a world in which no star rushes to help a younger ingénue.

While Anne is chasing bad boy Lyon, Neely cunningly marries a good man, a man who will support *her* career. He's a press agent, just like Susann's husband, who made her first book, *Every Night, Josephine!*, a bestseller, despite the fact that it was an extended love letter to her poodle by a woman famous for wanting to be famous. Neely's husband gets her to Hollywood.

Once there, she 'unloads' him and marries someone even more useful: a costume designer. Work always comes first for Neely. She spends her nights at home, studying scripts with her hair smothered in lanolin and cream slathered over her face, and (for the cameras) puts up with her second husband cheating on her. But when she wins an Oscar she decides she's earned the right to play the diva. She gets a divorce, goes to work late or not at all, ignores directives from the studio, feasts on caviar and takes dolls to lose weight, or just to numb the loneliness. For a while, the studio put up with this; after all, she's very talented. But then they fire her, and she takes an overdose.

Like her tears in Anne's office, Neely's overdose is real, but when she comes round a week later, woozy but miraculously alive, she immediately takes charge of her career. She grins when she sees how much weight she's lost. Still hooked up to a drip, she summons her lawyer and agents to her bedside and soon she's making threats and demands and fighting her way back. It starts a saga of disastrous crack-ups and glittering comebacks – Susann based Neely on Judy Garland.

In the best scene in the book, Neely runs into Helen again, in the bathroom of a swanky club. Helen has clawed her way back into the limelight more than once, and she doesn't think Neely's got her talent or her staying power. When she calls Neely a 'washed up little has-been', they have the bitch-fight to end all bitch-fights. Neely wins by grabbing Helen's lustrous hair, which turns out to be a wig, right off her head. She gleefully dances round with it, then flushes it down a toilet, leaving Helen to sneak out ignominiously, and Neely to prove she's not washed up by doing what she does best: believing in her talent, putting it first, and clawing her way back to the top.

If only I'd had a fraction of her self-belief. Instead, I did job after job that took me further away from writing. I edited other people's writing, not even at a proper publishing house but at a vanity press (allegedly the one that inspired Martin Amis's *The Information*). It was like the boarding school I never went to – the editors were all young women, mostly Oxbridge blondes, and we'd pad about the office in laddered tights, drinking tea and taking turns on the office phone, swinging our legs, having semi-secret, half-whispered conversations with mysterious men. Each editrix sat in a tiny cubicle with blue padded walls. I found proof-reading soothing. I liked the clean white spaces. I liked the arcane proof marks. I liked making things right. But it was long, laborious work (Anne would have loved it), and I longed to be slapdash, chaotic, creative.

The work also scared the living daylights out of me. A lot of the writing was shockingly bad (they were called vanity presses for a reason). Characters changed sex halfway through (and not in a postmodern way), the poems were all o'ers and e'ens, there were obnoxious far-right political tracts, vainglorious memoirs and anatomically incorrect erotica. We laughed at the howlers, but it was also a glimpse into the abyss. These writers were mostly puffed up and deluded but what if I was too? How did I know I wasn't fooling myself that I could write?

Valley's third heroine, the staggeringly beautiful (secretly sad)

Jennifer North, is the opposite of Neely. She believes she has no talent but that she can become a famous actor anyway, by telling lies. And she does it too. Jennifer terrified me. What if I had no talent? And what if I made it anyway? Would that mean I was just like Jennifer?

At the start of the novel, she is claiming she's five years younger than she is, and later she subtracts another decade. She does breast-tightening exercises, massages cocoa butter into her skin and wears frownie plasters to bed, trained by her parasitic mother who warns her that 'Big breasts like yours are going to drop soon enough, and then they'll be an eyesore. Make them pay while you have them. Men are animals.' The men Jennifer meets *are* animals. She's only ever enjoyed sex with a Spanish girl she loved way back when. But women don't have power, so she sleeps with men. She doesn't enjoy her time on the casting couch. On the night of her wedding, to a sexy Italian crooner, he tells her to turn over. 'She ground her teeth in agony as he tore in to her. She felt his nails ripping down her back. Smile, Jen, she told herself. You've made it – you're Mrs Tony Polar.'

Jennifer has the worst time of all the *Valley* women. At the end, she's 40 but looks 25, and she's had to resort to more drastic and mendacious methods to look younger – like a sinister-sounding 'sleep cure' which involves spending a week sedated in a Swiss clinic to lose weight, as well as a painful facelift and hormone injections to keep her breasts firm. Then she finally thinks she's found a man who loves her for herself. So when she is diagnosed with cancer she tries to tell him, and she hopes he'll support her. But as he creepily caresses her breasts and calls them his 'babies', she realises there's no point telling him she's got to have a mastectomy. He doesn't love her for herself at all. So she kills herself.

Susann had just been diagnosed with breast cancer when she wrote this, and she'd been told over and over that she had no talent. She writes Jennifer with great tenderness, and gives her all her worst fears. Yet in real life, once she'd decided writing was her talent, Susann never doubted herself. She pushed herself to the limit promoting *Valley* and its successors, *The Love Machine* and *Once Is Not Enough*, schmoozing critics, booksellers and even the truck drivers who delivered her books to shops. She pushed herself, day and night, in her Pucci print frocks and lacquered wigs, caked in kohl, tripping on hairspray, and of course on dolls. She had no shame. About anything. In *Once* she helpfully explains how to catch semen in a glass and refrigerate it for use as a face mask. But most of all she was fantastically open about her aspirations. She pursued what she wanted with bravado and pizzazz, which makes it all the more perplexing that she structures her book so that apathetic Anne seems to be the top heroine. Looking back, I find it hard to see what I liked about Anne. She's a WASPy ice queen who gets more and more sanctimonious as the book goes on. She spends most of it pining for Lyon, although when she gets another job, modelling cosmetics, she dates her boss there too, as though it's all she can think of to do. Even though sex with him is 'absolutely antiseptic' she doesn't leave him until dastardly, squalid Lyon returns, bleating that 'If I had any character, I wouldn't see you after tonight' – and saying it *while* he's having an affair with her. And it's a fling, mind, not a relationship, let alone a marriage, because Lyon is a free spirit who can't be tied down. God forbid, it might hurt his precious writing.

It makes me sad to see what Anne does next. She loves Lyon so much that she resorts to ugly scheming to keep him in New York, even sneakily buying him a business. She makes sure to get a ring on her finger before he finds out the truth, and seals the deal by getting pregnant. Lyon's furious. He feels he's been castrated, and consoles himself by sleeping with more pliable and (Susann is merciless about ageing) *younger* women.

Worst of all, he sleeps with Neely. Then, I blamed her. I thought Anne was an angel, and Neely was a disloyal man-stealing junkie. Now I'm not so sure. Neely's got grounds for hating Anne: Anne got her committed to a mental hospital. All right, it got Neely clean, but tough love is never endearing. When Neely gets out, she's off the drugs but she's box office poison, and *fat*. So it's a kick in the teeth to find Anne loved-up with Lyon, swimming in money and about to have a baby. Neely gets Lyon to manage her comeback tour, and while they're on the road she gets back on the dolls, loses weight, and takes her revenge. Lyon likes his women skinny as reeds, and can't understand why his wife seems to have put on a bit of weight *having his baby*. Soon he and Neely are having a very public affair.

Class is what Anne started with and it's all she's left with. Lyon goes back to her, but their marriage has been exposed for the sham it is. When she finds out he's shagging a teenage starlet, she takes a doll, brushes her hair and freshens her make-up so she can cling on to her dignity.

It's a bleak ending to a bleak, bleak book. In *Valley*, love is never equal or mutual or trusting, women are betrayed by their bodies, and men are weak, cruel and shallow. Anne and Jennifer try to escape their mothers' lives of joyless housewifery, but end up no happier. Neely can't remember her mother, and she's not happy either. It isn't that they make the wrong choices: there are no right choices, the world is unfair, and they can never be happy.

I'm sad that Susann gave her talent – writing – to Lyon. And that she didn't give any of the dolls a marriage like the supportive, sustaining one she had. And that she didn't find a way to give even one of them a happy ending. In the 1967 film, Anne leaves Lyon. But the Anne of the book is too lovesick, and too stuck on being 'classy', to go anywhere.

Susann was clearly terrified she was talentless like Jennifer, and she knew she had Neely's drive, but I wonder if, when people called her vulgar and brazen, she dreamed of being 'classy'. Maybe that's why Anne hogs the first half of the novel. It seems that Susann started finding Anne more and more vapid – what else can explain the vitriol of Neely's attacks on Anne in the second half? The film critic Pauline Kael famously said a good girl artist was a contradiction in terms. Anne's a good girl and she'll never be a star. But Neely thinks her talent justifies any amount of bad behaviour. Told off for sleeping with her friend's husband, she replies, 'my talent makes the world happy. And Lyon makes *me* happy . . . I need Lyon.' A grown-up, gutsier version of Posy in *Ballet Shoes*, Neely will behave monstrously if she has to, because she's just following her talent. Neely delivers what I think is *Valley*'s real lesson: 'Guys will leave you, your looks will go, your kids will grow up and leave you, and everything you thought was great will go sour; all you can really count on is yourself and your talent.' It's not terrible advice.

Instead, scared of claiming to have theatrical talent, let alone counting on it, I fell into journalism. No one was more surprised than I was when a few days' filing at the *Evening Standard* turned into research, which turned into writing, and by the time I was 25, I had my own page. And although it wasn't what I wanted to do, at least journalism was *fun*.

Every morning, I'd ride the gleaming escalators through the massive, glass atrium, past palm trees and ponds stocked with koi carp, to the cacophonous office, with clocks on the wall showing the times in New York, Beijing and wherever the most important war was on. There were war reporters in flak jackets, a cigar-chomping editor and a style writer who kept a hatbox on her desk containing a passport, pearls and a little black dress, just in case. It was not unlike the *Daily Planet* office in the *Superman* films, and I tried to make my phone manner as quickfire and efficient as Lois Lane's. Like her, I was a girl reporter. And I loved it. Messing about with words, sparring with the subeditors about whether *hip hop* was two separate words or one or hip dash hop and what about when it was adjectival?

It was brilliant getting paid for being curious, and having the licence to ask anything I wanted. After I put my page to bed, I'd go to a gallery opening then a play, then a gig; my page was the Insider's Guide to Going Out, and I was the Insider, so Going Out was my job and London was my oyster. But there was no time to write. So I went freelance. And immediately went nuts. Now, instead of writing, I was researching and pitching ideas, panicking, eating peanut butter out of the jar and watching double bills of *ER*, kidding myself it was useful to watch drama because it would embed brilliant ideas about story structure in my head. My evenings were dedicated to obscure fringe theatre, some of it brilliant, most of it not. A low point was watching an avant-garde puppet play about vampires with rock songs blared out in Catalan while puppet Draculas bit puppet virgins and puppet cherubs frottaged merrily above.

By now I also had another distraction from writing. I was going out with a graffiti artist. We met in the bookshop he worked at, and, uncharacteristically, I set out to seduce him. It took a month or two, and several visits to the shop. First I tried wearing short skirts and reaching for books on high shelves, then I started ordering books with flirtatious titles. When I turned up in red lipstick and asked for Darian Leader's pop-psychoanalysis book *Promises Lovers Make When it Gets Late*, he finally asked me out. We went out for nearly a year. A brilliant year, in lots of ways. He played me old records, which we danced to, in his garden. He tagged my books. The other day, looking up a recipe, I found, on the inside cover of the cookbook, a lazy, lolling pear with twinkly eyes he'd sketched in fat blue pen, now slightly faded. On holiday in Paris, instead of going to the Louvre, we wandered the *banlieues* looking at graffiti he'd heard was particularly good. It was romantic at the time. But it wasn't *love*. When we broke up, I still didn't commit to theatre. Instead I threw myself into work. I interviewed the President of Moldova, in the icy capital, Kishinev, and flew to Genoa to meet James Thiérrée, who looks just like his grandfather, Charlie Chaplin, has his own circus, and can play the violin on roller skates. But it had never been my dream to be a journalist, and I felt I was floundering.

If only I'd spent my twenties trying to be more like Neely than Anne. If only I'd read other books. I wish I'd been a fan of lady detectives; one career where women are almost *over*-represented in fiction is crime-fighting. But most of all, I wish I'd read *Lace*. I've always avoided Shirley Conran's novel because I thought it was just another bonkbuster. It's a curveball to read it now and find out it's really a career woman's handbook.

Although the story runs from 1943 to 1980, *Lace* was published in 1983 and is catnip to anyone who grew up in the Eighties. The hair is huge, money equals happiness and glitz is king. Take, for example, 'Kate's huge, quiet living room. Leopard-skin and tiger-skin cushions were strewn on the couch, which ran thirty feet along the depth of the room. Above them hung a collection of paintings and engravings of tigers and leopards . . . The wall opposite consisted entirely of panels of smoked-mirror glass, each concealing liquor, games, TV, stereo, projector and other valuable clutter.' So airy, that 'other valuable clutter'! It's all very Bret Easton Ellis (no relation). *Lace* makes me crave the sharp, heady scent of Elnett hairspray, and leopard print. A look I've never liked. But I do now own a leopard-print scarf. I got to the end of *Lace* and just couldn't help myself.

To get the filth out of the way, yes there's plenty. I'll never look at a lemon meringue pie in the same way again, and I will never, ever date a man who keeps a goldfish. But the filth is not the point. The point is work.

Conran's four heroines meet in Switzerland where Judy is studying French and waitressing to pay her way. She doesn't have rich parents like Maxine, Pagan and Kate, who are at finishing school dreaming about boys, and she wants money, independence and challenging work. Conventional Maxine tells her if she marries well she won't need to work. 'Wanna bet?' replies Judy. That's how hardboiled she is. They vow to stick together through thick and thin (in Maxine's thick French accent it comes out as 'sick and sin'). Slowly they come round to Judy's view that work is what counts.

Conran lards the novel with lovingly detailed descriptions of how to run an interior design consultancy and turn a crumbling champagne estate into a multimillion tourist destination (Maxine), raise a fortune for cancer research (Pagan), become a top publicist (Judy), a war reporter (Kate) or start a magazine for new, independent women (Kate *and* Judy). She gives the fifth heroine, enigmatic Lili, a success story too, as she beats poverty, neglect and exploitation to become a serious actress and international film star. Lili drives the novel with her explosive opening question, 'Which one of you bitches is my mother?' You have to read all 700-odd pages to find out. Now *that's* storytelling.

At first I like Maxine best. She travels, first class, with nine maroon leather suitcases, stamped in gold with her initials and coronet (she's a countess). She eats a little caviar (no toast), a tub of home-made yoghurt, a peach from her hothouse and drinks a glass of champagne. She brings her own silver spoon to eat with (well, she's got to fill those nine suitcases with something). She makes notes, in a duplicate book and on a tape recorder. Conran devotes whole paragraphs to expounding Maxine's tried and tested method for taking notes, not forgetting to tell us that her pencil is solid gold.

Maxine has come a long way since she was a chubby teenager hoping to attract a husband. Encouraged by the others, she gets her teeth done, has a nose job and a radical haircut, plucks her eyebrows, diets and spends hours rolling away her plump thighs with a rolling pin (does this even work?). Newly svelte, she attracts a sexy skier but decides she doesn't want to marry. She wants to be '*une sérieuse*'! She persuades her father to let her spend her dowry on studying interior design and leasing a shop, and eventually she marries a client who admires her business acumen as much as her beauty. Though he does also fancy her. They have a lot of rampant sex, and when she wears underwear to a party after he's told her not to, he stops the car, throws her knickers over a hedge and spanks her. I did say there was filth.

Pagan is more ramshackle, i.e. less intimidating. She evolved her 'carelessly marvellous' style during the war when she ran out of clothes and started plundering her dead father's wardrobe, and then her grandmother's. Now she's eccentric, vintage, thrown-together, fabulous. She bags an Arab prince as her first lover, dark and flashing-eyed and every other cliché. Abdullah's been taught the arts of love by a wise old man in Cairo, and is expert in deferring his own pleasure and giving women undreamed-of delight. This is not a skill shared by Pagan's first husband, a bad banker called Robert. Robert first goes out with Kate. When he decides Pagan is a better investment, he lies to both women and manipulates Pagan into marriage. He is icy, snarling and a terrible lover, and when Pagan asks him to take a bit longer, he calls her 'frigid' and a 'castrating bitch' (how I *don't* miss those Eighties insults). She uses the kitchen egg-timer to establish she can masturbate to climax in only five minutes and confronts him. He responds by raping her. (This is not the only rape in the book – Conran is very clear that some men really do hate women.) She leaves, but her spirit is broken and all she can do is hide in a gloomy cottage and drink herself into oblivion. She's eating baked beans laced with vodka out of the dog bowl, dressed in gumboots, old riding breeches and nothing else, when Kate rides to the rescue. Women are, pleasingly, always rescuing women in *Lace*, which makes a nice change from the backbiting and husband-stealing that go on in *Valley*. Pagan falls in love, then, with Christopher who is definitely a Good Man – he is so good that he has dedicated his life to trying to cure cancer. While Robert just wanted her to be a society hostess, Christopher encourages her to find her vocation, so she starts raising money for his research and soon realises she loves work too. And – women helping women again – Judy mentors her.

Kate also starts out floundering and uncompetitive, perpetually attracted to men as overbearing as her father. After Robert, she marries an architect who criticises her underwear from a design perspective. And while she's with this knickers snob she has *not one orgasm*. She always fakes.

Judy (again) helps Kate out of the marriage into (obviously) work. Kate becomes a journalist and a writer, with Judy acting as life coach and cheerleader. She gives Kate an alarm clock (a gold one, from Tiffany's) to help her get up two hours earlier every morning to write her books. One is called *Danger! Women at Work*, which could almost be an alternative title for *Lace*. Then Kate dreams up a magazine. Her pitch is: 'It's 1970 and the Sleeping Princess is waking up. She's got her own job, her own money, she can make her own rules and run her own life.' I wish *VERVE!* really *was* a magazine – I'd buy it. Editing it gives Kate the confidence to seek her own pleasure – and she gets it. Never have I read a book in which the female orgasm is taken so seriously as a right worth fighting for. It does make *Lace* a jubilant read.

But sex is still not as important as work. Which is why *Lace* makes *Riders* (which came out three years later) look deeply old-fashioned in the way it presents women's roles, and *Valley* positively antediluvian. It's also why career girl Judy is *Lace*'s real heroine. Growing up with a father who was often out of work, Judy 'thought about financial security the way other girls did about Prince Charming'. She doesn't want to end up having no life, like her mother. She doesn't believe marriage guarantees anything: work will bring her security, money, independence and impact. She starts out as a secretary in Paris, always on the lookout for opportunities and living as frugally as she can. With admirable ingenuity she uses an electric iron as a stove (the linen setting for eggs or toast, the wool setting for stews). She becomes a couturier's manager and publicist but doesn't want to play second fiddle to anyone so off she goes to New York. It's Maxine's husband who assures her she's old enough to set up her own PR agency. 'You're nearly twenty-three, Judy,' he says. 'A woman of that age is not too young to be responsible for little children, so why not for a little business?' Perhaps Conran is using her character as a mouthpiece but who cares, when it's such good advice? Judy's soon the hottest press agent in the world.

Through all this, she's been supporting and empowering other women. Her vision for *VERVE!* is that it will 'give its readers the support that she had found in Kate, Maxine and Pagan . . . Alone their frailties might have overwhelmed them. Together they had strength and speed and style.' They are also all fabulously immodest about their ambitions, and I love the scene where they're honoured with tea at Buckingham Palace, and go round saying what they wish they'd been taught when they were

younger. (This is Conran on her soapbox again, but it's entertaining – and useful.) Pagan wishes she'd been taught to earn
her own living, Kate that she'd learned to handle her finances,
Maxine would like to have been warned there would be trouble
ahead, and Judy wishes she could have *unlearned* the idea that
a woman needs a man for status or protection.

She does want a man in her life, though. Publishing magnate
Griffin Lowe does not seem to be the answer when he approaches
her at a work do and suggests they run away to dinner. She can't,
she says; she's working. He replies 'No need to, if I say you're
not.' The rotter! Judy walks away, but at the end of the evening
when she leaves last, like the consummate professional she is, and
finds Griffin waiting outside in his Rolls-Royce to offer her a lift
home, she takes it. And doesn't ask him in. Cool as a cucumber
is Judy. They do end up going out. And she makes him respect
her by punishing him for acting thoughtlessly; she leaves him tied
up, his clothes slashed to ribbons, on her bed, covered in lemon
meringue pie, and when he protests, she tells him he was once a
Boy Scout and ought to be able to work out how to free himself.

She is honest about her mixed feelings. Although she doesn't
want to be dependent for her happiness on anyone, she does
fantasise about marrying Griffin. Yet when his wife gives him
a divorce and he rushes round to ask her, she doesn't jump to
say yes. She reasons it out. She loves him, but she loves her
independence too. She worries that he's got into the habit of
cheating on his wife, and doesn't want to become that wife.
And – massive, capital-letter SPOILER ALERT – she also has
another reason to say no. It turns out *she* is Lili's mother – as
a teenager, in Switzerland, she got pregnant and paid for the

baby to be fostered. But Lili's foster mother took her on holiday to Hungary, they got caught up in the revolution, and Lili went missing, presumed dead. It's incredibly moving when they are reunited. Judy decides this is a 'firmer bond' than any marriage could be, and so she'll stay with Griffin as long as it lasts but won't marry him. Because, you know, since feminism, who needs to be bound by the marriage plot?

Although Judy is wonderful, I worry that I'm choosing the wrong heroine again. Judy says herself that Kate's the only one with any talent, while her role is to push her into using it. Yet again I've been attracted to the handmaiden not the princess, the cheerleader not the star. For a moment I have the alarming thought that maybe I want heroines so I can be their best friend and loyal sidekick without ever facing the challenge of becoming a heroine myself.

Towards the end of my twenties, I started a theatrical history column for the *Guardian*. It meant several heavenly hours a week in the sepulchral gloom of the Theatre Museum's underground archive, rummaging through old playbills and programmes and photographs of long-forgotten starlets and matinee idols. One afternoon, I was reading about the premiere of *A Taste of Honey*, a play which shocked audiences in 1958 with its story of a working-class white teen who goes out with a black sailor, gets pregnant and, after he goes away to sea, sets up house with her gay friend, who will be a surrogate father to the baby. Critics thought the playwright Shelagh Delaney was trying to be like the Angry Young Men, and that women shouldn't really be angry. But the play's firebrand director Joan Littlewood said at least Delaney knew what she was angry about. I gazed at a picture of Delaney in a big coat, collar up, cigarette dangling, staring fearlessly at the camera – an image Morrissey loved so much that he used it as the cover of the Smiths' album, *Louder than Bombs*. Delaney looked like she knew what she wanted and could take on anyone. Her rage and sense of purpose suddenly made me feel that I was doing everything all wrong. Just as Anne had supported Lyon's and Neely's ambitions instead of developing her own, here I was, delving into archives instead of breaking new ground; writing about theatre instead of making it.

Delaney threw herself at *A Taste of Honey*, and Susann gave everything she had to *Valley*. I tried to do the same. I wrote a play and gave it a title from one of Sylvia Plath's strange, intense love letters. 'I am living now,' she wrote, 'in a kind of present hell and god knows what ceremonies of life or love can patch the havoc wrought'. My play *Patching Havoc* was inspired by my first relationship – its heroine's fiancé was in love with God. In my favourite scene, she challenged him to make a bush burn, and he set fire to a pot plant. The play was jagged and messy, but it had more sincerity than all my previous safe, careful, perfectionist plays put together. I'd written it seriously, and selfishly, and sitting in the dark at the final performance I thought I'd finally worked something out. I watched my heroine, who also had a cake saved from her bat mitzvah, decide to change her life, and take The Cake out of the freezer, actively choosing to wreck it and start again. She ended the play watching it defrost. I had a stack of plays I wanted to write, but that wasn't what was making me feel so free. I'd worked out how to work. Now it was time to work out how to love.

CATHY EARNSHAW

If this were a novel, I wouldn't let my heroine fall tempestuously in love three times in a row. It would make her seem fickle and unserious. It would strain credulity. But I had a lot of catching up to do. Since Cambridge, apart from the graffiti artist, there'd been only flirtations, unrequited crushes and the obligatory fling with an actor. But I was one year off thirty, most of my friends were in relationships, and I was conspicuously not. And I'd been reading *Wuthering Heights*.

I've read *Wuthering Heights* every year since first finding it at twelve. In the run-up to my birthday I get out my copy and sink into it like a hot bath. Often actually in a hot bath, with a glass of wine. *Wuthering Heights* is, for me, so synonymous with love that reading it is almost as satisfying as having a romance. Cheesy though French film posters are, I have one of the 1939 Laurence Olivier and Merle Oberon film on my bedroom wall; in French it's, pleasingly, *Les Hauts de Hurlevent*. When I dress up for parties or dance around my kitchen, my soundtrack is always Kate Bush's heart-lifting song. *Wuthering Heights* is a book I think about, one way or another, every day. At 29, I tried to live by it.

I thought my Cathy moment had come. I wanted intensity. I wanted to be swept off my feet by avalanche love. Love that would make me dance like a moonstruck sprite; Bush based her video on Oberon's wild, wired performance in the film. I was trying to ditch my inner good girl. I was doing more theatre, at last, and I loved the late nights, drinking red wine and banging tables and talking about stagecraft, and the deep concentration of the rehearsal room, where we would unpack the characters I'd dreamed up alone in my room. I wrote a play about a puppet called Martin and three angry women – his best friend, his enemy and his ex-lover; the women were also the puppeteers so poor, hapless Martin couldn't escape them. I was binge-writing until dawn. I was even being cavalier about the washing up. I was also powering through my *Sopranos* box set and lusting after Tony Soprano even though I knew he was a bad man (possibly because he was a bad man). I liked the glint in his eye, and I thought going out with a man like that would help me be a bit more wild. To which end I was writing a play about rewilding Scotland, and reintroducing wolves. I was inhaling Clarissa Pinkola Estés's *Women Who Run with the Wolves* and trying to find the incorrigible, dangerous wild woman she promised was in me somewhere. When I interviewed a gamekeeper on a remote Highlands estate, he invited me into an enclosure of wild boars. I hesitated, and he laughed at me for writing about wild animals when I was so obviously scared of them. I'd even been scared of his dog. And the dog didn't have tusks. I said I'd always tried to write about what I fear and what I desire. He turned off the electric fence for a moment and in I went, and the wild boars roared. It was researching this play that made me start eating meat again after eighteen years. I was pushing at the boundaries. Things were shifting.

The seizures gave my life a general air of chaos. They'd grown more rococo, harder to manage, and the medications I tried mostly made things worse. One made me unable to form coherent sentences. One made me stop eating. One sent me to sleep for twenty hours at a time. None of them worked. Fed up, I got reckless. At one party I fell and crashed through a windowpane. I lay on the floor as my friends swept up the broken glass and joked that my head had made a hole that was the exact shape of Africa. Then '99 Red Balloons' came on, and I was up and dancing, until dawn. The next day I had concussion, but still, I felt glad I hadn't let my seizures define or limit me.

I met a political researcher, tall and very erudite on the history of the pineapple. When I had a seizure on our first date, he scooped me up off the pavement, got me home, hauled me up four flights of stairs, held my wrists till the spasms stopped, then sat on the edge of my bed and stroked my hair until I fell asleep. I was smitten. And he wooed me. With champagne and chocolates and trips out of town in his battered old car, complicated jazz and simple dinners. But after all that, he said he didn't want a big relationship. I wanted a love that would tear us apart! So I got needy, I played the damsel in distress. Like the Disney princess in *Enchanted*, I expected him to catch me every time I fell. It was a relief when we broke up. But as I walked home that last morning, I felt hungrier for love than I had ever been.

Next came an alcoholic – very charming and never without a bottle of whisky. I wanted to go to the dark side with him, and I wanted to save him – but he wisely and elegantly broke up with me. So, all in all, I wasn't doing that well at tempestuous love. Then I met the oud player. And what happened next only happened because of *Wuthering Heights*.

It's time to read it again. I get out my copy and before I even know it, I've got a bath running and a glass of wine in my hand. It's a Pavlovian response. Am I really going to read in the bath, with a glass of wine, on a cold grey Wednesday morning? I am.

Immediately, I'm on the moors. And Heathcliff is black eyed and gazing ferociously, sneering diabolically. The trees are slanted and stunted by raging gales. Dogs snarl. A 'bitter whirl of wind and suffocating snow' traps the coxcomb Lockwood at his landlord's house, and he lies, insomniac, in a wooden bed with a shelf full of books. They're worn and scuffed, their margins dense with scrawling. (Another reason to love Cathy: she treats her books as familiarly as old friends.) The scribbles are her diary: 'H. and I are going to rebel.' That's Cathy, already a vixen, up and slugging. Moments later, she's there, an icy hand banging on the window to be let in. She's lost her way on the moor, she's 'been a waif for twenty years!' Idiot Lockwood smashes her wrist on the broken windowpane and rubs it back and forth until blood soaks the bedclothes. And Heathcliff, gruff, grim Heathcliff, opens the window and sobs out to his heart's darling to come home.

Best start to a novel EVER.

Nine-year-old Heathcliff, found starving on the streets of Liverpool by Cathy's father, and bold, saucy, eight-year-old hoyden Cathy, are so lovely at first. So tender. So understanding. When her father dies, they sit up in the bed they share (at eleven and twelve), consoling each other. They imagine heaven so beautifully they almost feel better. It's adorable. It's the sweetest glimpse of love in print. But it sours. Cathy's jealous older brother Hindley separates them, works Heathcliff like a slave and tries to turn Cathy into a lady with fussy ringlets and clothes she can't tramp the moors in. Cathy says Heathcliff's been brought so low that it would degrade her to marry him, and Heathcliff hears only that bit and not that she loves him, and he runs off, in a thunderstorm, and Cathy's all alone.

I wish Cathy were stronger. I wish she'd refuse Edgar Linton's proposal. I wish she'd trust Heathcliff to come back for her. I wish she didn't have so many incentives to leave her drunk, miserable brother and their disorderly house. And I wish Edgar wasn't so good on paper – rich, adoring, and (for a romance hero this is damning with faint praise) 'cheerful'.

All this I knew already. But for all the times I've read *Wuthering Heights*, it is very different, reading it with Emma's words from our trip to Haworth ringing in my ears. Every other time I read it uncritically, for comfort; that was the point. Every other time, I suspended my disbelief. But this time, I want to keep waking myself up, keep thinking. This time, I've sworn really to think about Cathy. It takes some effort. I get out of the bath, swap my wine for coffee, and try to honestly examine my own feelings about this heroine I thought I knew so well. And what I feel is surprising. Cathy seems haughty. She seems petulant at times, solipsistic, and violent. I don't feel like Edward from the Twilight novels who damned *Wuthering Heights* as a book about 'ghastly people who ruin each other's lives' (which is *rich* coming from him), but this time I do struggle with Cathy's decision to marry Edgar. Why does she do it? Is she just remarkably naïve? She seems to think she can have

Heathcliff as a friend and Edgar as a husband – as if sexual jealousy doesn't exist, as if she doesn't know the two men detest each other. When Heathcliff returns, three years later, mysteriously rich, and, finding her married, asks '*Why* did you betray your own heart?', I'm wondering the same thing.

A word in her defence. Heathcliff didn't leave a forwarding address. We never do find out where he spent those three years. Nelly thinks he has been in the army because his posture is better, which is just the kind of boring thing Nelly *would* think. But he could as easily be dead. So Cathy's options are to marry Edgar, to marry someone else (though there doesn't seem to *be* anyone else), or to stay in her brother's house. Marrying Edgar is really her only viable choice.

But, still, Cathy, *why* do you betray your own heart?

Later, Cathy falls into 'brain fever', which is one of those amorphous diseases fictional Victorians get all the time, and not one my neurologists recognise. I have asked them. This is when Cathy sees how lost she is. She pulls the feathers out of a pillow she's ripped up with her teeth, and arranges them on the bed sheet, naming the birds they come from – turkey, wild duck, pigeon, moor-cock, lapwing. 'I wish I were out of doors,' she cries. 'I wish I were a girl again, half savage and hardy, and free . . . I'm sure I should be myself were I once among the heather on those hills.' This line breaks my heart. Because after betraying *her* heart, she's never herself again. She never can be.

But could she have redeemed Heathcliff, if they'd married? I'm not sure. Particularly as I am forcing myself, though it pains me, to admit that Heathcliff is a bad man. He raises a hand to strike a woman (his daughter in law) on page 28. It's deeply disquieting. I never thought of Heathcliff beating up women, but he does. Repeatedly. Never exactly a jolly, even-keel character, he gets so twisted up by bitterness and hate that he becomes more villain than hero. I hate the way he wreaks revenge on Hindley and his innocent son Hareton, and the way he gloats over his enemies' misfortunes. I hate him beating Isabella, calling her a 'slut', hanging her dog, goading her to hate him, sneering that the more brutal he is to her, the more she loves him. It's hard to root for a man who rages about saying things like 'I have no pity! I have no pity! The more the worms writhe, the more I yearn to crush out their entrails.' It's savage stuff, but it's also just so . . . can I say it? . . . melodramatic.

But here's the thing: *Wuthering Heights* isn't really about Heathcliff as a hero, or Cathy as a heroine. Heathcliff himself cautions against 'picturing in me a hero'. It's about love. Transcendent love, operatic love, excessive, abandoned love. It's unreasonable, this love. It is angsty and probably immature. But tornado love is more appealing than postmodern love, the mealy-mouthed love Umberto Eco wrote about when he defined postmodernism as the attitude 'of a man who loves a very cultivated woman and knows that he cannot say to her "I love you madly", because he knows that she knows (and that she knows he knows) that these words have already been written by Barbara Cartland. Still there is a solution. He can say "As Barbara Cartland would put it, I love you madly". At this point, having avoided false innocence, having said clearly it is no longer possible to talk innocently, he will nevertheless say what he wanted to say.' All those caveats and equivocations make me want to scream. That isn't love, it's nit-picking.

Wuthering Heights is a novel that comes out strongly against small-mindedness. Cathy and Heathcliff may be monstrous but at least they aren't like Edgar, who disowns his sister like a fat-headed patriarchal buffoon. They're not like Joseph who wants to impose his boring, narrow view of God on everyone else. Or like pernickety, patronising Nelly. Or loser Lockwood idiotically going out in a snowstorm and thinking all the women fancy him (we do *not*). Cathy and Heathcliff are not sensible in their love. But the novel holds out the hope that their love could have survived if the world weren't so petty and stupid.

I was brought up on high drama. An Iraqi Jewish endearment, *fudwa*, means 'I would die for you'. In a five-minute phone call about yoghurt my grandma can offer to die for me ten or fifteen times. So the *Sturm und Drang* of Heathcliff and Cathy's love made sense to me. I wanted a love so intense it could send me into a brain fever or cause the man who loved me to gnash his teeth and dash his head against a tree till he bled. To dig up my grave and be so blinded by love that he'd swear that even after seven years in the ground my face was still my face, uncorrupted.

I met the oud player at a Kurdish community centre where I was researching my first radio play, about a Kurdish teenager who avoids being married off to a Nice Kurdish Boy by joining the freedom fighters in the mountains of Kurdistan. I was still writing the story about a girl who doesn't want to marry the man her family chooses for her – but I was trying to find different endings for my heroines, new things for them to do.

Over glasses of tea, under maps of Kurdistan (maps that are acts of faith, wishes that one day the Kurds will get their country and the sketched-out borders will be real), the oud player told me the story of his life. He was born on a boat, at sea, in a storm, where his father delivered him in the raging waves. His name means 'liberty' in Kurdish. The rest was no less romantic. He'd been with the freedom fighters, he'd been a refugee on the run. He'd arrived in England with only his oud, cigarettes and a copy of Friedrich Nietzsche's *Beyond Good and Evil*. I'm not even making this up. 'Do you know the saddest thing that's happened to the Kurdish people?' he asked. I shrugged; chemical bombings? Having their language banned and being denied a country? No. 'We've lost all our love songs,' he said. 'When we got political, we changed all the songs. Instead of "I love you", "I want you", we sing "I love you Kurdistan", "I want you Kurdistan". It's impossible,' he said, gazing at me, 'for a man to say to a woman "I love you".' I thought he was doing fine.

He played me Kurdish songs, translating the lyrics. As in the Arabic songs I grew up with, the songs are narrated by lovesick swains tormented by unattainable ice queens. One man waits for years in the garden of a woman's house and, just once, smells her perfume in the evening air. By the time I found out the oud player had a girlfriend, it was too late. I was already in the garden.

We tried to be friends. And when, a year or so later, they broke up, and we ended up in his bed, I half knew they'd get back together. I was behaving badly. But in *Wuthering Heights,* everything is justified by love. And that first night, I had my recurring dream again, again I was being chased through the desert by mustachioed men, but this time the oud player turned up in a getaway car and saved me. It felt like a sign. But things got a lot more tangled and confused before, many months later, he was single and I was single and we tried again. And then it was sometimes beautiful.

We watched black and white films, we brewed thick, sweet coffee, we went for long walks late at night in London, just us and the foxes. There was a frisson of star-crossedness – my family would not have been happy to know I was dating a Muslim. Which was ironic, because it was the first time I'd gone out with someone who spoke the language of my child-hood and it was unbelievably intimate. I felt as if my previous relationships had been lost in translation. He felt like home. And just as I'd always tried with my family, I wanted to make up for all the bad things that had happened to him. But you can't rescue people; you can only help them rescue themselves. And he didn't love me the way Heathcliff loves Cathy. He didn't love me enough to commit to me. I wasn't Cathy, adored by Heathcliff. I wasn't even Heathcliff, adoring Cathy as she married another man. I was Isabella, fawning on Heathcliff. And no one wants to be Isabella.

As I'm writing this book, I'm also writing a play, about a woman who goes out with all the wrong men because her paradigm for a romantic hero is Heathcliff. When I show it to my writers' group – all men, all better feminists than me – over chips and wine at our usual Tuesday night in a skanky pub in Soho, they tell me 'you can't really still want Heathcliff!' My heroine doesn't work in the first draft, or the second, and I'm wondering if she ever will. And then I think, I must be writing her because I need her, and if I need her, someone else will too. She ends up summoning Heathcliff's ghost to meet her on the moors so she can persuade herself that he really, finally, definitely isn't The One. Maybe reading and reconsidering *Wuthering Heights* is my attempt at a similar exorcism. And I feel weepy. Not pleasurable-weepy but very sad. Because Heathcliff and Cathy feel remote, and I feel as if I'm saying goodbye to a book that meant so much to me.

I wonder if *Jane Eyre* will pick me up. I wonder if Emma is right.

My copy of *Jane Eyre* is pristine, not battered, not defaced, not trashed by the fury of my affection. But I'm surprised on the very first page. Jane is so *present*. While Cathy was muffled, dead for most of the novel, glimpsed through her names scratched into paint, her scribbles in old books and a series of nested narrators, Jane addresses us boldly, vividly from the start. This culminates, of course, in her famous 'Reader, I married him'. In her very first words she questions authority and in her opening scene she speaks her mind, and gets a book thrown at her head for it. Some men (like her horrid cousin) can't take a woman being cleverer than them; that would have been a useful thing to know. As a teenager I found her impassive, dejected. When she ruefully imagines that her aunt would like her if she was 'sanguine, brilliant, careless, exacting, handsome, romping', I thought those were all things I wanted to be myself. (Yes, romping.) Instead she's plain and awkward. I was too, but I didn't *want* to be. Back then, I wanted my heroines to show me new ways to be, like heedless, selfish Cathy. I didn't want heroines who mirrored my own anxieties too accurately. But maybe I've changed. Or at least: maybe I am changing.

Jane could have taught me that you don't have to be beautiful to value yourself. She could have taught me to find my own faith – at school, she rejects the founder's false pieties and her friend Helen's angelic renunciation, but she hangs on to her own ideas about religion. She could have shown me how to seek out female mentors, like Miss Temple, the headmistress, who clears Jane of the false accusations against her, comforts her with seed cake, and helps her become a teacher.

I've always resented what I saw as Jane's placid preternatural calm but now it seems like enviable self-possession. And she does get angry sometimes. In one amazing passage she seethes, 'Women are supposed to be very calm generally: but women feel just as men feel; they need exercise for their faculties, and a field for their efforts, as much as their brothers do; they suffer from too rigid a restraint, too absolute a stagnation, precisely as men would suffer; and it is narrow-minded . . . to say that they ought to confine themselves to making puddings and knitting stockings, to playing on the piano and embroidering bags.' Is there a better articulation of discontented Victorian womanhood? Oh Jane, I've misjudged you.

When Rochester, her foxy, brooding employer, needs her to deal with crises (a stranger with blood pouring out of his arm, his bedroom going up in smoke), she's calm, unhysterical, brave; I wish I could be as cool under pressure. She's not coquettish like her pupil Adèle or haughty like Rochester's admirer Blanche (supposedly elegant, yet always played by an actress in sausage curls). When Rochester asks Jane if she finds him handsome, she bluntly says no. She's more interested in his 'original . . . vigorous . . . expanded mind'. (Later she decides he's not bad looking after all.) She stands up for herself and when she thinks he's going to marry Blanche, she hands in her notice.

How can anyone not love a Jane who demands,

'Do you think I can stay to become nothing to you? Do you think I am an automaton? – a machine without feelings? and can bear to have my morsel of bread snatched from my lips, and my drop of living water dashed from my cup? Do you think, because I am poor, obscure, plain, and little, I am soulless and heartless? You think wrong! – I have as much soul as you, – and full as much heart! And if God had gifted me with some beauty and much wealth, I should have made it as hard for you to leave me, as it is now for me to leave you. I am not talking to you now through the medium of custom, conventionalities, nor even of mortal flesh; – it is my spirit that addresses your spirit; just as if both had passed through the grave, and we stood at God's feet, equal, – as we are!'

Wow, just wow. It's quite a speech. No wonder Rochester proposes. I wish she hadn't let him dress her like a doll and load her with jewels and I wish she'd insisted on knowing why he doesn't fire the weird, laughing, apparently homicidal servant. But she becomes a proper heroine when, her marriage ruined by the discovery of Rochester's mad wife in the attic, she refuses to stay and be his mistress.

This didn't always strike me as heroic. I used to think she was cowardly and skittish, a prude without the guts to flout convention. I thought *she* was the one betraying her heart. Why bang on about passion if you're not going to defy society? He's offering her a love nest – and it sounds brilliant: a whitewashed villa in the south of France, on the shores of the Mediterranean. I'd join him there in a heartbeat. And they love each other. Why *can't* she go? I thought it was because she was still trapped in the self-abnegating faith she'd learned at school.

Plus, my allegiance was to the anti-heroine. With her wild hair, her passion and her justifiable rage at the husband-stealing governess, Bertha seemed a lot more interesting than Jane. I liked the way she ripped up Jane's wedding veil like a Fury out of Greek tragedy. I'll never forget the image of her at the end, on the battlements of Thornfield, black hair streaming against the flames, leaping out of her prison. My favourite literary critics Gilbert and Gubar made me think any right-thinking feminist had to prefer Bertha because she embodies everything Victorian society makes Jane suppress. Jane isn't keen on the fancy wedding veil – so Bertha rips it up. Tiny Jane wants to be Rochester's equal though he's always saying he could crush her – but Bertha is tall and strong enough to wrestle with him. And Jane doesn't exactly say it but she wants to be wanton, and Bertha just *is*. In Shared Experience's Gilbert-and-Gubar-tastic stage adaptation, bawdy Bertha is constantly on stage, trying to shove plain, sober Jane aside as she moans, writhes and grabs at Rochester. She's got my hair – dark, curly, unmanageable: curly hair is so often a shorthand for unruliness and this just gave me another reason to like her.

I'd got more ammunition against Jane from Jean Rhys's *Wide Sargasso Sea*, her intoxicating 1966 prequel to *Jane Eyre*. Rhys's heroine – basically Bertha, but called Antoinette – grows up in a Jamaica evoked in hot, sensuous, *longing* prose. The novel is scented with cinnamon, vetiver, lime and frangipani. But it is no romance. Antoinette is forced to marry a cold, uptight Englishman; Rochester reimagined as a racist, misogynist coloniser of women who changes his wife's name, curbs her rebelliousness and represses her sensuality. He makes her feel foreign, exotic, wrong. She is driven mad by the pressure to conform to his white, male, English world. I've felt that pressure myself. I still love *Wide Sargasso Sea* but now that I'm rethinking Jane, it no longer feels like a threat to *Jane Eyre*. It is its own book, and wonderful. I like it separately.

Now, Jane seems so bold that I have to completely reconsider my feelings about her decision to leave Rochester. These pages are so gripping; Charlotte gives us a blow-by-blow account of a heroine making the decision of her life. In the hours after she's dragged from church, up to the attic to face her nemesis, Jane is alive to every feeling, and her mind is racing. She finds the compassion to tell Rochester to be kinder to Bertha, who can't help being mad. She finds both pity and forgiveness for Rochester – and the dynamic here is fascinating because for all his wealth, and for all that he's a man, she is freer. He was sold on the marriage market and is still chained to a wife he doesn't love, but Jane can choose whether to marry or not. In itself, this is subversive. Jane won't listen to any sophistry from Rochester, and when she has the weaselly thought that she *could* throw away her reputation because no one would care, her heart sings out: '*I* care for myself. The more solitary, the more friendless, the more unsustained I am, the more I will respect myself.' It's a pretty fearless manifesto. And it sustains her once her decision is made. She knows she will have to be the strong one; Rochester can't resist her. She's already had to push away his caresses. She is tempted, too – she frankly admits it would be 'rapture' to stay – but she's made up her mind. She doesn't waver when he threatens to crush her and tear her. (This is terrifying in the 1943 Orson Welles film. He's so bear-like and hulking that when he towers menacingly over doe-eyed Joan Fontaine, he really does look as if he could rip her in two.) Finally, Jane copes with his sadness, which is worst of all: 'I had dared and baffled his fury; I must elude his sorrow.' She steals away in the night without asking him for money for the journey (not even the wages he owes her), resourcefully oiling the key and lock so that no one will hear her leave. And she's not remotely smug about her decision: 'I abhorred myself. I had no solace from self-approbation: none even from self-respect. I had injured – wounded – left my master. I was hateful in my own eyes.'

She goes on to do other brave and brilliant things: sharing her inheritance with her new-found cousins, not letting St John tell her how to believe in God ('God did not give me my life to throw away') and refusing to marry without passion, snapping 'I scorn your idea of love.' I thought Jane was cold, but she's not; she says she's terrified of 'those cold people' who stifle their feelings.

Charlotte rewards her heroine with a marriage that is sanctioned by God and also equal. Rochester has changed. He doesn't want to be just a 'giver and protector' but will let Jane help him. And he doesn't care about jewels and dresses any more. As an orphan girl, years before, Jane demanded a voice ('*Speak*, I must'); now she sums up ten years of marriage with 'We talk, I believe, all day long'. It's a charming picture of companionship. It's very far from Cathy and Heathcliff's thwarted, afflicted love. I believe Jane and Rochester are happy.

As I finish *Jane Eyre*, I text Emma saying she was right. She is thrilled. Compared to Jane's strong decision to leave Rochester, Cathy's decision to marry Edgar feels ignoble. *She* seems the conventional one, marrying Edgar because 'he will be rich, and I shall like to be the greatest woman of the neighbourhood, and I shall be proud of having such a husband'. Cathy *is* a snob, refusing to marry Heathcliff because he has been denied education and status and 'brought low'. Later, when her daughter Catherine is faced with a similar dilemma when she falls for illiterate Hareton, she doesn't reject him; instead she teaches him to read. (You can argue, and people do, that Cathy and Heathcliff's histrionic love resolves into the quieter romance between Catherine and Hareton, but Catherine's not the heroine of *Wuthering Heights* and never will be. Her father's milk-blood runs in her veins.)

Hardly anyone likes both novels. In the battle of the Brontës, it's not just 'wild, wick slip' Cathy versus 'poor, obscure, plain and little' Jane, it's also Emily versus Charlotte. I'd always thought Emily was the tempestuous genius, and Charlotte was her try-hard, mumsy sister. In her dazzling poem, 'The Glass Essay', Anne Carson casts them just this way, imagining:

> . . . Emily Brontë's little merlin hawk Hero
> that she fed bits of bacon at the kitchen table when
> Charlotte wasn't around.

I resented Charlotte for what she said about *Wuthering Heights* after Emily died. Her preface to the posthumous edition is full of barbs like, 'Whether it is right or advisable to create beings like Heathcliff, I do not know; I scarcely think it is'. Some Emily fans even think she wrote a second novel which Charlotte burned! I really, really hope this isn't true.

But equally, if Charlotte hadn't talked her odd, reclusive sister into publishing, and done all the hard work of making it happen, we wouldn't even have *Wuthering Heights*.

Once the novel was out there, and Emily gone, and all the critics calling it coarse and unwomanly, it must have been hard for Charlotte to know what to tell people about it. No wonder she sometimes said Emily was an unsophisticated country lass who had no idea what she was writing, and sometimes said she was a crazed mystic. At least she didn't claim their brother Branwell wrote *Wuthering Heights*. This rumour, started by Branwell's drinking pals, is surprisingly tenacious. It supposedly answers the question of how a woman who died a spinster at thirty, having never been in love, could have written one of the greatest love stories of all time.

This, of course, assumes that *Wuthering Heights* really is one of the greatest love stories of all time. I certainly read it that way, and I wasn't the only one. The 1939 Hollywood swoonfest is partly to blame, hacking off the second half of the story so that it ends with Cathy's death – and we never have to cope with seeing luminous Olivier go from hopeless romantic to wife-beating, grave-digging, dog-hanging psychopath. But is the love in *Wuthering Heights* really that great? It obliterates the people who experience it. Cathy says it best: 'I *am* Heathcliff.'

And their love is *impossible*. Even if miscommunication, heinousness and bad luck hadn't kept them apart, the idea of

Heathcliff and Cathy getting married and settling down in some cosy cottage, growing old together, does not compute. This is not one of those romance novels where a kind, daring heroine sees the kernel of good in an edgy, dark-hearted hero and redeems him (for which read most of Mills and Boon and, oh, about half of nineteenth-century fiction). Cathy is as moody and savage as Heathcliff, and she couldn't save him if she tried. She doesn't want to. She doesn't want to be kind and sweet and good: she dreams that she goes to heaven and hates it so much that she cries until the angels throw her down to the moors where she belongs. Cathy and Heathcliff's love is too raw and rarefied to exist in the real world, and they know it; they can only be together as restless ghosts. *Wuthering Heights* fan fiction is obsessed by casting Cathy and Heathcliff as vampires, but even without making them undead (and usually in such deathless prose), their love is just not realistic. It is the kind of love, in fact, that could only be written by someone who had never been in love. Which makes me certain Branwell never wrote a word of it – and also means that *Wuthering Heights* is a terrible template for actually conducting a love affair. The longer the oud player and I went on, the less myself I felt. Like Cathy, I lost myself. I can't help thinking that a heroine should be able to love without being erased. But, then, I didn't know how.

I don't know if *Jane Eyre* would have given me the answers either. Charlotte knew love, it's true. She had her crush (not wholly unrequited) on her professor, a flirtation with her publisher and eventually she married her father's curate. Apparently they were happy. I hope they were, but I worry. I read that he campaigned to stop the impious housewives of Haworth hanging up their washing in the graveyard. There's something ridiculous about a curate ranting and raving at women laden with wet petticoats. I think he might have been a bit of a prig.

And for all that Jane and Rochester's love is based on experience, the more I think about it, the less I like it. Rochester is twice Jane's age, he's domineering and he has behaved very peculiarly. He apologises for lying, but he doesn't apologise for flirting with Blanche to make Jane jealous. And there's something very troubling about equality coming because he's lost a hand and one of his eyes. Can a woman not be equal to her husband unless he's wounded? And while *Wuthering Heights* doesn't shrink from the horrible truth that Cathy is dead and Heathcliff has to live and struggle on alone, Charlotte has to bring on the Gothic in a big way to give Jane her happy ending – with the fire, madness and even supernatural voices, is the ending of *Jane Eyre* really more realistic than the ending of *Wuthering Heights*?

Even Jane, lovely Jane, can't entirely hold my affections. She's a heroine who does everything right – but what's interesting about a heroine who never makes mistakes? There's a perverse pleasure in loving Cathy. The more holes I pick in *Wuthering Heights*, the more my stubborn heart clings to it. And struggling with it is, of course, a pleasure in itself.

I do wish, though, that Emily had experienced love. Imagine what she might have written then! She might have given her heroine more of a chance at happiness. She might, in fact, have written *Jamaica Inn*. Daphne du Maurier's 1936 novel plays with both *Wuthering Heights* and *Jane Eyre*, with its moorland setting (in Cornwall, not Yorkshire) and its heroine drawn to darkness. But du Maurier gives Mary Yellan a better choice of men. Cathy's only alternative to Heathcliff is bland Edgar, and Jane's only alternative to Rochester is severe St John. But Mary can acknowledge her attraction to her aunt's drunk wrecker husband, Joss Merlyn, and deflect it by going off instead with his brother, Jem, who is just lawless and wild enough, but not black-hearted; and not embittered either. If only Cathy had had a sexy horse-thief to whisk her away. If only Emily had.

If I were playing Snog, Marry, Avoid (let's face it, I sort of am), I'd still snog Heathcliff but I'd never try to marry him. I'd still avoid Rochester, because I don't think he'd make me happy. And maybe (thank you, Ms du Maurier!) I'd marry Jem.

I don't really want to have to choose between Rochester and Heathcliff, or Cathy and Jane, or Emily and Charlotte. At Haworth I get worked up over Charlotte's darned stockings and when I see a closed-down wedding shop on the high street, the white dresses hanging ghost-like on the rails, refracted in the rain spattering the glass, the Cathy in me sees it as a forlorn image of both sisters never really finding the love they wrote about. But the Jane in me knows it's probably a casualty of the recession. And while my inner Cathy thinks I recognise Haworth because of my subliminal connection to the Brontës, my inner Jane points out it's actually because of the Hovis advert. The charming olde apothecary where I browse rose petal lip balm and bath salts shaped like cupcakes is where Branwell got the laudanum that killed him. It's probably unwise to romanticise everything – and I'll probably always do it.

Back then, though, tempestuous love was making me unhappy. A dear friend broke up his relationship and came to stay, filling my flat with sadness and rage. Writing lost its savour – though I kept plugging away, and my drawer started to fill up with unproduced plays. I sent off for prospectuses for law school, thinking that if I was going to be miserable I might as well be miserable doing something lucrative.

And then I got a fellowship at an artists' colony in New Hampshire.

10

FLORA POSTE

The snow was deep and thick in New Hampshire, and there was always a fire lit in my log cabin, and woodsmoke in my hair. In the evenings, reading in the rocking chair, it all felt very *Little House in the Big Woods*, and for all that I was 32, I still held a candle for Laura Ingalls Wilder. I'd first read her autobiographical novels about her pioneer childhood years ago, so when I heard howling at night, I'd remember Pa carrying an excited, tiny Laura to the window to see wolves, and how later, at twelve, sliding on a frozen lake, following a moonpath, she encounters a wolf in the flesh, gleaming in the moonlight, wind rippling through his fur. The other artists said the howls were coyotes, not wolves, but they did teach me a mnemonic for when the bears woke up, in case any should venture this way. It went, 'Bear brown, lie down. Bear black, fight back.'

I'd never seen so much snow. I had a shovel for the mornings when I'd find it banked up against the door and have to clear a path. It made me think of Laura's baths of melted snow, and the candy she'd make by pouring maple syrup on to plates of snow. Walking in the woods, everything froze: my eyelashes, my hair into stiff little ringlets. The snow fell fresh every night, a clean white canvas for the black-and-white birches. When the photographer Francesca Woodman was at the artists' colony in 1980, she peeled off strips of birch bark and wrapped them around her wrists like manacles or bandages, to make portraits of herself as Diana perpetually turning into a tree. I made photocopies and pinned them up above my desk for inspiration.

It wasn't just the snow; I also kept thinking about how the *Little House* books are all about self-sufficiency. I wasn't particularly interested in hunting, trapping and fishing, still less in making my own fishing rods and bullets, I didn't want to salt or smoke, or churn butter, or braid straw, or sew endless calico dresses. I've never really wanted to pack up my life in a covered wagon and take off for the unknown, as Laura does over and over as a child, and then again as a young bride, embarking on her own pioneer adventure. But I did want a different kind of self-sufficiency. I didn't know if my relationship with the oud player would still be there when I got back, and I had started to think it might not be disastrous if it wasn't.

Two artists got married in a snowfield. We all held sparklers, the groom played his guitar and the bride wore a mermaid dress covered in sequins and peacock feathers. They didn't seem erased by love; instead, they seemed to be making something together; their love seemed a collaboration.

I was researching a play about Gertrude Bell, the British bluestocking, traveller and diplomat who played a major role in the creation of the state of Iraq. My grandfather had seen her ride along the banks of the Tigris at dawn, dressed in white. He'd said that she fell in love with Iraq's first king, but as a child I'd been much more interested in her career. Yet now I was finally writing about her, I became fascinated by the idea that Bell, thwarted in romance, had thrown her love at Iraq – not the king but the country. It was a deeply unconventional love, but for much of her life it sustained her. In her pearls and long Edwardian lace dresses, Bell was very different from the artists in the snow-field, and she also made me think that there were different ways of being in love.

Or not being in love. I'd stashed Stella Gibbons's 1932 classic *Cold Comfort Farm,* in my suitcase as a salve for homesickness. I'd heard it was the most quintessentially English novel ever. What I didn't know was how much it would help me with my questions about the possibility of living without love. I'd waited so long to read it because, as a rule, I don't like parodies. I worry they'll be cruel and that the jokes will get in the way of any empathy I might have. But *Cold Comfort Farm* is more gleeful pastiche than savage take-down. As I got stuck in, it became clear that it was too good a novel to dismiss. Its sparkling heroine Flora Poste was my first comic heroine since Lizzy Bennet. I hadn't realised how much I'd been longing for a funny leading lady. From the moment she arrived on the page, orphaned but not heart-warming, I knew I'd found a cooler, tougher Anne Shirley.

Flora's been left a hundred pounds a year, not enough to live on, so she decides to go and live with her relatives. She writes to them all, and chooses to go to the Starkadders first, because they have a spare room for her and she won't have to share. How sound and sensible she is! And not just about choosing accommodation. Flora is a very *cosy* heroine. She's always surrounding herself with creature comforts. Not fancy things, but bread and butter and jam, hot baths and warm rugs. And despite her enviable *sprezzatura*, she does have a sort of plan;

'when I am fifty-three or so,' she says, 'I would like to write a novel as good as *Persuasion*, but with a modern setting, of course. For the next thirty years or so I shall be collecting material for it.' In the film, which is blissful, Kate Beckinsale is constantly scribbling. Her writing inspiration is Austen, who she thinks was just like her: 'She liked everything to be tidy and pleasant and comfortable about her, and so do I. You see . . . unless everything is tidy and pleasant and comfortable all about one, people cannot even begin to enjoy life. I cannot *endure messes*.'

Flora hopes her relatives will have messes or miseries for her to tidy up, and wow, they don't disappoint. At decrepit Cold Comfort Farm everyone is kept just this side of suicidal by Aunt Ada Doom who once saw something nasty in the woodshed and has been off her head ever since. She runs the farm from her bed, where she finds time to enjoy five meals a day. Flora tartly observes that if she *is* mad, it's a very pleasant and convenient sort of madness. In fact, she suspects that the melodramatic Starkadders rather enjoy 'doors being slammed, and jaws sticking out, and faces white with fury, and faces brooding in corners, and faces making unnecessary fuss at breakfast, and plenty of opportunities for gorgeous emotional wallowings, and partings for ever, and misunderstandings'. Flora does not enjoy these things. She is poised and tranquil. One of her first innovations is to introduce afternoon tea to Cold Comfort Farm. She's as cool as the eau de cologne she dabs on her temples at tough times.

She was the perfect antidote to my unsuccessful experiments with tempestuous love. Gazing out at falling snow from my studio, I daydreamed an encounter between Flora Poste and

Cathy Earnshaw in the kitchen at Wuthering Heights. It would be snowing there too. Cathy would race in, soaked to the skin, hair wild, neglecting to shut the door. Flora would get up from her chair by the roaring fire to do it. She'd bring Cathy warm, dry clothes, and a restorative cup of tea. If Cathy dashed her head against the furniture and made long speeches, Flora would wait. Perhaps she might sigh. Or use the time to freshen up her lipstick. Cathy would think her empty-headed, but Flora wouldn't care. She would be sympathetic but firm. She would slash through the muddle and help Cathy see clearly. She might even help her to be happy. Because Flora's great skill is to find out what is gnawing at people and make it stop.

She solves all the Starkadders' problems, starting with Meriam, who thinks she's doomed to get pregnant every time the sukebind is in flower; Flora breezily introduces her to contraception. (The sukebind, incidentally, is a fictional, smelly flower, invented by Gibbons, along with such ruralisms as 'clettering' and 'mollocking'; part of the book's pleasure comes from knowing it must have been so much fun to write.) Flora pokes gentle fun at the Starkadders, from wildfire preacher Amos (*'there'll be no butter in hell!'*) to Mr Mybug, who has come to Sussex to write. Men who write in books by women are usually villains, and Mr Mybug is worse than most because he's (*again!*) trying to prove that Branwell wrote all his sisters' books (even *The Tenant of Wildfell Hall*). Mr Mybug's so sex-obsessed he can't go for a walk without pointing out phallic trees, bosomy hills and nipple-like buds. Flora faces all this preposterousness with lucid calm. When she asks her cousin Judith about getting her curtains washed, Judith replies (first sinking into a reverie):

'Curtains? Child, child, it is many years since such trifles broke across the web of my solitude.' Flora briskly asks if she could have them washed all the same, then pragmatically organises it herself. She is not the kind of heroine to put up with dirty curtains.

At dark moments I fear I am more Judith than Flora. Judith has hair like black snakes (yes, dark and curly) and always looks as if she's on stage. Like all the Starkadders she is in the grip of a painful *idée fixe*: her unhealthy obsession with her ludicrously handsome son Seth. (In the film, Rufus Sewell leavens Seth's lazy beefcake insolence with an ironic glint in his eye that makes him even more irresistible.) Flora dispatches Judith to be psychoanalysed by a helpful friend – Flora has a friend for every occasion, as every single woman should, and is always getting her pals to send her amusing letters, or gumboots, or magazines, or to deal with unhappy relatives. Another friend is a film producer who whisks Seth off to Tinseltown to make him a matinee idol; which is, conveniently, Seth's dream come true.

Like Anne Shirley but with more style and less chatter, Flora is an altruist. She transforms the Starkadders' lives. Even the farm ends up clean and pretty, and she's so pleased, she says to herself, 'I did all that with my little hatchet'. Which makes me want to cheer, and perhaps buy her a fortifying fruitcake. At the wedding at the end of the book (not *her* wedding, I hasten to add), she's delighted to see the Starkadders enjoying themselves – and for normal, happy reasons, not because they are in the midst of self-made melodramas. Her main aim is for people to enjoy themselves. When, later that evening, she feels a bit flat, she calls an amusing and attractive man she's been flirting with by letter all the way through, and he picks her up in his plane. As they fly off literally into the sunset, she joyously praises his 'heavenly teeth'. It's a very Flora thing to notice and derive pleasure from, and it struck me that being single would mean taking responsibility for enjoying myself, not waiting to be entertained, or trying to live my life by entertaining someone else. That Purim at the colony, another playwright and I held a party. We read from our plays, and cross-dressed (dollar-shop tiaras for the men, charcoal moustaches for the women) and obeyed the Talmudic injunction to drink till we didn't know the difference between good and evil. I felt a lot more like Vashti than like Esther. Even better, I felt like Flora, too.

Back in London, the oud player and I broke up. I emerged from the wreckage determined to learn the art of being single and happy. Flora would show me how.

On Valentine's Day, I bought a power drill, to mark the new can-do, self-sufficient me, and when I gouged an enormous hole in the wrong bit of my wall I wasn't downcast but did what Flora would, and called a friend. He sorted out the wall, I made us dinner, and we both had a lovely time. I felt that Flora would approve. I aimed for enjoyment. I tried new recipes. I walked miles every day, I played with my friends' children. I wrote a play about my seizures, and it went on at a theatre in Cambridge. Just writing it was enormously clarifying and helpful. So much so, that a friend suggested I call it How I Learned to Stop Standing Up And Fell In Love With Falling Over. (I did not.) But I did stop trying to get the seizures cured, and started trying to learn to live with them instead, which meant that for the first time in fifteen years I wasn't at the mercy of each new drug with its unpredictable side effects, and I was out of the hope–despair–hope cycle too. I got a commission to make a play with twenty-four actors-in-training who challenged and provoked and inspired me all at once. I learned to knit. I stopped watching old episodes of *Sex and the City* and instead my comfort programme became *30 Rock*; it felt good to abandon Carrie Bradshaw, who now felt sappy and boy-crazy, for Liz Lemon, who, in a seminal episode, becomes terrified that she will choke alone in her flat and die. But when she does start to choke, home alone, she bravely launches herself into the back of a chair, dislodging the food stuck in her gullet, and with it the fear of being single.

But still, I felt sad, sad that my relationship hadn't worked, and sad that my idea of love had proved wrong. *Cold Comfort Farm* couldn't help me. Its sunny ending started to seem forced and fake. It was practically *deus ex machina,* with a hero literally descending in a plane to rescue Flora. It was all too convenient to be true, and too perfect. There was a smugness about it I didn't like. There was a smugness about Flora too. I started resenting her modernising and sanitising and tidying everything up – especially the way she makes her cousin Elfine, a fanciful girl who likes dancing on the Downs in fog, 'groomed and normal' and marries her off to the local squire. Like he's such a catch. And why does Elfine have to stop writing poetry? Her work may be bad but she's only seventeen, and has plenty of time to improve. And isn't it hypocritical of Flora to squash Elfine's creative ambitions while nurturing her own? When Flora congratulates herself, after Elfine's makeover, on being 'an artist in living flesh', and when she tells the squire's mother that Elfine 'can be moulded into exactly what you would wish her to be', she sounds superior and manipulative. It's all a bit *Emma*, and Emma Woodhouse is my least favourite Austen heroine – so interfering and know-it-all, so mean to spinsters! Replaying my daydream of Flora and Cathy in the kitchen at Wuthering Heights, I realised that the person Flora reminded me of most was Nelly Dean. And I never, *ever* wanted to be Nelly Dean.

So I turned to the eponymous heroine of Sylvia Townsend Warner's transgressive 1926 debut *Lolly Willowes*. At 47, she escapes being a maiden aunt by selling her soul to the devil and becomes a witch.

Laura (her real name) has a quiet country childhood, then keeps house for her father, and wants nothing more than to go on long walks, find herbs in hedgerows, make cures and ointments, and read. But when she is 28, her father dies, and she is parcelled off to live with her brother and his wife. Life there is stultifying. Laura thinks her sisters-in-law look dead. One resembles a memorial urn, and the other keeps her linen preternaturally tidy because she wants to emulate the way Christ's grave clothes were folded. Laura is repulsed, but doesn't say anything. She's not a rebel. She doesn't escape into marriage, either. She scares off her only suitor (a snob who wants a well-trained wife) by telling him she thinks he might be a werewolf (a line I fully intend to try one day). After that, she lives 'an existence doled out' by her family. She copes by constructing 'a sort of mental fur coat' of small pleasures like roasted chestnuts eaten in bed, fancy soaps, *marrons glacés*, extravagant bunches of flowers, second-hand books. All single women should have a 'mental fur coat'; after reading *Lolly Willowes*, I compiled my own list of small pleasures, like reading a book in a hot bath scented with orange flower water, walks on Hampstead Heath and pistachio baklava.

Twenty years go by. Laura's niece who, as an infant, nicknamed her Lolly in the first place, is all grown up. She has married twice and driven lorries in the war, and thinks her aunt is terribly un-enterprising for living such a limited life, on the margins of everyone else's. Poor Laura has been tamed and subdued into becoming an indispensable maiden aunt. A bit odd, maybe, but still so useful that she's never allowed to stray. She looks likely to moulder on for ever that way.

But one day she's at a greengrocer's, buying flowers, and suddenly has a vision of an old woman, alone, picking fruit in her own orchard. The grocer gives her a spray of beech leaves with her flowers and says they're from the Chilterns, and something in Laura ignites. She buys a guidebook and a map and announces that she is moving to Great Mop. (Sadly there is no such village, but there is one called Mop End, and I can confirm that its beech woods are divine.) Her brother blusters, 'Lolly! I cannot allow this. You are my sister. I consider you my charge. I must ask you once and for all to drop this idea. It is not sensible. Or suitable.' But she insists 'Nothing is impracticable for a single, middle-aged woman with an income of her own' – go, Laura! – and that's when he pales and starts mansplaining that he's lost most of her inheritance on a bad investment. She goes anyway, with what money she has, and soon she's settling in at Great Mop. She doesn't bother being bitter, or having regrets. And she doesn't waste time on trying to nobly forgive her 'tyrants' as she calls them. Instead, she rejects all masculine institutions – including the law, the Church, the Bank of England and (startlingly) prostitution. She doesn't need or care about them. She pleases herself. She goes for walks. She sleeps outdoors. She bakes scones in the shape of the Great Mop villagers. If there's one thing a lone ranger can and should do it's indulge her idiosyncrasies. It's quite an achievement to make even scones subversive.

Laura has to show her strength when her independence is challenged. Her nephew Titus comes to visit and likes Great Mop so much he decides to stay there and write a book. As I said, men who write in books by women are usually villainous, and Laura immediately feels the weight of her chains, doomed to become 'the same old Aunt Lolly, so useful and obliging and negligible'. In despair, she cries out loud for help and a kitten bites her. She realises at once what it means (and why everyone in the village is so weird and always up so late): Great Mop is a witches' village and, in accepting that bite, she's sold her soul to the devil and she's a witch too. Her first act of magic is both mischievous and to the point: she sours Titus's milk.

She dances at a witches' sabbath, and tingles all over when her alluring dancing partner's red hair brushes her face. Titus's milk curdles, day after day. He can't keep it fresh, no matter what he does. And who can write with sour milk in their tea? No one. Finally, he skedaddles, and Laura is free.

Warner wrote the novel quite consciously as a feminist fable, inspired by the idea that sixteenth-century Scottish witches may have turned to magic as a release from their dull, proscribed lives. Her devil is somewhat romantic, 'a kind of black knight, wandering about and succouring decayed gentlewomen', and (pre-empting *Lady Chatterley's Lover*) dressed like a gamekeeper. Laura thinks she must be 'a witch by vocation': why else would she have made all those herbal remedies and gone on all those country walks? Warner, who supplemented her income by selling home-made chestnut jam, rhubarb chutney and pickled nasturtium seeds, played up her affinity with her heroine, telling Virginia Woolf she knew so much about witches because she *was* one, and claiming that modern witches flew on vacuum cleaners instead of broomsticks.

But *Lolly Willowes* is not just whimsy. It's a cry for freedom, for 'a life of one's own', as Laura says – three years before Woolf called for a room. Warner wrote it ten years into a relationship with a married man. She was sick of being the other woman, living in the interstices of other people's lives, in a small London flat where she subsisted on black coffee, cigarettes, winkles and scrambled eggs. But after she'd written *Lolly Willowes* and rehearsed self-sufficiency, Warner decided to try it for real. She broke up her relationship. Later she spent forty years with the androgynous poet Valentine Ackland. Love saved and reinvigorated her, and although her daring novel *Summer Will Show* is more directly about her relationship with Ackland (its heroine goes to Paris to track down her unfaithful husband and ends up falling for his mistress instead), it is in *Lolly Willowes* that she expunges her fear of living half a life and explores how she might change.

The tough message of *Lolly Willowes* is that women turn witch to show their 'scorn of pretending life's a safe business'. Laura comes to feel part of a community of angry, outsider women: 'When I think of witches,' she says, 'I seem to see all over England, all over Europe, women living and growing old, as common as blackberries, and as unregarded . . . Nothing for them except subjugation and plaiting their hair . . . But they must be active.' Yes we *must*. Laura's clarion call echoes right down to Mira in *The Women's Room* saying all the women she knows feel like outlaws. When I read *Lolly Willowes* I was struggling with a play about an Orthodox Jewish girl who starts doubting her religion and her relationship. I wrote draft after draft with happy endings that didn't ring true. I was keener than any Jewish mother to marry off my heroine, keener than Mrs Bennet to marry off her daughters, keener than my mother had been to get me under the *chupah*. Laura gave me the guts to try a different tack. In *Cling To Me Like Ivy*, I sent my heroine up a tree to kiss a boy during an anti-road protest, and brought her down again to confront her family, to tell her fiancé the truth, and to end the play single, questioning and hopeful. At the opening night party, I felt just the same.

I still love *Lolly Willowes*. It's a joy to reread – so buoyantly funny, so unrepentantly weird and so lyrical. Acerbic, unprepossessing Laura helped me keep my feet on the ground instead of wanting to be swept off them. She helped me worry less about meeting The One. She helped me feel I was living, not *waiting*. But now, I wonder if it wasn't a bit perverse to switch from ingenious, witty Flora, who ends up flying off with her dream man, to Laura, who ends up sleeping in a hedge. I didn't want to sell my soul to the devil. I wanted to be happy.

But where *are* the happy fictional spinsters?

Miss Havisham lives the single life with a certain batty panache, but much as I see her point, I don't want to rot in my wedding dress, with my wedding feast covered in mould, spiders and mice, my cake cobwebbed, adopting a daughter and raising her as a feminist avenger. I go back to *Persuasion*, an old favourite, and am shocked to find that Anne Elliot is only 27! As a child, I thought she was ancient and her happy ending nothing short of miraculous. But no. And while I still think she's brilliant, she can't be my spinster heroine, because I have the biggest crush on Captain Wentworth so I'm willing them to marry all the way through; as, of course, is she.

Both Flora and Laura emerged in the 1920s and '30s, which, as Virginia Nicholson shows in her rigorous, encouraging *Singled Out*, was the golden age of spinsters for the tragic reason that because of the First World War two million 'surplus women' had lost their sweethearts, or missed the chance of ever having sweethearts. The women coped, and some even thrived. Those who had never wanted to marry a man anyway, but didn't have the confidence to rock a suit, tie, cropped hair and monocle like Radclyffe Hall (whose novel *The Well of Loneliness* came out in 1928), took the opportunity to quietly move in with their partners.

E.M. Delafield's 1919 shocker *Consequences* showed what could happen to those who weren't so brave and resourceful; her naïve failed debutante enters a convent, spends ten miserable years being a nun, finally asserts herself and is released from her vows, but still feels so wrong and out of place as a single woman that she puts stones in her pockets and drowns herself in a pond on Hampstead Heath. It's unremittingly bleak. I think of her every time I swim in the ponds – but she's a warning, not an inspiration.

Luckily, the 1930s threw up other heroines who didn't define themselves through men, like Agatha Christie's indefatigable Miss Marple, who debuted in 1930, and P.L. Travers's unflappable, imperious magical nanny Mary Poppins (first in print in 1934), and Lady Slane, the heroine of Vita Sackville-West's 1931 novel *All Passion Spent*, who is ecstatic to finally be single, when she is widowed at 88 after years of blameless duty as a diplomatic wife. And then there's Sarah Burton, the heroine of Winifred Holtby's 1936 novel *South Riding*.

For a while I borrow Sarah's mantra: 'I was born to be a spinster, and, by God, I'm going to spin.' She arrives in Yorkshire, battle-weary from bad, sad love affairs, determined to throw herself into work as the headmistress of a girls' school. Almost immediately, she is derailed by a hero straight out of the Gothic. Robert Carne is her Rochester, and she knows it. Parallels abound. He's rich, with a mad wife (in an asylum, not an attic), a little girl (his daughter, not his ward) and a lot of anger. Sarah really doesn't want to fall in love with him. But she does. Head over heels, the whole business. And he loves her back, in his irascible, tormented way. Then he dies in an accident. Just dies. Just like that. And he's gone.

I couldn't *believe* Holtby had killed him off. I was so caught up in the love story that I didn't much care that Sarah's good work was being scuppered. But as I read on, with bad grace, Sarah showed her mettle. I realised what kind of heroine Holtby really wanted to write: a heroine who learns to survive without love – which was exactly the kind of heroine I needed.

Sarah finds a mentor. The sprightly Mrs Beddows is an iconoclast from way back; for years she's been the only alderwoman on the local council (as was Holtby's own inspiring mother). Beddows tells Sarah she'll be a better teacher than ever because before she was invincible, now she understands shame and sorrow and frailty. But it's not enough to save her. It's only when Sarah is nearly killed in a plane crash that her will to live surges back. Bruised and bandaged but not defeated, she makes a stirring speech to her girls about how they should question everything from the arms race to poverty to misogyny. At the end, Sarah knows she's found what she's been looking for: not a gorgeous, stricken hero but Mrs Beddows whose 'gaiety . . . kindliness . . . valour of the spirit [is] beckoning her on from a serene old age'.

Holtby wrote this knowing *she* wouldn't live to a serene old age. She was in the throes of Bright's disease which killed her at 37; *South Riding* was published posthumously. But in her cruelly short life she worked out lots of ways to be single and happy. She threw her formidable energies into writing, into campaigning for pacifism, socialism and feminism, and into friendship. When her best friend Vera Brittain invited her to live with her and her husband, she also became joint parent to their children. Brittain was so keen to give her friend a big romantic finish that she dragged Holtby's on–off lover to her deathbed and made him propose. I wonder if Holtby was more touched, as I am, by Brittain's ardent attempt to make her best friend happy than by that last-ditch, half-hearted proposal from a man who didn't really love her. Friendship, work, self-belief, and the values Holtby gives Mrs Beddows – gaiety, kindliness and valour – seemed a good basis for the single life.

These qualities are not much in evidence in the single women in more contemporary fiction. It makes me sad to compare the intrepid spinster heroines of the 1920s and 1930s (including, of course, both Flora and Laura) with their modern sisters. I cringed at bitter Barbara Covett, in Zoë Heller's fantastic, terrifying *Notes on a Scandal*, who destroys a young, pretty colleague out of loneliness and jealousy. And Bridget Jones made me laugh, a lot, but she didn't help me discover how to live. Bridget talks the talk, but spends most of her time in love (mostly unrequited), chain-smoking, counting calories and sabotaging her own happiness, going back to the bad boy even after she's got Mr Right. I know love is complicated but I wish she knew her own mind, I wish she wasn't always choosing between the same two men, and I wish she was a bit more *capable* – I hate the scene where she makes blue string soup. No one's that helpless in the kitchen. My favourite Helen Fielding heroine is not Bridget but her ranty friend Shazzer who calls herself a 'singleton' because 'there's more than one bloody way to live' and sees herself as part of 'a whole generation of single girls . . . with their own incomes and homes who have lots of fun and don't need to wash anyone else's socks'. Quite.

Barbara Pym is often called the patron saint of spinsters, and *Excellent Women*, her 1952 debut, is hilarious too. But it's also so *sour*. Her heroine Mildred Lathbury is so mordant and vinegary that it makes me weep. When she says she is 'not at all like Jane Eyre, who must have given hope to so many plain women who tell their stories in the first person', I feel the ice close around my heart. This is going to be one of those laceratingly honest books where Rochester marries Blanche while Jane hangs around, condemned to being the eternal governess, in musty tweed. There is, it's true, a lot of Mildred wearing bad clothes and eking out a tin of baked beans over several meals, and being imposed on dreadfully and everybody taking umbrage.

But I'm being mean. There is lots to love about Pym. She is as funny as Austen, employing the same delicious irony on the same tiny canvas. Her spinsters are 'excellent women' – sturdy, energetic, capable, helpful – while the married women are debonair and incompetent. Men need 'excellent women' to smooth over life's rough edges, but they marry women who don't know how to wash a lettuce. The grey (in all senses) vicar in *Excellent Women* doesn't go for Mildred but for Allegra Gray, a glam widow who manages to charm a bevy of spinsters into hemming her curtains for her. Mildred reads cookbooks when she is insomniac, and knows everything there is to know about stain removal. Her dazzling neighbour, Rockingham Napier, asks her to help around the house, but his wife is an anthropologist who cheerfully calls herself a slut and revels in being woefully undomestic.

Is Mildred destined always to be an excellent woman? And if she is, will she never find love? She rebels a tiny bit – she makes the odd bold statement, she flirts (*very* mildly) with Rocky Napier, she buys new lipstick and makes herself some slightly more fashionable clothes. But mostly she is cynical about herself, and other women. A running gag is that Mildred is a shrewder social observer than the anthropologists whose job is to observe. She knows that one reason she's been chosen to work at a charity for impoverished gentlewomen is because she may one day become one. She reprimands herself for caring about her appearance, because no one will notice. Arguing with her spinster friend Dora, she suddenly feels desolate as she imagines the two of them 'in twenty or thirty years' time, perhaps living together, bickering about silly trifles'. Ruthlessly she observes herself wolfing down her dinner, without dignity. When she goes to a pub, she tries not to be schoolmarmish and orders a bitter, but she finds it, well, *bitter*.

There's something so helpless about her. Her ugly, serviceable underwear makes her feel dejected, but she doesn't replace it. She doesn't know how to eat spaghetti. She can't enjoy Rocky's teasing because she worries so much. When Allegra offensively asks what spinsters *do*, Mildred gives the dreary, surrendered reply: 'Oh, they stay at home with an aged parent and do the flowers, or . . . they have jobs and careers and live in bed-sitting-rooms or hostels. And then of course they become indispensable in the parish and some of them even go into religious communities.' She doesn't try to stick up for her life. She doesn't point out that Allegra has no inner resources and would be sunk without a man. She doesn't present her life in a flattering light. She doesn't even have the pride to make something up. When she bravely tries to buy a new shade of lipstick she is embarrassed into buying a colour that doesn't suit her, and humiliated by having to say its name, 'Hawaiian Fire'; it's funny but it makes Mildred seem pathetic, and why does she have to leave the shop with the wrong shade of lipstick, feeling absurd and ashamed? Why can't she just buy a nicer colour? She does too much for people and ends up feeling resentful and bitter. She finds the idea of getting married 'a little fantastic'. But why? She does have the odd suitor – with perhaps the emphasis on 'odd', but still . . .

When the anthropologist Everard Bone invites her to dinner,

she assumes she will have to do the cooking, pre-emptively imagines how this will make her back ache, and declines. Later, she does go, and finds he has organised dinner. But she's not pleasantly surprised. She can't seem to let herself be surprised any more, or experience pleasure.

She doesn't seem to like women either: she watches them in the ladies' room at a shop, 'working at their faces with savage concentration, opening their mouths wide, biting and licking their lips, stabbing at their noses and chins with powder-puffs'. It's so judgmental. She resists true friendship; when she feels sad that she's not really first in anyone's life, she swallows down the words because she doesn't want to have a heart-to-heart about it with her spinster friend Winifred.

Mildred is at her best when she lets herself hope. She tries to talk about love, and her desire to be with someone splendid and romantic, but her repressed confidantes don't respond, or don't encourage her. She does value her independence – she refuses to share her flat, or move in with friends and, unlike Winifred, she makes her own clothes rather than dress in swag from parish jumble sales which would 'swamp whatever individuality I possess'. She calls spinsterhood 'a positive rather than a negative state', but when Everard asks if that means excellent women can't have feelings, she shuts down again and says they may have feelings but they mustn't act on them. But why not?

The novel asks what constitutes a full life. Rocky Napier says, in his teasing way, that Mildred lives 'what is known as a *full* life', but his wife snorts, 'I thought that was the kind of life led by women who *didn't* have a full life in the accepted sense'. At the end, Mildred thinks that helping Everard with his proof-reading, and defending the vicar from predatory women might give her a full life, but it doesn't feel very full to me. She's relieved that the Napiers are leaving. She's found them too exciting. After one night out, she reflects, 'Love was rather a terrible thing, I decided next morning, remembering the undercurrents of the evening before. Not perhaps my cup of tea.' (Tea is very serious in Pym's novels. There is food and drink, or the promise of food and drink, or the denial of food and drink, on every single page. You can even buy *The Barbara Pym Cookbook* and cook your way through all the food mentioned in the novels, from toad-in-the-hole to railway pudding and rabbit with forcemeat balls.) In church one sunny morning, Mildred feels so peaceful she wishes the Napiers had never moved in and disturbed her life. But life needs disturbing sometimes, doesn't it? I can't help feeling that Pym never quite got over working as a censor during the war, and never quite shook the habit of putting a red line through anything that might be dangerous.

My disappointment in Mildred brings me back to Flora. I've been single for five years now and the ending seems very different. Flora's rescuer doesn't just turn up like a magical rescuer; she *summons* him. She has spent months solving other people's problems, and now she brings that same charm and intelligence to bear on her own situation. She secures her own happy ending. And it's really a new beginning. I wish I hadn't given up on Flora. Maybe I should be trying to summon a rescue of my own. At my writers' group, I panic that my life isn't progressing smoothly towards its happy ending. 'It's the marriage plot,' they say, 'it's exerting its pressure on your life.' I feel I somehow need to guarantee that things will work out. Flora wouldn't just sit in Soho, moaning about the marriage plot. She'd do something. I'm seconds away from agreeing to go on a disastrous-sounding blind date when it occurs to me to revisit *To the Lighthouse*.

I first read Woolf's slender novel at seventeen but I completely missed its pleasures and its point. It was written, of course, in 1927, and it's a happy spinster novel. It actually is.

At seventeen, I admired Mrs Ramsay's polymorphous creativity, the way she makes food, makes marriages, makes people happy. Now I think I'd hate holidaying with her on Skye and her coming into my room at night to say 'an unmarried woman has missed the best of life', as she does with Lily Briscoe, the thirty-something spinster painter. Mrs Ramsay thinks Lily is a little fool and what with another guest, Charles Tansley, droning on that 'Women can't write, women can't paint . . .', Lily feels oppressed and uncertain and thinks maybe she should marry William Bankes as Mrs Ramsay says. Oh I know that feeling!

And then comes the happiest page of the novel. Lily works out how to finish her painting, and exults: 'she would move the tree to the middle, and need never marry anybody'. This glorious flash of creative power illuminates the rest of her life. She and William become friends, and their friendship becomes, she says, one of the pleasures of her life. She dismisses Charles as a man who always sits blocking the view. She rejects the inner voice that says she's 'not a woman, but a peevish, ill-tempered, dried-up old maid'. And then she draws the line that finishes her painting.

She finishes the painting! She ends her novel single, and she gets sustenance from something that isn't a man. I'm so glad to have finally found a happy fictional spinster that I go on about it, at great length, to a friend of mine, my sometimes writing-partner, whose friendship is, like William's for Lily, one of the pleasures of my life. But he laughs. 'It's *phallic*,' he says. 'Have you never *seen* a lighthouse?' I make such an extravagantly Middle Eastern gesture of outrage that I knock half our lunch off the table. Later, one of my book group stalwarts, one of the most intelligent and witty single women I know, startles me by saying 'It's not a phallus, but a dildo, and Lily can use it to pleasure herself.' At least this is a *feminist* Freudian reading but still, I'm outraged. Who knew all my friends were Mr Mybugs? I'd like to bring Flora in to back me up. Because I don't think it's a phallus *or* a dildo. I can't believe I'm even typing that sentence. A lighthouse is a symbol of self-sufficiency. Like the lighthouse keepers who live there, not needing anything from the mainland, Lily has become self-sufficient. And like the lighthouse beam that stops shipwrecks, she saves lives: she has saved her own life.

Of course, Lily also breaks free of Mrs Ramsay. She stops trying to please her, and instead she claims her as her muse. Woolf based Mrs Ramsay on her mother, who died when Woolf was thirteen. After that, they stopped summering in St Ives under the beam of Godrevy Lighthouse and Woolf had her first breakdown. When she finished *To the Lighthouse*, Woolf felt she had exorcised her obsession with her mother. Just as Lily stops trying to please Mrs Ramsay, so Woolf immortalised her mother as Mrs Ramsay. It's breathtaking. But it also makes me wonder: do I need to break free of my heroines, too?

SCHEHERAZADE

I don't want to give up my heroines. The idea makes me feel bereft. For a few days I consider it. I imagine a life without heroines. I even read a Lee Child novel with a tough title, *Killing Floor,* as a sort of palate-cleanser, thinking it will be the most male book I've ever read. But there's a heroine in it too, a small-town cop whose supposed strength is constantly undercut by her dependence on the hero; nevertheless, I find myself trying to work out what I can learn from her, and realise I'm doing it again. Maybe I'm too addicted to heroines to stop. But is this addiction damaging? If I don't give up my heroines, will it mean I can't become a heroine myself?

I turn to Patti Smith's mesmerising memoir *Just Kids*. It is crammed with heroines and heroes but that doesn't stop her becoming heroic. In fact, *Just Kids* tells the story of how she went from being a teenager in New Jersey, living with her family, working at a factory and accidentally pregnant, to becoming the iconic punk poet on the black-and-white cover of her first album, *Horses*, released the year I was born. I love every wrecked and passionate song on *Horses*.

In New Jersey, making the difficult decision to put her baby up for adoption, Smith already knows who is in her pantheon.

She loves Arthur Rimbaud, Nina Simone, Joan of Arc and William Blake. She speaks of them with reverence. She copies them and she learns from them. Like them, she has a burning desire to express herself, but she doesn't know how. Will she write poetry like Rimbaud and Blake, sing like Simone, or start a revolution like Joan? She heads for New York to try to find out. It's 1967. She befriends Robert Mapplethorpe, and together they turn themselves into artists.

Smith experiments with painting, drawing, acting and writing. Mapplethorpe hasn't yet settled on photography. But they have faith that they will find their way. They're so skint that when they go to galleries they buy just one ticket, one going in while the other waits outside to hear a description of the show, but they tell each other that some day they'll go in together and the work will be theirs. Meanwhile they keep exploring, ecstatically: 'We gathered our coloured pencils and sheets of paper and drew like wild, feral children into the night, until, exhausted, we fell into bed.'

As she's experimenting with art, Smith also experiments with different selves. And yet, this is not at all like the myth of Sylvia Plath painfully shedding her false selves until she reached an impasse that could only end in suicide. Smith (who is, anyway, making her own myth) is trying on different selves, putting them on and taking them off, seeing how they suit her. It is life as costume drama. She says Mapplethorpe 'approached dressing like living art'. And she is forever donning a striped boatneck shirt and red throat scarf in the manner of Yves Montand in *Wages of Fear*, or channelling Audrey Hepburn's *Funny Face* beatnik bookseller. When someone says she looks like a folk singer, she decides to change her image. She studies pictures of Keith Richards and cuts her hair to look like his. It's transformational; 'I miraculously turned androgynous overnight'. For a fancy dress ball she wears an all-black outfit of pegged trousers, silk shirt, tie and jacket, with pristine white Keds. She leans against a wall like Buster Keaton and when people ask, she says she's come as a 'tennis player in mourning'.

This justifies my many hours poring over *Vogue* – style is serious! – but, when she's dressing as Montand or Hepburn or Richards or Keaton, Smith is also saying something profound about hero(ine) worship. When she dresses like Keaton and gives her look a funny name, and looks beautiful and singular as she's doing it, she isn't mindlessly stealing, she's honouring her heroes and heroines, remixing them, pastiching them and making something new.

Maybe we all find our style through homage – just as I learned to put on make-up from watching my mother at her dressing room table all those years ago. And some of my best-loved heroines are mash-ups. The Fossil girls in *Ballet Shoes* are rewrites of *The Whicharts*. Emily Byrd Starr is Anne Shirley rebooted. Mary Yellan is Cathy Earnshaw, but with better choices. And maybe this means I don't have to feel so guilty about the heroines I've misread. Lucy Honeychurch has been on my conscience. But Smith makes me think that perhaps I didn't misread so much as exuberantly appropriate her. And maybe it's by appropriating our heroines that we become heroines ourselves. That's how it happens for Smith. After many turbulent times – she and Mapplethorpe weather illness, disappointment, poverty and the shift in their relationship as he discovers he is gay – she finds out she wants to be a rock and roll poet, and he takes the picture of her for *Horses*, and ever since she's been one of the heroines other women want to dress like and learn from.

After *Just Kids* I feel hugely relieved. I don't need to give up my heroines after all. I won't go cold turkey, read only books about men. I won't edit my bookshelf. Even *What Katy Did* is still up there. After all, I loved Katy once.

Inspired by Smith's commitment to hero worship, I decide to visit the grave of Aphra Behn. Smith is always visiting graves in *Just Kids*. She crosses the Atlantic to visit Rimbaud's grave. I thought the least I could do was go four stops on the tube to Westminster Abbey. Virginia Woolf, no less, said all women writers should let flowers fall on Behn's grave. And I am helping to found a women's theatre company which we've called Agent 160 – Behn's code name when she was moonlighting as a spy. She was the pathbreaker: the barber's daughter from Kent who was supposed to enter a convent, but instead became a spy, a dedicated libertine, a pioneer playwright and the woman who introduced milk punch to England. The Abbey staff have no idea where, or even who, she is. But I find her. Not among the dead white male poets but in the cloister, by herself. As I put down the flowers, I remember how in Behn's preface to her 1686 play, *The Lucky Chance*, she rants at the critics who said her work was unwomanly: 'I value Fame as much as if I had been born a *Hero*,' she says. She wasn't born a hero, or a heroine. But she asserts her right to become one.

At home, I make Behn's milk punch. In green tea I steep cinnamon, cloves, coriander, lemon juice, sugar, brandy, rum and (oddly) pineapple, then mix it with hot milk, letting it curdle, and straining it. The translucent, golden punch tastes velvety, voluptuous and not off-puttingly milky. Under its influence, I stage a party for my heroines in my imagination, and in my flat. It's less like the glowering encounter I imagined between Cathy Earnshaw and Flora Poste, and more like the riotous bash in *Breakfast at Tiffany's*.

Not everyone is going to like milk punch. So there are also dirty martinis, and bagels and baklava, and my mother's *masafan*, Iraqi marzipan. The Little Mermaid is in the bath, with her tail still on, singing because she never did give up her soaring voice. Anne Shirley and Jo March are having a furious argument about plot versus character, gesticulating with ink-stained hands. Scarlett is in the living room, her skirts taking up half the space, trying to show Lizzy how to bat her eyelashes. Lizzy is laughing her head off but Scarlett has acquired a sense of humour, and doesn't mind a bit. Melanie is talking books with Esther Greenwood, who has brought her baby and also the proofs of her first poetry collection. Franny and Zooey have rolled back the rug and are doing a soft shoe shuffle in rhinestone hats. Lucy Honeychurch is hammering out some Beethoven (in this scenario I have a piano. A grand piano. Well, why not?). Marjorie Morningstar is gossiping about directors with Pauline and Posy Fossil. They've come straight from the shows they're in, still in stage make-up and full of stories. Petrova, in a leather aviator jacket, goggles pushed back, a chic scarf knotted around her neck, is telling the thrilling story of her latest flight and how she fixed an engine fault in mid-air. Mira, in her paint-stained jeans and poncho, is listening, fascinated, asking a thousand questions. Mildred has been persuaded to drink a tiny glass of sherry, then another tiny glass, then another and now she and Lolly are doing a wild, strange dance in the hallway, stamping their feet, their hair flying wild and electric. Lolly's cakes, in the shape of patriarchs she hates, are going down a treat. The Dolls from the Valley are telling Flora some truly scandalous and unrepeatable stories, and she is firmly advising them to get rid of their men and find worthier paramours. Celie is modelling trousers of her own design and taking orders from the *Lace* women; Judy is giving her a ten-point plan on how to expand her business to an international market. She is quite drunk but nevertheless the plan seems quite coherent, even if it is punctuated by her bellowing 'More leopard print, more leopard print!'

Cathy looks tumultuous and on the edge of violent weeping and just as I think she's either going to storm out or trash my flat, Jane arrives, late, with an unexpected guest. Cathy turns in anticipation: is it Heathcliff? Once I would have joined her, but now I'm glad it isn't him. It's a better surprise. It's Emily's hawk. Hero or Nero. Jane's found him at last, and has him on her arm, perched on her glove; small for a bird of prey, he is dashing and patrician looking, brown and white, observing the room with dark, flinty eyes. When Cathy sees him, she looks at Jane and smiles.

And in the kitchen is a heroine I probably should have had when I was four and sitting on my parents' carpet, wishing it would fly. In the kitchen is Scheherazade.

Why didn't I come to Scheherazade sooner? She's perfect:

Middle Eastern, a storyteller, a feminist. And she's not born to be a heroine but she definitely becomes one. At the start of *The Thousand and One Nights*, she's defined only by whose daughter she is, by having a vizier for a father. She is sheltered to quite an extraordinary degree. It's been three years since the king, Shahriyar, caught his queen being unfaithful and murdered her. Every night since, he has married a virgin, deflowered her, and murdered her in the morning. That's over a thousand dead women, and Scheherazade's father has been procuring them. But does Scheherazade notice? Does she say something? Does she take her sister Dunyazad and run for the hills? No. It's only when her father comes home despairing that there are no virgins left (they've either fled, or are dead) that she thinks to ask what's been going on. But she does make up for her myopia after that. Quickly she formulates a plan. She's going to be the king's next virgin bride. Her father isn't keen. You can see why. But Scheherazade is so persuasive that he agrees to let her marry the royal serial killer, and take her sister along for the ride.

Poor Dunyazad never really gets any heroine points but she absolutely should. For Scheherazade's plan to work, Dunyazad has to be in the room for the deflowering and has to stay unruffled enough to remember to ask for a story at the end. And she does. And so it begins.

Scheherazade tells stories so marvellous that the king doesn't want her to stop, and keeps deferring her death sentence, so she can keep going. Every story has a cliff-hanger. And, for all their tricksiness, a moral too. The very first story is about a merchant who eats a date and throws away the pit, only to find a terrifying jinn threatening to kill him because he claims that the date pit struck his (invisible) son a fatal blow in the chest. The merchant begs for his life but the jinn won't relent – until three old men appear and make a deal with him. They will tell stories, and if the jinn thinks them marvellous enough, he will let the merchant live. He agrees – just as Scheherazade hopes the king will spare her life in return for her stories.

Most translations leave out the frame narrative between the stories, because it gets repetitive, but when I find a translation that leaves it in I'm struck by the fact that Scheherazade's father, the vizier, arrives every morning, a thousand and one times, with a shroud folded under his arm, in case today will be the day the king kills his daughter. Scheherazade is telling stories with a gun to her head. She's like a souped-up Esther. No fainting and fasting for her; Scheherazade becomes a heroine by fictioneering. And while Esther saves the Jews, Scheherazade saves her people too; her people are the women. She says she's doing it to save herself and her sisters. And she doesn't just mean her actual sister Dunyazad. She uses the plural: she means *all* the women who would otherwise be forced into marriage and then murdered. And she manages it. She saves them, she saves herself and she becomes the queen.

As a child, I was told stories from the *Nights* but I found them too fantastical. They made me anxious. I've always felt uncomfortable with stories that too flagrantly defy logic; I've tended to prefer mimesis to fancy, closure to open-endedness. I've worried about heroines who can do magic or stop time or transcend realism, because how can I learn from them when I so blatantly can't do any of these things? But while Scheherazade has her head in the clouds, her feet are planted firmly on the ground. And so it's through her that I fall under the spell of *Nights*.

The stories *are* fantastical, it's true. Carpets fly, women turn into gazelles, men into dogs, jinn into clouds of smoke, a severed head speaks, a book poisons its reader, fish raise their heads from a frying pan and speak, the caliph wanders the city disguised as a merchant. A man is turned into an ape. He is rescued by a princess who fights a demon to free him. The fight is, of course, a shape-shifting fight.

First the demon turns into a scorpion, so the princess turns into a snake. He turns into an eagle, so she turns into a vulture. He turns into a cat, so she turns into a brindled wolf. He is losing so he turns himself into a pomegranate and bursts, scattering bright red seeds. She turns into a cock and eats all the seeds, missing just one, which turns into a fish and dives into a fountain. She turns herself into a bigger fish and dives in after him. He emerges from the fountain as a firebrand, and she emerges as a huge burning coal. As they go on fighting, flames and smoke engulf the palace. A spark catches the ape in the eye. And then the princess wins. The demon is dead, and she magics the ape back to human form – except he has lost the eye that was burned by the spark. And the princess is so depleted by the fighting and the spell-making that she only has time to say goodbye to her father before collapsing into a pile of ashes. It's dazzling. That's the kind of princess I think I could cope with becoming even now: a shape-shifting, magic-wielding warrior and saviour of men.

The thing that used to worry me most about fantastical heroines – the fact that I couldn't learn from them because I couldn't be like them – was also what made me dissatisfied when I thought my heroines were being too obviously *written*, or manipulated, pushed around – as when L.M. Montgomery doused Anne Shirley's spark, or (even though it was a happier example) Jane Austen arranged Lizzy's wedding. I felt let down when I could see the writer too much at work on a character because it reminded me forcefully that of course I don't have a writer working on my story, guiding me to safety, bending the laws of reality for me, bringing in a hero to rescue me or transporting me to a happier life by the stroke of her pen. No writer is writing me a better journey. No writer is guiding me through my misunderstandings and muddles and wrong turns to reach my happy ending.

And then I realise I am the writer.

I don't mean because I write. I mean because we all write our own lives. Scheherazade's greatest piece of storytelling is not the stories she tells, but the story she lives. The best transformation in the *Nights* is Scheherazade transforming herself from vizier's cosseted daughter to queen, mother, storyteller and saviour.

And all right, Scheherazade is herself a story. We don't know who really wrote the *Nights*. It could be a phalanx of men. But whoever came up with the frame narrative must have needed a heroine like Scheherazade. And she needs heroines too; she writes heroines who will help her cure the king. Like a detective analysing a criminal mind, she works out what heroines will change him. First, she flatters him with stories about fickle heroines, that confirm his view that all women are as faithless as his first wife.

Once he's hooked, she wheels out good, kind, loving heroines. Finally, she invokes heroines who are unashamed of their sexual desires. By the end, the king repents having killed all those women, and may even understand why his first wife strayed. Scheherazade has given him precisely the heroines he needed to learn from.

She's also understood her own life. In her version of 'Sleeping Beauty', she spins her own story into a mischievous, playful, magical tale, with an ending that is part-punchline, part-moral. She isn't just telling a story about the events that have shaped her life; it's more active than that. She's shaping the inchoate events of her life into a story. And it's about a woman who educates a prince.

Sittukhan is not a princess, though she is very beautiful. When she wakes from her flax-induced coma to find a prince kissing her (and not just kissing), she freely takes her own pleasure. But after forty days and nights, he leaves. Because he's a prince, and a snob, and she's just a very pretty girl with a flax allergy.

But Sittukhan isn't going to just let him go. (Scheherazade wastes hardly any words on her time asleep; this beauty is more interesting when she's awake.) She enlists a demon to enhance her beauty and build her a palace. Soon the queen comes begging Sittukhan to marry her son. Sittukhan says no. She plays these status-obsessed royals at their own game. The queen brings gorgeous brocades and Sittukhan has them cut up into floor cloths. The queen brings emeralds, and Sittukhan feeds them to her pigeons. She says she'll only marry the prince if he feigns death, and they wrap him in seven winding sheets, carry him in sad procession through the city and bury him in her garden. The lovesick prince agrees.

Once everyone has gone, Sittukhan digs him up, unwraps

him and laughs at him for being so keen on women that he'll go so far as to be buried alive. He realises she is the same woman he spent forty days and nights with, and now she very much has the upper hand. *Then* they live happily ever after. Maybe Scheherazade does too.

And yet, I worry about Scheherazade's ending.

Not that I've read every story in the *Nights*. Legend has it that if you get to the end of the *Nights*, you die. There are an awful lot of them; my edition runs to three hefty volumes. I skipped to the thousand and first night to find out what happens to Scheherazade. I knew she survived, but there's more: she also presents the king with three sons. During the thousand and one nights, she has not only been telling stories but has gone through three pregnancies, without the king having noticed. At no point does he comment on her changing shape. She never has to break off the stories to go into labour. And she doesn't think, say, after the first baby, or even after the second, of telling the king it's surely time this farce of a marriage becomes real. When she *does* tell him, she asks him to commute her death sentence purely on the grounds that he won't find a better mother for their children. She's arguing for him to value her as a mother, not as a storyteller; not even as a wife. It's very peculiar.

When she suddenly produces her three sons for the king, she just as suddenly produces, for her readers, the idea that she has had a shadow life all along, that while we've been relating to her as a storyteller, she's secretly gone off and changed roles, becoming a mother. I don't know what to think about it. Is she having it all, stories *and* sons? Or is she going to stop telling stories now? Is this like Anne Shirley giving up writing all over again? Or, even worse, does this story, so far-fetched, even compared to the most absurd and sensational stories in the *Nights*, suggest she's not believable herself, that she's just a framing device, a cipher?

And then I turn the page. Scheherazade's stories don't end on the thousand and first night. Some of the most famous stories – like 'Aladdin' and 'Ali Baba' – come after. The story of Sittukhan comes after. Her stories burst the bounds of the frame. She doesn't stop telling them.

I don't find Scheherazade's stories too fantastical any more. I find them liberating. These wondrous, curious heroines, with their magic and their dreams and their twists and turns of fate, make me feel that anything is possible. I write a short play for the opening show of Agent 160, about a heroine who feels miserable and blocked in her life, tied to her past, home-sick for Baghdad, where she's never been and can never go. (I call her Noura, but the play hugs the shore of my life.) She learns to belly-dance, and as she makes her arms move like a snake and like a swan, she starts to feel she can be anything she wants.

All my heroines, yes, even the Little Mermaid, even poor dull listless Sleeping Beauty, have given me this sense of possibility. They made me feel I wasn't forced to live out the story my family wanted for me, that I wasn't doomed to plod forward to a fate predetermined by God, that I didn't need to be defined by my seizures, or trapped in fictions of my own making, or shaped by other people's stories. That I wanted to write my own life.

When I first told my mother about meeting my heroines

again, she said 'And at the end, you become the heroine.' I objected, vehemently. To be fair, all our conversations are vehement – we're Middle Eastern drama queens, and we can't help it. But also: *she's* the heroine, not me. As a child I thought her life was fascinating but that mine would be safe and boring. My whole quest for fictional heroines began because I wanted to be a heroine like her. But I didn't understand what heroism was. I thought my mother was heroic because things had happened to her. It's taken me till now, at 37, after two years of thinking about my heroines, to realise that my mother is a heroine because of what she did. For all her superstition, my mother defied fate. She was flung across the world, ripped away from everything she knew, but she went on coping and hoping and making a new life for herself, living in a new place and in a new language. Like Scheherazade, when bad things happened, she didn't become a victim. Instead, she wrote and rewrote the story of her life. That's how she became a heroine. She improvised.

There are no regrets in improvisation, and no mistakes. All accidents are happy accidents, invitations to go in a new and exciting direction, to change the game. There's a principle of improvisation that I think about a lot: it's called *yes and*. When one performer makes an offer, the other must accept it (*yes*) and offer something of their own (*and*). Otherwise the improvisation gets blocked. And *yes and* feels like the secret of life, not just improvisation. We have to keep making choices, keep transforming. Scheherazade's stories never end. Every story in the *Nights* opens a door that leads on to another story. I don't know if I'll get a happy ending. But why worry about a happy ending? Why worry about any ending at all? I don't know where I'm going next, and for the first time in forever, I don't want to. I want my life to be picaresque. Fantastical. I want to say *yes and*.

POSTSCRIPT

If I can't exactly tell you how to be a heroine, I can (in affectionate homage to Nora Ephron, who put recipes in *Heartburn*) tell you how to make Iraqi Jewish marzipan: *masafan.* Of course, it's my mother's recipe. And it is heroically good.

Preheat the oven to 200°C and grease an oven tray really well. Mix 200g ground almonds, 200g caster sugar, two egg whites, some bashed-up cardamom seeds and a few drops of orange-flower water. Fill a bowl with water and another drop or two of orange-flower water, and dampen your hands in it, then roll the mixture into little balls. Pinch each one to shape it into a star. Sink half a pistachio into each centre. Bake for eight minutes, till they're golden.

BIBLIOGRAPHY

Introduction

Austen, Jane, *Northanger Abbey* (1817)
Campbell, Joseph, *A Hero with a Thousand Faces* (1949)

Chapter 1: The Little Mermaid

Andersen, Hans Christian, *Fairy Tales* (1837)
Anon., *The Story of Henny Penny* (n.d.)
Basile, Giambattista, *Il Pentamerone* (1634 and 1636)
The Book of Esther
Carter, Angela, *The Bloody Chamber* (1979)
Dworkin, Andrea, *Woman Hating* (1976)
Grimm, Jacob and Wilhelm, *Grimm's Fairy Tales* (1812)
Perrault, Charles, *Stories or Fairy Tales from Past Times With Morals* (1697)
Sexton, Anne, *Transformations* (1971)
Shakespeare, William, *Titus Andronicus* (1594)
Warner, Marina, *From the Beast to the Blonde* (1994)
Wolf, Naomi, *The Beauty Myth* (1991)

Chapter 2: Anne of Green Gables

Alcott, Louisa May, *Little Women* (1868)

—*Good Wives* (1869)

—*Little Men* (1871)

—*Jo's Boys* (1886)

—*A Long Fatal Love Chase* (written under the pseudonym A.M. Barnard in 1866; first published 1995)

Burnett, Frances Hodgson, *A Little Princess* (1905)

Ephron, Nora, *When Harry Met Sally* (1989)

Francis, Richard, *Fruitlands: the Alcott Family and Their Search for Utopia* (2011)

Gilbert, Sandra and Gubar, Susan, *The Madwoman in the Attic* (1979)

Montgomery, L.M., *Anne of Green Gables* (1908)

—*Anne of Avonlea* (1909)

—*Anne of the Island* (1915)

—*Anne's House of Dreams* (1917)

—*Rainbow Valley* (1919)

—*Rilla of Ingleside* (1921)

—*Emily of New Moon* (1923)

—*Emily Climbs* (1925)

—*Emily's Quest* (1927)

—*Anne of Windy Willows* (1936)

—*Anne of Ingleside* (1939)

—*The Selected Journals of L.M. Montgomery Vol 1.* (1985)

Porter, Eleanor H., *Pollyanna* (1913)

Rubio, Mary, *Lucy Maud Montgomery: the Gift of Wings* (2008)

Chapter 3: Lizzy Bennet

Austen, Jane, *Pride and Prejudice* (1813)
—*Mansfield Park* (1814)
Blume, Judy, *Are You There, God? It's Me, Margaret* (1970)
Cooper, Jilly, *Riders* (1985)
—*Rivals* (1988)
Dickens, Charles, *Oliver Twist* (1838)
Meyer, Stephanie, *Twilight,* (2005)
Orbach, Susie, *Fat is a Feminist Issue* (1978)
Shakespeare, William, *Romeo and Juliet* (1597)
—*A Midsummer Night's Dream* (1600)
Spence, Jon, *Becoming Jane Austen* (2003)
Tomalin, Claire, *Jane Austen: a Biography* (1997)

Chapter 4: Scarlett O'Hara

Carter, Angela, *Nights at the Circus* (1984)
Collins, Suzanne, *The Hunger Games* (2008)
Flaubert, Gustave, *Madame Bovary* (1856)
French, Marilyn, *The Women's Room* (1977)
Greer, Germaine, *The Female Eunuch* (1970)
Ibsen, Henrik, *A Doll's House* (1879)
Jong, Erica, *Fear of Flying* (1973)
Larsson, Stieg, *The Girl With The Dragon Tattoo* (2005)
Mitchell, Margaret, *Gone With The Wind* (1939)
Pyron, Darden Asbury, *Southern Daughter: the Life of Margaret Mitchell and the Making of Gone With the Wind* (2004)
Shakespeare, William, *The Taming of the Shrew* (1594)

Tolstoy, Leo, *Anna Karenina* (1878)

Whedon, Joss, and others, *Buffy the Vampire Slayer* (1997–2003)

Woolf, Virginia, *Orlando* (1928)

—*A Room of One's Own* (1929)

Chapter 5: Franny Glass

Donne, John, *Songs and Sonnets* (1601)

Dunn, Jane, *Antonia White: A Life* (2000)

Maynard, Joyce, *At Home in the World* (1999)

Parker, Dorothy, *The Portable Dorothy Parker* (1944)

Salinger, J.D., *Franny and Zooey* (1961)

Shakespeare, William, *Antony and Cleopatra* (1623)

Slawenski, Kenneth, *JD Salinger: A Life* (2010)

White, Antonia, *Frost in May* (1933)

—*The Lost Traveller* (1950)

—*The Sugar House* (1952)

—*Beyond the Glass* (1954)

Chapter 6: Esther Greenwood

Alvarez, Al, *The Savage God* (1972)

Coolidge, Susan, *What Katy Did* (1872)

Hardy, Thomas, *Tess of the d'Urbervilles* (1891)

Hughes, Ted, *Birthday Letters* (1998)

Malcolm, Janet, *The Silent Woman* (1993)

Plath, Sylvia, *The Bell Jar* (1963)

—*Ariel* (1965)

—(with a foreword by Frieda Hughes) *Ariel: The Restored Edition* (2004)

—*The Journals of Sylvia Plath* (1982)

—(edited by Karen V. Kukil) *The Unabridged Journals of Sylvia Plath* (2000)

Richardson, Samuel, *Clarissa* (1748)

Walker, Alice, *The Color Purple* (1982)

—*In Search of Our Mothers' Gardens: Womanist Prose* (1983)

Chapter 7: Lucy Honeychurch

Albee, Edward, *Who's Afraid of Virginia Woolf?* (1962)

Brecht, Bertolt, (edited by John Willett) *Brecht on Theatre* (1964)

Brook, Peter, *The Empty Space* (1968)

Chekhov, Anton, *Uncle Vanya* (1897)

Coward, Noël, *Private Lives* (1930)

Euripides, *The Bacchae* (405 BC)

Forster, E.M., *A Room with a View* (1908)

—*Where Angels Fear to Tread* (1905)

—*Maurice* (1971)

Moffat, Wendy, *E.M. Forster: a New Life* (2010)

Parker, Dorothy, *The Portable Dorothy Parker* (1944)

Streatfeild, Noel, *The Whicharts* (1931)

— *Ballet Shoes* (1936)

Wouk, Herman, *Marjorie Morningstar* (1955)

Chapter 8: The Dolls (from the Valley)

Conran, Shirley, *Lace* (1982)

Delaney, Shelagh, *A Taste of Honey* (1958)

Kael, Pauline, *When the Lights Go Down* (1980)

Littlewood, Joan, *Joan's Book* (1994)

Seaman, Barbara, *Lovely Me: Life of Jacqueline Susann* (1987)
Susann, Jacqueline, *Valley of the Dolls* (1966)
—*The Love Machine* (1969)
—*Once Is Not Enough* (1973)

Chapter 9: Cathy Earnshaw

Barker, Juliet, *The Brontës* (1994)
Brontë, Emily, *Wuthering Heights* (1847)
Brontë, Charlotte, *Jane Eyre* (1847)
Carson, Anne, *Glass, Irony and God* (1992)
Du Maurier, Daphne, *Jamaica Inn* (1936)
—*The Infernal World of Branwell Brontë* (1960)
Eco, Umberto, *Reflections on the Name of the Rose* (1985)
Estés, Clarissa Pinkola, *Women Who Run With The Wolves* (1992)
Miller, Lucasta, *The Brontë Myth* (2001)
Rhys, Jean, *Wide Sargasso Sea* (1966)

Chapter 10: Flora Poste

Austen, Jane, *Emma* (1815)
—*Persuasion* (1818)
Christie, Agatha, *The Murder at the Vicarage* (1930)
Delafield, E.M., *Consequences* (1919)
Dickens, Charles, *Great Expectations* (1861)
Fielding, Helen, *Bridget Jones's Diary* (1996)
Gibbons, Stella, *Cold Comfort Farm* (1932)
Heller, Zoë, *Notes on a Scandal* (2003)
Holtby, Winifred, *South Riding* (1936)
Ingalls Wilder, Laura, *Little House in the Big Woods* (1932)

—*Little House on the Prairie* (1935)

—*On the Banks of Plum Creek* (1937)

—*By the Shores of Silver Lake* (1939)

—*The Long Winter* (1940)

—*Little Town on the Prairie* (1941)

—*These Happy Golden Years* (1943)

—*The First Four Years* (1971)

Nicholson, Virginia, *Singled Out* (2007)

Pym, Hilary and Wyatt, Honor, *The Barbara Pym Cookbook* (1988)

Pym, Barbara, *Excellent Women* (1952)

Sackville-West, Vita, *All Passion Spent* (1931)

Townsend Warner, Sylvia, *Lolly Willowes* (1926)

—*Summer Will Show* (1936)

Travers, P.L., *Mary Poppins* (1934)

Woolf, Virginia, *To the Lighthouse* (1927)

Chapter 11: Scheherazade

Anon., (translated by Lyons, Malcolm and Lyons, Ursula) *The Arabian Nights: Tales of 1001 Nights* (2010)

Behn, Aphra, *The Lucky Chance* (1686)

Child, Lee, *Killing Floor* (1997)

Capote, Truman, *Breakfast at Tiffany's* (1958)

Smith, Patti, *Just Kids* (2010)

Postscript

Ephron, Nora, *Heartburn* (1983)

ACKNOWLEDGEMENTS

Thanks to my fantastic editor Becky Hardie and my fabulous agent Judith Murray, for championing the book from the start, and to everyone at Chatto & Windus, especially Katherine Ailes, Kate Bland, Alice Broderick, Parisa Ebrahimi, Beth Humphries, James Jones, Susannah Otter and Ruth Warburton.

Thank you also (for cheerleading, tea and sympathy, wise advice, and more) to: Robert Anasi, Hephzibah Anderson, Jonathan Beckman, Marina Benjamin, Tom Berish, Michael Caines, Maddy Costa, Ezra Ellis, Edmund Ellis, Aida Hakim, Paul King, Robert Macfarlane, Alexander Masters, Neel Mukherjee, Roskar Nasan, Ruaridh Nicoll, Nick Quinn, Amy Rosenthal, Rachel Shabi, Jonathan Thake, the wonderful women of my book group (Mary Agnew, Natalie Gold, Rebecca Hughes, Katherine Knight and Heloïse Sénéchal), the Dog House writers (Robin Booth, Nick Harrop, Matthew Morrison and Ben Musgrave), and my god-daughter Audrey Quentin (for mermaid lore).

And with my love, thanks to my best friend Emma Ayech, and my mother Amanda Ellis.

Acknowledgements

I'm very grateful for permission to quote from the following:

Howl by Allen Ginsberg. Copyright © 1956, Allen Ginsberg, used by permission of The Wylie Agency (UK) Limited.

Words from 'Glass, Irony and God' by Anne Carson, published by Jonathan Cape. Reprinted by permission of The Random House Group Limited

'Fever 103°' taken from *Ariel*, the Restored Edition © Estate of Sylvia Plath and reprinted by permission of Faber and Faber Ltd

'Cut' taken from *Ariel*, the Restored Edition © Estate of Sylvia Plath and reprinted by permission of Faber and Faber Ltd

Extracts taken from *The Journals of Sylvia Plath* © Estate of Sylvia Plath and reprinted by permission of Faber and Faber Ltd

Extracts taken from *The Bell Jar* © Estate of Sylvia Plath and reprinted by permission of Faber and Faber Ltd

'The Minotaur' taken from *Birthday Letters* © Estate of Ted Hughes and reprinted by permission of Faber and Faber Ltd

INDEX

Index

Index